By George F. Butterick

EDITOR

Poetry and Truth by Charles Olson (1970)
Additional Prose by Charles Olson (1974)
The Maximus Poems: Volume Three by Charles Olson, with
    Charles Boer (1975)
Selected Poems by Vincent Ferrini (1976)
Muthologos: The Collected Lectures and Interviews by
    Charles Olson (1978-79)
*Charles Olson & Robert Creeley: The Complete Correspondence
    Volumes 1 & 2* (1980)
*Charles Olson & Robert Creeley: The Complete Correspondence
    Volume 3* (1981)
The Postmoderns: The New American Poetry Revised, with
    Donald Allen (1982)
*Charles Olson & Robert Creeley: The Complete Correspondence
    Volume 4* (1982)
*Charles Olson & Robert Creeley: The Complete Correspondence
    Volume 5* (1983)

AUTHOR

The Norse (1973)
Reading Genesis by the Light of a Comet (1976)
A Guide to the Maximus Poems of Charles Olson (1978)

JOURNAL

OLSON: The Journal of the Charles Olson Archives (1973-78)

CHARLES OLSON & ROBERT CREELEY:

THE COMPLETE CORRESPONDENCE

VOLUME 5

EDITED BY

GEORGE F. BUTTERICK

BLACK SPARROW PRESS
SANTA BARBARA   1983

CHARLES OLSON & ROBERT CREELEY: THE COMPLETE CORRESPONDENCE. *5/1984 Eng. Cont>*
VOLUME 5.

ACKNOWLEDGEMENTS

A number of Charles Olson's letters in this volume were first published in whole or in part in *Mayan Letters*, ed. Robert Creeley (Palma de Mallorca: Divers Press, 1954); reprinted in Olson's *Selected Writings*, ed. Robert Creeley (New York: New Directions, 1967). The originals of these letters are in the collections of the University of Connecticut Library, Storrs, and Washington University Libraries, St. Louis, and are printed here with those libraries' kind cooperation. Grateful acknowledgement must continue to be made to Donald Allen, who provided encouragement along with typescripts of many of Charles Olson's letters; to Holly Hall and Timothy Murray of Washington University Libraries; to Edith Jarolim for providing a copy of Paul Blackburn's poem "l'education sentimentale" from among his papers; to Diana Woelffer for her photographs of Lerma; to Seamus Cooney, who meticulously helped to read proofs; and to Linda Press, who tirelessly coordinated things at Black Sparrow.

Cover photographs by Gerard Malanga.

LIBRARY OF CONGRESS CATALOGING IN PUBLICATION DATA

Olson, Charles, 1910-1970.
    Charles Olson & Robert Creeley : the complete correspondence.

    Includes bibliographical references and indexes.
    1. Olson, Charles, 1910-1970—Correspondence.
2. Creeley, Robert, 1926- —Correspondence.
3. Poets, American—20th century—Correspondence.
I. Creeley, Robert, 1926- II. Butterick, George F.
III. Title.
PS3529.L655Z544   811'.54 [B]   80-12222
ISBN 0-87685-561-3 (v. 5)
ISBN 0-87685-562-1 (deluxe : v. 5)
ISBN 0-87685-560-5 (pbk : v. 5)

PS
3529
.L655
Z544
1980b
v.5

TABLE OF CONTENTS

Editor's Introduction   vii

The Correspondence, February 13–April 26, 1951   11

Notes   189

I. Index of Persons Named in the Letters   213

II. Index of Works by Charles Olson and Robert Creeley
    Cited in the Text   217

Photographs follow page 100

Editor's Introduction

In this volume, Olson comes into his own. His restless energy is given focus by the new and appealing subject spread before him, at times literally underfoot. Olson is free, as he says, after "22 yrs in the Pen"—the relatively conventional life before desks, as scholar, bureaucrat, and writer. He has room to follow his larger instincts and to investigate alternatives to the inherited culture, with no particular outcome in mind. All is discovery.

The Olsons are settling in at Lerma, a small fishing village about four miles south of Campeche, on the Yucatan coast, within sight of Mayan ruins. They have rented an attractive adobe house with pillared terraza overlooking the sea, which their friends from Black Mountain, Emerson and Dina Woelffer, had told them about. Creeley, on the other hand, is still in New Hampshire with his young family. By a turn of circumstances, in this volume he assumes a slightly subordinate role—simply because, for the first time in the series, fewer of his letters are available for publication.

Earlier volumes may have suffered somewhat by the loss of several of Olson's letters, particularly those from the final months of 1950. This time, it is a number of Creeley letters that did not make it. Actually they did survive, but in no condition to be read and reproduced. The letters, some in their original envelopes, were part of a trunk-load of papers, along with a few cardboard cartons of material, that Olson had stored upon returning to Gloucester from Black Mountain in the basement of a house that Vincent Ferrini then occupied. There was a flood during a storm, however, leaving the papers in brittle bundles, for the most part unable to be peeled away without damage. The Creeley letters in particular, typed on the thinnest onionskin and airmail sheets, fared poorly; the sizing of the paper had become bonded together and it was not possible to render the content available, even though local paper conservators were consulted. Perhaps five or six letters, or as many as ten (some are very likely still buried among larger heaps of fused material in the trunk), were lost this way—at least until better recovery techniques become available.

Thus, a more daily account of Creeley's activities from this time will have to be filled in from his letters to Cid Corman, Paul Blackburn, and the others he was in steady communication with. (It must be remembered, through the extent of this series, that both writers kept up letter writing with a number of other correspondents, in addition to usual business matters, though none with the same frequency and intensity as each other.) Still, there is enough surviving from Creeley here to make plain that he was not merely the hollow echo of a sounding board.

The letters in this fifth volume begin with Olson seeking to discover precisely "what the Maya were." He had done little, if any, reading beforehand by way of preparation—though a good deal while on the path of discovery, as the editor's notes make evident. More detrimental to his efforts, he made no language preparation; consequently, he finds himself "imprisoned," as he says, by his American speech—though the result (these letters) is all our gain. Creeley has some background to understand it all, having visited India and Burma during the War, as he engagingly reveals in his February 18th letter.

Some of Olson's major topics are culture (including the imperialization of culture) and primitivism, an intuitive methodology, and the role of the private investigator (seen especially in the contrast of Olson with Raúl Pavón, director of the local museum). There is also the poet's frustration with the professionals, the increasingly desperate search for money to sustain the venture (which will be more evident in the next volume, as time runs out), and plans for trips to various sites, often unfulfilled. Occasionally, strains of publishing efforts mix in: *Origin* is not yet off the ground and Richard Wirtz Emerson's Golden Goose Press continues to cause frustration.

Theories are raised—the relationship of the Maya to the sea, the identity of the god Quetzalcoatl with the planet Venus—but repeatedly Olson comes back to language, especially language as he found it embodied in the ancient Mayan glyphs. The glyphs represent an archaic imagism, units of intimate meaning, not simply astronomical configurations or anthropomorphic constructs. (Oddly, Olson does not seek to apply Fenollosa's Chinese ideograms to them, comparatively, even though "The Chinese Written Character as a Medium for Poetry" was of inspiration when formulating "Projective Verse"—probably because at this point, as he admits, he does not fully grasp the meaning and role of the glyphs, though their possibilities provoke him thoroughly.)

Creeley encourages him, biding his own time, until he can make his way with growing family into new possibilities abroad. During the course of the letters, Creeley announces his intention to leave Rock Pool Farm for France, where Mitchell Goodman and his wife Denise Levertov were living and where the income from Ann Creeley's small trust fund could be stretched more comfortably.

Readers familiar with Olson's work will recognize a number of the letters from his *Mayan Letters*, the careful selection that Creeley published from Mallorca in 1954. Fifteen of the thirty-one letters that follow were published in that collection, either in whole or in part. As a volume, *Mayan Letters* offers a more concentrated impression of Olson's Mexican experience than the often interrupted view displayed here. Now, however, we have the full context, including significant omitted material and current literary concerns that carry over from the previous volumes, especially Olson's continuing impatience to establish reliable and sympathetic outlets for his work.

Olson's oft-quoted observations on the "ego-beak" of Pound and on Williams' not knowing "what a city *is*" occur in his March 8th letter (although the total correspondence makes it clear that he had a good deal more to say about both predecessors). Another passage in that same letter might be taken as leading toward a redefinition of modernism: "that the time has come when, a bunch of men . . . are already disposed, by bias of attention born in them, away from ego but without loss of cutting edge, to themselves & others as, fresh critters going about daily business with some certain differences from the way immediate predecessors have gone about any business, including ART." There is as well the important letter on Rimbaud (March 15th), no doubt omitted from *Mayan Letters* because not germane to the designated subject, and the significant April 1st letter in which Olson explores an alternate humanism (a postmodernism?) that he was to propose with greater elaboration in "Human Universe." Also in April, he goes off to attend his first bullfight with eagerness and writes a poem about it (as a young man he had reviewed Hemingway's *Death in the Afternoon*). In terms of literary output, Olson rewrites his essay "The Gate & The Center" for Cid Corman's *Origin* and revises his bullfight poem, "This," with help from Creeley; while Creeley manages the poem "Helas," later collected in *The Charm*, amid his apparent preoccupations with making a break.

Olson and Creeley continue to "swap principles," as Olson describes their business. The instinctive bond between the two men remains as firm as ever. Olson, for instance, this early on, recognizes that it is "movement" that gives "echo" to his friend, whereas he himself confesses a need, a "weakness" he calls it, for "place" in his life (in his February 18th letter). Neither man is ever a disembodied voice. From this point on, Olson is in full form; Creeley will reach his powers after he is positioned in Europe and the poems begin to flow with seeming regularity. Olson thrives in the tradition of the amateur—like Schliemann of Troy or linguist Benjamin Lee Whorf—following his instincts and curiosities, testing the strata, leaping towards conclusions. He becomes the embodiment of the historian in the Herodotean tradition (as he would recognize a few months later, reading J. A. K. Thomson's *Art of the Logos*), where history is a verb, finding out for oneself. He is able, by a directed gaze of imagination, to shift vast blocks of theory off established foundations. His investigations are an early exercise in what he will call at Black Mountain two years later, the "New Sciences of Man." Having practiced them, he could teach them.

Above all, there is a sense of immediacy, the constant activism, live unrehearsed action, perhaps best exemplified by Olson's February 24th letter in which the breakdown of his typewriter (under the drive of his fingertips) occurs, only to have the thread picked up and continued by pen. The letters when taken together, as much as anything else that Olson ever wrote, display the fullest sense of the man—dynamic, dauntless, incautious, exploitive, and, above all, "hot" for the world around him, as he found the ancient Maya themselves to be. The result, for the reader, is the crackling of a highly contagious energy.

George F. Butterick

Charles Olson & Robert Creeley:
The Complete Correspondence

Volume 5

Notes to the letters begin on p. 189.

tuesday feb 13

robert:

more nits in eden—am just beating back migraine attack, sixth, as I count, in my experience. Came on an hr ago as i was sounding off to Con on this Martinez (who comes *every* evening) and how he seems a clue to what the Maya were (still most obscure, precisely what usage they put life to (((was then speaking of you, and how "nice" yr mind was to put that question mark after "temple," was it Uaxactun (wah-shark-toon))))

i remain unconvinced that these archeologistas (lacking any prime taste) have caught hold of this nigger by his toe propre

My delight at licking this attack so fast is boundless (I have, what my wife with her pretentious medical knowledge says, is one form of migraine, a peculiarly wretched one for one of my drives: suddenly one eye starts a whir very much like a pinwheel, at which point I begin to go blind, and as the sping [sic] increases (it is a black-out by light alone, both eyes starting to spin contrariwise, that is, the light in them starts to spin—something like those worm images that come normally before sleep) the stomach starts a Dean Swift's torture[1]

nothing you can do (for a laugh, the 1st one i ever had was, when, a[g]e 15, working for construction co., barrowing cement out over a plank (over water) filling in a pier, suddenly this crazy biz, and you will imagine, knowing what a wheelbarrow of cement is like to run, trying, with such wild breaking down of sight, to hit that plank! Jesus, was I puzzled!)

Anyhow, this day, so far, it's licked—and a further joke, maybe, forever, the cure: this old woman of mine comes in to see how I am, settled, in this hamacka (was), and, suddenly, the touch of her, and I grab, the blood starts down, and—beatissimo! the fucking whirring leaves off!

Only: was just settling to push off, the two of us, down the road here-abouts to a ruinas (as they call em, hereabts) I uncovered yesterday by a careful map reconnaisance (nobody breathed a word of same—probably, reasons—but it is within walking distance of the house, abt 3 kilometros! name: CHUM–PICH (choom-peach)

Probably screwed (this stomach, aftermath) fr going out in the noon-day sun, hoy. But will report further results.

(Even to find a map in Campeche was practically a day's operation, with my ignorance of their language plus their (the Campechanos) almost total intellectual defunctness:

one reason (MAYBE) for, another time, settling, as Barlow, in Telchac, is, to be near Merida, even tho it is a shit town (trying to be both mexico city & americano). For I am already bitched here by two things: (1) Maya not in much use, Lerma & Campeche being for so long Spanish Colonial plus pirate ground (the pirate danger causing Mayan peoples to lean more heavily on Spanish—guns, thus speech); and ()) not a bookstore excusing name, in Campeche (cam-pich, as was)—fantastic, the vulgarity (tho it has its side: the bookstores (3) are notions, or stationery stores, and, in two of em, it comes out this way: same case, candy & books, with the words written thus, above: DULCES   LI-BROS[2]

I sd, flies, in the honey: Sat. woke with both trunks of this tree covered with red pimples! (Scared pissless, of course! Turned out to be nothing more than, sez the queer doc. (both pharmacist & medico, as most), non pathologica, climata, Senor, climata!

But, counting advances, one was what, as kid, I knew, as CREOLINE (was base disinfectant in states, before barton barton & bullshit.[3] Con, yesterday, while I was in town, dragooned a couple of these kids (who stare in windows, walk in doors, climb over walls, lean out the school windows and yell, in chorus: griing-GO, grrrriiing-GO [added in margin: unbelievable, the underground hate for Americans (all over)—talk abt soft underbelly! Am with them, of course, all the way, only it makes you sore, they don't (the mass) let you extricate yrself fr the antagonism]) such as, and sd, por favor, go get me some petrol (to you, kerosene), which, so far, she had found was best to keep cutting away at this limestone still covering our tiles. Now these kids start talking too fast among themselves, pointing, laughing, confusing the wits out of her who is, as they make clear, cleaning (not, we figure now they meant, lighting lamps or starting carbona fires). Anyhow, off they finally set (confusions confounded between them & Con) with the bottle and 2 pesos (which, they insist, is necessary for what they are going for (Con suspicious, knowing, petrol, here, 20 cents, or, 2¢, a bottle). And come back triumph with "creolina." Which of course turns out to be just what Con needed, making a shine on some of the better tiles, but, above all, licking, as my mother used to, all such SUSIUS,[4] of human droppings as, this particular toilet seat hereinunder

(it stands by itself, no seat cover (as Mexico generally), no pipes but with all the proper american holes, through which holes, of course, when the flush system is pails of salt water carried in to cause detritus to, eventually, take itself down, through chief back hole comes slosh (or did, before CREOLINE!

all of which precisely, like a Frobenius law (as well, the records the little growing mexican-american squirt in the house across the street tosses me out of my hammock with every morning, his radio-victrola combo) declares the date & progress lag of this hyar present day mexico (o lost jar of ointment):

a.e. a.d. p.barton 1920 (1st radio program,
KKWK, or something Pittsburgh, John McCormick [*sic*]
& some movie star, ALL ALONE (by the telephone,
of course—and me with a cats whisker set of
my own making) and (the move star, Grace
Moore or thereabouts) SALL-Y eeeeee[5]

You see, Creeley, you are also right (beside the question mark) to conceive of yrself and family transported direct to Uaxactun, there living, properly, with the iguanas, and the look of that Mayan city, which was, in this moonlight, what we wised-up (as is not the rest of the world, looking in, thru, those shining Vel[6] windows) advantaged AMERICANS know, reasonably guess, was a thing of some
DIGNITY

ONE HOPE: yesterday, going in to have a beer before catching bus back here, I was introduced to one Joaquin Tico del Saz

PILATO AVIADOR (as his card reads), in other words a pilot of chicle planes (the way of transportation just back of this hill which rises along the coast, all the way to Guatemala has he mapped RUINAS—and has offered me his charts!

a hope, i say, my friend, for you & me, that, maybe, one day, some time, ahead, we will be set down, and take up a usage of life, there (yr picture)

temple (?)   Uaxactun

love, for now,

o

Charles

yr letter in yesterday, with
Corman on 18, which, by god,
gives ORIGIN, some little more
hope, yes?

———————————————

[Littleton, N.H.]
Sunday [18 February 1951]

Dear Chas/

Very great to have yr letter, but the migraine biz sounds altogether miserable. Will hope yr done with it; can't stand anything having to do with the eyes—just that having one gone, etc., get very fucking nervous. Hope to christ it's over.

Thinking of yr notes on how it goes there—somewhat shy of the fact, there is that undercurrent. And what the hell else could there be—what I come to. I expect it wd seem, troubles enough without holding up whatever slop the american tourist, &/or: american, had dropped off there. Anyhow, finally shoves you out, if that is the fix. What saved it in either

India or Burma—that fact we were, usually, beyond those edges, where such has got hold. And, more, that some can swallow that biz whole, & still spit it back. Thinking, particularly, of the Sikhs, or like this: was sitting one day, in the back of the ambulance, drinking some rye & close to where I was, was another bunch of ambulances, with Sikh drivers, etc., & one, seeing me drinking, ambles over & stands close to where I'm sitting, etc. After a time, of watching, he starts to smile, then laughs, & says—how does it taste? And, because it was one hell of a hot day, myself soaked with sweat, etc., mouth like fur, etc., I answered: like hell. And he says—wait a minute, & goes off, & comes back with an onion, takes out a real crazy knife, chops off an edge of sd onion, & hands it to me. He tells me to just rub a little on my tongue, which I did, & then, taking some of the rye—too much! I.e., the onion cuts all the shit taste out, & it tastes very damn good. What I miss here, or what, telling it, doesn't come thru—fact of this man's goddamn infinite grace, thruout/ fact he does, all of this, with a fantastic presence. A very weird kind of 'kindness.' Cannot spot for you, as precisely, or at all, as I wd wish: this presence they have. Frankly, there is a goddamned subtlety in them, a grace, that just is goddamn well UNKNOWN in the US, or in any of the western countries. The english, then, at that time: were shy of them, as why not? I mean, one or two times, playing bridge with an old Sikh (him, say, a major) & two english, call them: yng captain & the fatherly colonel, etc. Anyhow, you wd flip, to watch the goddamn play. Sikh: just covers the whole damn table, people, with his fucking BEING/ dominates it all, AND not a damn bit but that FIX IN/ just seems to pull the works, to his center. Punjabis, or others: rough, & childish against the english, or placed against them, how they seem. Not so/ Sikh. Make the continental gentlemen, look like he was stealing apples. Can do more with a gesture, a single word, than usual european with an evening's talk. IF they take to you, i.e., find you pleasant (as it turned out I got along with some)—you feel like you've been pulled into a completeness, something puts a fix on everything around you. That makes balance.

Also, remember hindu, used to tell me these stories, & how it came then: wd get reference, so to call it, from, jesus, 10 centuries, like a fucking piano. I mean/ every damn thing, coming in, trees, sky, birds, earth, man/ all played against a continuum of a fantastic length.

Well, no matter. One thing more: wd keep bumping into 'priests,' or those who had begun the yr of going from place to place, making a worship, & supported by whatever they were given. They wd be dressed in a deep fine orange cloth, cape-like, well, the longi. And with them, usually, one disciple, who cooked, etc. Foraged. The man himself: you'd find way the hell from nowhere, sitting in a hut of sorts, just damn well: thinking! Machine-gun fire, sometimes, fifty yards away, & this man: not a fucking sign.

I don't know. The feel of them, from them: shaking to one from this country. Going into these giant pagodas/ with little low tunnels, & all the noise, sound, of hundreds of people, & these little booths, cut out, into, the sides, people yelling & squatting, & kids, dozens, running around, playing. And only light of these lamps, oil, or something, and at the center, these Buddhas, going way the hell up, some 150 ft., static, with all this fucking movement around them, at their feet.

                                                                    The
greatest thing happened to me. One night, in Hyderabad. I was walking thru the side-streets of the town by myself, abt 10 at night, and the place is pitch-black. No one around, but a few in doorways. Call out, as you go by, etc. Kids, now & again, shooting out of doorways. Am walking along so, when I turn on, abruptly, to another street, & looking down, catch this look of a glow, coming toward me, & with it, the weirdest damn drums, you ever heard/ & now & again: off-sounds, of some kind of horn. But this very damn wonderful beat, looping, of the drums, & as it had been: pitch-black, & only this glow, way off, and coming, with these sounds. I was standing, waiting, and it comes closer, until finally, see it is a procession, & at that same moment, catch this deep full smell of flowers, hundreds & hundreds of goddamn flowers!! And, then, the whole thing breaks out, down, on me, and am caught, literally, and dragged along, for abt 2 blocks, in this crazy parade, lights, and this music, & the goofiest SOUNDS you ever heard. See toward the back, the drummers, loping along, these things caught to their waists, which they slap at, with little sticks, off-beat, and the low yelling of them, & the lights, all flaring, shadows fucking well dancing, faces, long, on the goddamn walls around us. And COLOR. The end. And so, pulled, those

two blocks, am pressed back, off, and the damn truth, in a second, it was not a goddamn inch longer, GONE. Not a trace.

I think, because I don't know, it was a funeral procession, but then, in the fucking whirl of the thing, cd only tear out, the sounds, the color, & the movement, the rush of the thing, breaking in on that goddamn absolute darkness, in the middle of that damn strange place.

Well, wonder, etc.

What I had started off to say, was that, reading what we just got, The Telegraph, New Directions, etc., come on this in the appendix, which is too much:

"I write out the plan after having written the story . . . to make the plan first freezes me, because after that, memory is the active agent instead of the heart."[7]

Fuck YOU, EZRA POUND.

Every damn time, I think of that biz in MAKE IT NEW, on James, i.e., LISTEN:

(he's just given the nauseous biz of James' 'outline' (A spits at B; B spits at A; C comes in and spits at both, etc., etc., etc.))

"Here in a few paragraphs are the bare bones of the plan described in eighty of Henry James' pages. The detailed thoroughness of this plan, the complicated consciousness displayed in it, gives us the measure of this author's superiority as conscious artist, over the 'normal' British novelist, i.e., over the sort of person who tells you that when he did his first book he 'just sat down and wrote the first paragraph,' and then found he 'couldn't stop' . . . I give this outline with such fullness because it is a landmark in the history of the novel as written in English. It is inconceivable that Fielding or Richardson should have left, or that Thomas Hardy should leave, such testimony to a comprehension of the novel as a 'form' . . ."[8]

Somehow, that damn well turns my stomach. The biggest, the most blind example of idiocy, in all of Ezra Pound—(who ever practised, in this case, what he preached??? Bullshit!)

He damn well MISSES the point, does NOT know what FORM IS IN THE NOVEL.

Well, to hell with it. But damn well believe, Pound never knew a god-damn THING abt prose, not one goddamn miserable THING.

(He 'knew' . . . good writing, etc., etc., etc. He did NOT know good prose.)

Sd he, IN this same article: "Most good prose arises, perhaps, from an instinct of negation; is the detailed, convincing analysis of something detestable. . . Neither prose nor drama can attain poetic intensity save by construction. . ."⁹ Up yr ass/ Mister Pound.

Abt it/ i.e., not much moving. But one thing, somewhat of a curiosity. Emerson wrote, asking me to do a tape for him, i.e., he'll send on the tape, & I, I expect, will trot over to the local station, to use their recording equipment. Ann laughs; which is finally, the point. I can't figure him.

Also, you may be hearing from Gordon Ringer, one who was in on the mag this past summer. Found via Pound, but not of a kind with Simpson, Cole, Horton, etc. Simply, some thought of his own. There may be some chance of a magazine starting out there, & that, I figure, wd be his reason for writing.

Cid has his hands full, I take it, trying to settle on a way to print. He gets a good response to the call for loot, i.e., had abt something over $500 the last letter. But here's the headache. He can print it, with print, for $650; and he can have it done, off-set, for something over $300. Now, obvi-ous, that the cheaper wd probably make it pay for itself; tho I have some doubts as to how it wd sell, so printed. The other is a pure gamble, but you have, finally, something to be looking at. I'm not for the fancy, certainly, but damn well do like a clean-looking page. And figure back-ing, or sales, will relate to just that. There's this hope—that once in France, I cd do something abt getting it printed there; not altogether dreaming, etc. I don't know, there being, certainly, no good argument against Cid's figuring, but that off-set, won't have the cleanness. Against that, or nothing: I figure he makes his point. Will see what he decides. Have written him two letters exactly on this head, so at least keep my oar in, etc.

A hell of a mess, getting out of here. Ann found all her papers were lost, i.e., she's both orphan & immigrant, before the law, & so all that to get copies of, etc. But somehow. Also, biz of settling on the house, a damn mess. But somehow, etc.

We booked passage for April 3rd, to arrive, the 10th, somewhere there. I figure a day's travel, will get us to Puyricard. I can't say I give a shit at this point.

Hell of a mess.

So, abt it. Write soon, & cheer us up! Begin to believe altogether, EITHER we wd set down, precise, at such a place as that in Uaxactun/ or: nothing. For what? The edges. No damn good, & if we were stuck, as we wd be, just there. . . slow death. Was thinking of Dave, for one, & that hate of americans. Wd not be very great.

Ok. And let me hear as soon as you can get to it. Will write if anything breaks, likewise.

> All love to you both/
>
> Bob

saturday   feb 18 (is it?)   lerma, campeche, mexico

my dear r. cr.:

>   birds, lad: my god what birds. Last evening a thing like our hawk. And that woman of mine (again) most alert to their

nature. It happened this way. I was down the beach bargaining to buy a piece of their best fish here, what sounds like madrigal, only it comes out smedreegal. [10] I had my back turned no more than three minutes, when, turning, to come back to the house (Con was on the terraza out over the sea, surrounded by a dozen of these gabbling kids), below her, on the water line, I noticed these huge wings fluttering wrong. My guess was, one of the kids, all of whom carry sling-shots, had brought down a zopalote (our vulture, "brother v," as Con named them). But when I came near, I noticed, just as Con cried down, that it was no vulture but another bird which is quite beautiful here, in Maya a chii-mi (chee-me): flies in flock over the water-line, soaring like hawks, high, and is marked by a long split tail ((by god, i was right: just checked dictionary, and is, as I thought, our frigate bird)) [11]

there it was, poor chii-mi stoned by one of these little bastards, and the others, throwing more stones at it, and a couple, kicking it. And it working those three foot wings, hard, but not wild: very sure of itself, tho downed. By the time I came up, it had managed to get itself over, and was already out into the water, to get away from the kids. But each wave was wetting it down, and the misery was, that it drown.

My assumption was, the stone had broken its wing. But Con had seen it happen, and seems to have known it was only its head that had been struck (it was out cold, she told me later, for a minute or so, and then, on its back, had disgorged its last fish). Anyhow, she had the brains to send down one of the older boys to bring it out of the water, and up on the terraza. And when I came up, there it was, quiet, looking hard at everyone, with its gular pouch swollen like my Aunt Vandla's goiter, [12] and its eye, not at all as a bird's is, when it is scared, or as, so quickly, they weaken, and that film drops over the eye. Not at all: this chii-mi was more like an animal, in its strength. Yet I still thought it was done for, something in the wings gone.

Just about then it started to work its way forward, pulling its wings in to its body, and making it look so much more like, say, a duck. What it had in mind, was to try to lift itself the two feet up to the wall that goes round the terraza. But it could not. It had worked itself into the inner angle of a corner. So I reached down and raised the right wing up to the top of the wall. Then the left. And, itself, it pulled its body up, perched for an instant, and swung off, off and up, into the sky, god help us, up and out over the sea, higher and higher, and, not like the others but working its wings in shorter, quicker strokes, it pulled off and off, out over the shrimp ship moored out in the deeper water, inside the bar, from which it swung inland again, and, as I watched it a good five minutes, kept turning more and more to the west, into the sun, until that peculiar movement of the wings began to give way to the more usual flight of a chii-mi. And I figure, as it disappeared, it was all right, all right.

God, it was wonderful, black, wonderful long feathers, and the wing spread, overall, what, five to six feet. Never got such a sense of a bird's strength, inside strength, as this one gave, like I say, more animal, seemingly, and sure, none of that small beating heart. That's why its victory, over these mean little pricks, was so fine.

(Its silhouette, anyway, above us each day, is a lovely thing, the fore part of the wing not a curve as in the gull, but angled, like a bat's a third out from the body. And this strange double tail splitting in flight like the steepest sort of an arrow.

How come "chii-mi" I can't yet tell you, though, last night, in my Dictionario Motul, which arrived yesterday from Merida and gives me a fair start in to the ride of this Maya tongue, I was able to locate "chii," as "margin" of the sea, a page, a dress, etcetera.[13] "Mi" I still can't find in the proliferation of double consonants, double vowels, and five extra letters beyond Western alphabets (I dare say if I had Tozzer's Maya-English dictionary[14] (the only one, I now learn), I'd be better off. To try to find anything through the screen of one unknown language to another! (this D. Motul is the base work, Maya-Espanol, done here in the Yucatan mid-16th Century, and not equaled since. My edition is by the one Mexican scholar whom I have yet had occasion to raise respect for, an 82 yr old citizen in Merida named Juan Martinez Hernandez.)

((You will imagine what excitement that was, to get the book yesterday, Creeley. Wish me, please, the power & constancy to do more than riffle its pages: i feel so hung & halved, confronted with the necesity to use Spanish when my whole urge is to cut straight fr English to Maya.

But I've been happier, by an act of circumvention, the last three days: I have been in the field, away from people, working around stones in the sun, putting my hands in to the dust and fragments and pieces of those Maya who used to live here down and along this road.

And the joy is, the whole area, within the easiest walking distances, is covered with their leavings: I already have in front of me as I write to you the upper half of an owl idol's (?) head, which I picked up on a farm five minutes from the house! And two half plates, among other fragments of pots, quite fine in the working of the clay, though the painting is average.

The big thing, tho, is the solidity of the sense of their lives one can get right here in the fields and on the hill which rises quite steeply from the shore. Thursday afternoon Con and I went back in, say, five miles, and ran into something which would take the top off yr head: on the highest hill, looking out over a savannah which runs straight and flat to the sea here, a sort of farm moor (it was maize once, but, due to the way of Mayan agriculture, grass defeated corn inside of seven years, and from then on, the grass is so durable, neither forest nor corn can come again), on that hill where the sea's winds reach, where the overlook is so fine, these Maya had once built what appears to have been a little city. I say appears, for now, after six years of the Sanchez Construction Co. crushing the stones of that city, we were able to see only one piece of one column of what (the Indian workers told us) was once, six years ago, many many such columns *in place*. My god what a whitened dump that hill top is: all gone, everything! ((The whole experience was like the deserts we found in and around Sacramento, where the Gold Cos. had, with their huge water shitting machines, spoiled the earth (in this case not men's work, but nature's soil accumulation, for ever, mind you, forever: they turn the top soil down under, and pile on top of it, as their crawling machine goes along, all the crunched gravel and stone their water-test has proven not to contain gold, or the dust, of gold)[15]

Crazy, "stupido," as the Indians at least, know it to be: it angers me two ways (1) that, the rubble beneath the facings, columns, worked facades, etc is the bulk of the stone, and there is no reason except laziness, that the worked things, so small a part of the whole, should not have been set aside; and (2) that this is the laziness, not of Sanchez & Co., which one has to grant its stupidity, but is the stupidity & laziness of the archeologists, both American & Mexican, which is that most culpable of all, intellectual carelessness.

I had the feeling, already in Merida, that the Peabody-Carnegie gang, whatever they may have done, 50, or 25 years ago, were, now, missing the job, were typical pedants or academics, and were playing some state & low professional game. Like this: that, at this date, it was no longer so important to uncover buried cities and restore same, as it was to strike in anew by two paths: (1), what I have already sounded off to you about, the living Maya language and what its perdurables, because language is, so tough, may well contain in the heads of these living farmers back one block from this street, or wherever, the deeper in, I imagine, the more

and (2), in the present context the important one (or did I also beat the drum of this to you?): a total reconnaisance of *all* sites (laugh, as they did at me in Merida, the "experts") instead of (as the Carnegie-Mexican Govt is about to launch) the recovery of the 3rd of the Maya Metropolises here in the peninsula, Mayapan.

The joker is, they are "advanced" enough to justify the Mayapan operation as a step to discover more abt the economic & political life of the ancient Maya! Which, of course, kills me. Here I am an aestheticist (or so I figure we might distinguish ourselves, yes?) (which I have yet to be convinced *any* one of them, from Stephens[16] on down, is). And now, when they, these professionals, are catching on (EP's 35 yr lag,[17] surely), to the validity of the total life of a people as what cargo art discharges, I am the one who is arguing that the correct way to come to an estimate of that dense & total thing is not, again, to measure the walls of a huge city but to get down, before it is too late, on a flat thing called a map, as complete a survey as possible of all, all present ruins, small as most of them are.

They'll cry, these fat & supported characters: "Oh, they are all over the place, these, ruins!" Which is quite, quite the big & astounding fact—so much so are they all over the place that Sanchez & Co, Campeche, Mex., is not the only sand & gravel company in business: already, in this walking area from this house, I have come to learn of four sites—and of some size more than "small"—which have been already reduced to white cement in bags! (That it has taken Sanchez six years of daily grinding at the site—no where, by the way, listed as a site—the natives here in Lerma call it *Casa Vieja*—to take only the face off the city, may be a gauge of ((what I had no way of knowing, in Merida)) is the extent of these ignored, or smiled at, spots where, 1500 years ago, for, o, say, 500 years, a people went about human business.

Robert, excuse me that I argue this out with you. But I am sharpening arms. I am not yet, of course, able to argue anything: I have only shots, no gun. You will, of course, see, how it bears in on our sort of interests, the vulgarization of culture, surely. Already I have figured out how easily this whole operation (what I have called a total reconnaissance) might be accomplished. But I need (1) Spanish; (2) the beginnings of a mastery of Maya; and (3) friends. I figure I'll keep at (1) and (2) here, at the same time putting this body of mine back in use ((already I am leaner, able to take days in this bitch of a sun; and my chest throwing off the incredible white dust all the ruins throw up—

this part of it delights me: it must seem funny to you to see the accent I put on this, but for seven—ten years, actually, I have let my system go (and you gather the incongruity of nature, in making a man of my size, an ass-worker!)

I swear, Rob't, if I could, fast, fill-in some ignorance on this particular front, of, what shall I call it, archeology plus, I'd take a flyer at raising some support for myself, some stake to enable me to do more than an alert tourist job here and in Guatemala, Honduras. Mexico. Nor—given my bases of verse—do I think such a demarche would be anything else than straight ahead.

But I'm dreaming. Where the hell would I turn, I've exhausted the Guggenheim. And the rest of the troughs are closed to me because of my abhorrence of modern academicism.

The whole trouble, again, is money. It goes fast, even here. I am already in to the money for our return! Not that that matters: I figure I can bum our way north fr Mexico City (drive some dame home, or something). Aw, shit, to hell with these notions. . . the thing is, get what I can, here, for a few weeks (these sites already have lifted the place into activity, and tomorrow we go by bus down the coast further, to a site sd to be still standing. . . Jesus, if I had a jeep! or could ride a horse, even. . . . stymied: the prick who is director of the Campeche Museum (a fine museum, by the way), has himself a beaut of a jeep, which sits all day in the street while he lets Sanchez & other cos take right out under his chair what other men, later, will wish he had the guts & brains to have kept. . . (fucking Mexican politics: which is no worse or better than any other, only, they work only five hrs a day, so the margin of good to be squeezed out, is that much smaller!)

oy, weh

And all this time I have been working, in the mind, over you, and your plans for movement—your two fullsome letters awaited us yesterday on our return with my owl's head, and pots: they were read, on the terraza, with, I swear, 30 kids looking on, in amazement, that one man, Robert Creeley, could write so many pages! Exclamations, as I held the pages, in the Gulf's wind! (It was a strange & nice sort of extra wonder you were offered, my friend!)

Con tends to agree, this place no spot for you, Ann & the kids in your present situation & need (sez she, last night: "You remember that friend of yrs who sd, the only trouble with the world is, that, the Americans—if they had only stopped with their improvements on plumbing? Well, here, we are at that stage *before* the Americans made their major advance!")

I don't know, Rob't, abt these things, kids, and what they can take, where there are the best amahs so that Ann could get a relief (why not Burma?), how many diapers make a pile. Certainly I know there is no grass in Mexico, that is, grass, as you mean it, for Thomas (funniest damn thing is, this, that there is no grass in Mexico!).

My only thot in this whole business is, (1), I wish to christ we might get together somewhere, if you are off for year or years, to places I don't see how I shall get to unless some patron turns his fortune over to me; and (2), concern, that you get what you want (which, as I read, seems to be North Africa, Iran, Burma, any outlandish place!)

(As Con also sd,
"France, my god, doesn't its civilized character sound luscious from
here—cream, blue trout, soups ((no soups of any taste in Yucatan—they
lash everything down with a pork fat you wouldn't shake a tongue at)),
ya, ya) ((yet do, Rob't, ask yrself, can't you find a place which is not a
way-station but such plus location?

Aw shit. It doesn't matter. I have
such confidence in yr accuracies, that, in fact, place is not of so much
importance to you, that it is movement that gives you back echo, that
any decision you make is right. ((Truth is, I am biassed, myself, out of
the weakness for place in me, against any place, these days, which is a
part of the withdrawing culture. Which is my cliche, and does not bear, I
feel, on you & your work.

((IDEA! Why the hell, if you want move-
ment: look! My whole impulse (Con's too), was not to leave that ship.
To keep going, with such stops as Vera Cruz. Even now, if I don't get off
to some new site each day, I begin to drop, lose impetus. IDEA: why not
carefully pick some cargo line (nothing better than that French Compag-
nie Maritime or whatever it was Joe Wehsberg[18] used to play on) which
wld give you & family movement around the whole world?

((Crazy,
Olson, crazy))

I see what I'm doing! I'm trying to get you to make a stop here in the
Gulf so that we can meet, and spend some days together at least!

But seriously: you might inquire (I will, too) into something I ran into
some time ago, and that my friend Riboud confirmed (K. A. Porter
wrote a novel which issued fr this very same fluke)[19]

That's this: that
the French ships sailing fr Vera Cruz for France are way cheaper than fr
NY to France (enough so, my impression was, to make the difference
plus).

When we pulled into V/C there, berthed beside us, was THE
SIEUR DE LA SALLE! One hell of a big boat. And the first thing I did in
V/C was to watch three passengers come down the cross-section of her
main house (abt five decks!), and go ashore (she had pulled in just ahead
of us, and the passengers were most interesting, out of our port-hole: a

couple, he in a black hat, looking very much like a French Jewish composer, his wife much younger, speaking Spanish and thus taking care of
custom men and porters ((much baggage((; the other was a bachelor,
sort of English, intellectual, dull.

If I'd thot, then, might have asked. Or
if Riboud was in NY instead of India, also (by the way the Ribouds left
for India with their seven months old baby, January. And had taken him
to France last summer at three months. But of course, he's French, and
she's a Tagore. So. Besides, they have dough.)

Well, keep us informed. Wish you might come here en route, anyhow.
Con says, "I can spare Ann, with the kids (while you and Creeley pack
into the back country," sez she, and meant it!) But I dare say you are all
more right than I abt this place, for any length of time (I am convinced of
one thing, anyway—that it must be no place, no place at all, for the five
months of the summer: not so much the rain, as the sun. And that's
already started, end of May, beginning of June, they tell me.

More that
than, for you, after three years, as you say, among people who are
forced to rise only against the minimums, the greater minimums here
would be killing, I fear. Even for me, with my special appetite after 22
yrs in the Pen, it is damn hard, the poverty, the lack of alacrity, the
pitiful cultural inertia ((to look in the face of even this owl, worked in
stucco, and to see the insides of even the wealthier Campechanos houses,
marks what a degradation the Spanish, the Catholics, and now the
Americans have brought))

Well, I'm done, for today. Enjoy so much being again in communication
with you. Keep writing, please. Let me have all news of our various
affairs. And of yr plans, yours and the family (I'll see what I can find out
about those French boats).

And do hold, yet, on the Guggenheim: the
fact that they have asked for further stuff is this sign: that you are over
the hump of the first eliminations, that you are going to be sat down to
in early March when the Committee meets with Moe in NY. Jesus,
wdn't it be wonderful! If, by any chance, Gerhardt's #2 comes in, with
yr things, before March 15 or so, ship it pronto to Moe (in any case, you

have proved what the application promised, and that's all to the very good).

This for today. And to end, on the birds, last night, after the chii-mi, a few minutes, when I did succeed in getting some medrigal fr another fisherman, overhead, suddenly, there was the handsomest flight I have ever seen of fowl going north, in that wondrous waving formation, v in v out. And all of the wings beating slow and alike: what they were I don't know. Looked like geese to me, too large for ducks and the wing movement too slow. The natives sd, one, ponto, the others, pelicano. But surely not pelicans. And what ponto are, I can't find out.[20] But sweet, sweet, against a half moon.

Love,
Charles

[monday feb 19 51 lerma]

with a rice bowl full of the cheap rum here (35¢, by god, the qt), the kerosene lamp (my barn & hayrack), and yr fine wonderful sending long letter (of last tuesday: still, the mails, too fucking slow, but, what matter), I to YOU, CREELEY, such greetings—christ, if my letter rode you, think, LAD, to me, here, coming in, slow, long off the beat, slugged from the body taking (like I wrote last) back, its power, I think, what all you say increaseth :

to start: (noting what you have noted that, the last two nights, the
            moon is coming to full) pick me up, thus—

by jeezus if he didn't, having talked to me as much as no common language permits—which is a very great deal, given such a subject as, what a handsome night it was, all these houses, and the rocks below this white terraza. And the fucking night spreading itself like a peee-cock, the birdless night, not a sound but dogs, and the beginning of cocks, and the last of men along the hill back off a bit. I, lying, like Cleo or some olden knichte in stone, on the stone bed the wall of the terraza makes, the head of the stair my fine pillow. Having just thought, that fine white cayucos, would make me a fine bed for the night, its sails, for some reason, still in it, the masts, of course, shipped.

by jeezus if he didn't, having sd, bueno noche, I, bonito, he, la luna, I, magnifico, he, presto—why, I still don't know, whether, he was whistling so, and came fr the direction of the cantina, down on to the beach

anyhow, with, hasta manana, if he doesn't walk straight out into the water to that magical boat, swing himself aboard, take up his bow line, haul himself off, by the stern line, a few twenty feet (enough to take care of the fall of the tide), heave off a heavier grab-iron, start moving around fixing the sails to his liking, light himself a cigarette, and lie right down there to sleep!

jee-zus—. o, creeley, it's handsome. I am like a kid. Tonight, swear, I never saw Venus lay down a path of light on water. She does. Has set, now. Stars: please make me a map of the handsomer constellations (I know Orion, the two dippers (stupid names). But what is that string of seven, or is [it] eight, which run down the sky to the west of Castor & Pollux? ((All I see is the movement of the west sky, we front the west so decisively. And the house blocks off, the other half. But enough, what is, to make me wild, wild (not like beautiful Lawrence, I don't mean, who, fr the full of the moon, is sd, to have got like the throat of his fringed gentians)[21] but wild as I am which is not wild but cool, real cool

God, give me a little more of this and I shall excuse what you say abt me, another time, my friend. For you have sd something so beautifully tonight (yr letter), in this business of force: it is (you see, I am still harping on this problem of mine, reference: constellations, Venus included (which, here, I will show can be called KuKulCan—abandoned such, as part of THE K's and THE PRAISES, discovering, this man's death, April 5, 1208 AD, who "rose" with Venus, 8 days later, was sufficient unto itself, so far as I was concerned) what you sd: that, force

STAYS, IS & THEREFORE STAYS, whenever, whatever:

that is what

is what we are concerned with

It breaks all time, & space.

muy bueno,

muy

[*in pencil:*] BONITO

━━━━━━━━━━━━━━━━━━━━━━━━━━━━━━━━━━

[Lerma, Campeche
20 February 1951]

tues.   (carlos, the letter carrier, abt due / sort of the village idiot, i take
it: walks like no fisherman, smiles like a gringo, and is altogether not native, is, "allegre," slap-happy, and of whom i am
most fond: yesterday, bringing yr letter, he holds out two us air
mail sts (enclosed)! I say, how come, and, as I understood, he
had noticed, that, they had not been cancelled. So he had carefully removed them from the envelopes, and brought them to
me! So here they are, for you.

You will imagine, knowing my
bias toward just such close use of things, how much all these
people make sense to me (coca-cola tops are the boys' tiddle-
winks; the valves of bicycle tubes, are toy guns; bottles are used
and re-used, even sold, as cans are; old tires are the base foot-
wear of this whole peninsula (the modern Maya sandal is, rope
plus Goodyear); light is candle or kersone [kerosene], and one
light to a house, even when it is a foco,[23] for electridad

and last night, at the store, for a beer, after they had closed, got
into one of those conversations one does, with storekeepers,

when they are sloping off: the wife was pinching off 8 pepper-corns per packet of newspaper (5 centavos)/ the page was open to a television ad (Mexico City)/ they both ask me/ I say MALO, MAS MALO QUE RADIO/ but then, sez the husband, the straight and surest question imaginable (Newsreel Companies please note, as well as the Dept of Disappearing Culture)— POSSIBLE TO SEE LA GUERRA?

by god, that kills me: Con tells me a kid on the beach went straight to the same, 1st question, too: possi-ble, to see, la GUERRA?

look, Rob't: allow me to let this sit, as what it is, a silly note, just to send you the fullest sort of greetings most loll-y today no push the sea outside/too much am a soup-head: on top of that the time has come to make final copy of GATE & CENTER, for le cid

i shall return same to, as close a version, as your original one: you make yr point completely, with me—my god, how i dropped the air, of that one! o o

love to you all, Robert, Ann,
David and Thomas Creeley

fr

Olsons

[*Added in pencil:*] but hold! one thing: know what I possessed myself of Sunday (at ruins, Cayal)? a fragment of stone, with the feathers, the feathered, headdress, the dominant image (the quetzal, as well as HE, KKC, or any redskin, N or S): dates, say (these parts, generally) 500-850, say, AD And *good,* besides. Also, a section of column. So now: 3 pieces of stone—these two, & the OWL gryphon or gargoyle I must have told you I picked up, 5 mins., fr the house (KID STUFF, like, I sd!)

[Lerma, Campeche
24 February 1951]

Rob't:

Yr letter yesterday (announcing yr departure April 3) either coincided or was a part of cause, of a bitter day & night. (Or was it the complete discouragement of the news (fr you & him) that ORIGIN 1 was to be in varitype (I won't bother to repeat my abhorrence—which I shot to him, as well as what might just turn out to be a save, turning loose for Corman one of the sharpest guys I know around Boston in such matters, Paul Williams,[24] in hopes he can aid Corman to find printer, type, and economies: you'd guess, anyhow, what varitype seems to me—and the use of it a giving-in to the very forces. . .) ((Or was it merely that bitterness, which comes, like "mother," in any solution?))

Anyhow, the news that you will be gone, to Europe, is such a cutting-off I can't, at the first of it, ride up: shall miss you, mightily. But there it is. And that it is a move, like you say, and what you want, of course, that, like you say, pleasures me, that you are. (I am an absolute fool, anyhow, about time: have never have any caliper in me to recognize how little is possible, how fast it disappears, how short it will be you are away, say. Was moved, the other night, to hear Con characterize a man here, as not seeming to have any sense of time, as taking it, he wld live forever. I suffer all the time from this fatal flaw in myself. Thus know no "realism." Or something. Shit; let it go: it's only the hangover from my chagrin, of yesterday. Got a little rid of it anyway, by way of an instant of Buster Keaton's gift: we saw last Sunday that a movie of his, El Moderno Barba Azul,[25] was to be shown last night. Figured it was an old one, fr the States. But not at all, a recent *Mexican* movie, with him speaking Spanish, no sub-titles. Not much, but a couple of moments, the one, of all, himself, alone, on a nag, going off, wonderfully slow, from one of these Mexican plazas: beautiful, the dignity of him, the horse, & time!

(/dash, here!)

(((Or was it the arrival, in the same mail yesterday, of Gerhardt's last
    letter, forwarded fr Washington, actually only a note enclosing the
    translation of the Praises, and a carbon of the Brief to you & me. For I

sat down in my own fucking shit & ashes, that, I don't even have
German (as you'd guess, my prison in American speech, & its
habits—and huge resistance to heave myself out of it—almost, nerv-
ousness, after all these years—is fucking intensified hereabouts.))

So, with the gripes dumped in yr lap, lad, let me forget it, and go ahead
to other things. (A sort of a shit week anyhow, picking up such literary
affairs as connecting back to Emerson to, somehow, manage, to wean the
bastard until he gets out THE PRAISES. And sloping up to the rewrite of
Gate & Center, by way of Corman. And general discouragement, I have
not been making anything new: this rear that work has, to publication, I
do not know how, ever, to remove. It is the dirtiest and most defeating
act of verse as business. Also in, this week, the news from Gallimard,
that they will definitely go ahead, that the translator is Max Beerblock[26]
(?), but that he can't possibly finish the translation until June (jesus, it
didn't take me that long to write the fucking thing), and, so, publication
will not come until, probably, October (which just abt finishes the deal,
the way I figure war, or at least the retrenchments preceding it, and their
effects in France.

You see, I am considerably off any hope!

But to forward things. Have moved ahead some on what I suppose I am
here for. And one badly damaged fresco at Chichen is a good part of
cause, joined to what I have been able to figure, from the number of
ruins here right back of me, & Martinez, my good fisherman who becomes the live object to spark it all. Figure—just to keep cutting in—to
go along on this notion: that none of the characters have spotted two
things (rather, they have suppressed one, and been blinded, by maize, to
the other):

(1) that the sea, precisely the FISH, was of first imaginative importance
    to the Maya (as well, of course, crucial to his food economy: I just
    might add a correlative to Sauer's beautiful shot, about maize[27]—he
    made clear to the boys that the very place where starch crops can be
    domesticated (moderate plateaus), where maize was (the inland
    slopes of the cordillera, Guatemala) cuts the people off from the most
    abundant source of protein and fat there is, the sea, that the earliest
    American farmers were just so cut off

based on Lerma, plus some
pots I have been looking over from the island of Jaina up the coast a
distance, here, plus the paintings at Chichen, I take it, I could, if I
wanted to, demonstrate, that the movement into the Yucatan peninsula might just have been a push for protein & fats (contradicting the
mystery abt same that all of these half-heads of great name keep
pushing along to perpetuate their profession)

the real proof may turn out to be one of those lovely curves of live
human connections. I must have sketched this bird Stromsvik,
whom Con and I got drunk with, in Merida? Well, in the midst of
his beer, Gus says, in Campeche, one guy, Hippolito Sanchez. The
1st day we walk into the museum here, we pick up, and take for a
beer, this Sanchez (who is worrying a white puppy, with a red
ribbon, that he was due to take to his girl friend, which taking I
delayed a good hour, which lad Sanchez, proving himself, did the
delay well by (how many you know who can take that kind of
pressing, eh?). So this week, I saw, why, Gus, had, what had caused
Gus to say, Sanchez (in fact the very same stuff which had led Gus to
get this kid assigned to go to Bonampak to aid the "artists" sent
there to take off copies of those newest discovered of all Mayan
frescoes): huge drawings, hundreds of them, of the GLYPHS on the
stairway of the major pyramid at Copan (Honduras)

my god, Rob't, those you must see, some day: I am already taking
steps to see if there is not some way to get them published. It is the
only time I have found the drawings of glyphs to begin to touch the
registration of the stone itself (and let me tell you the stones themselves are one hell of a job to see)

this boy has the hand, eye, heart, to get them over. And by god, if
right spang in the middle of looking over his pages do I see the most
certain demonstration of the power of the fish over these peoples
that I have yet oc
          [Written in ink:] God damn son of a bitch, if
the "f" in this machine didn't just go & bust—fuck it. Will have to
go Campeche, & hope to christ a fix possible

Well, to hell with fish—I obviously can't say much more abt them, today, without the "f" on this -ucking machine

One other thing, tho, while it's in my head, that I wanted to say to you:

don't let even Lawrence fool you (there is nothing in this Mexican deal, so far as "time in the sun"[27a] goes: the way I figure it, it must have seemed attractive at a time when the discouragement, that the machine world goes on forever, was at its height

but this is a culture in arrestment, which is no culture at all (to this moment, only Sanchez (& his function is, despite, secondary, gives a hint of live taste)

when I say that, however, I give these people much more head, than their recent slobberers

for the arrestment, surely, was due to the stunning (by the Spanish) of the Indian, 400 yrs ago ((the Indian has had the toughest culture colonialism to buck of anyone, much tougher than that which Parkman & Melville beat, 100 yrs ago, up thar

culture is confidence, & surely, Mao makes Mexico certain, ahead (Communism, here, by the way, is solid, but is, as not in the States, nor, so far as I have been able to judge, in Russia or Europe either, is a *cultural* revolution, or at least the weapon of same, the only one the Indian (like the Chinese?) has been able to get his hands on (this whole Peninsula—where Cardenas[28] got his familiar name: "The Old Man," in Mayan—is a muzzle rammed for firing)

The point is, the arrestment, is deceptive: it is not what fancy out-siders have seen it as, seeking, as they were, I guess, some alterna-tive for themselves (like DHL & his Ladybird).[29] Of course, now, it is easier to kiss off the States, than, even the 30's. Yet, they should not have misled us (which is the same as harming these Injuns: they have so fucking much future, & no present, no present at all. (Christ, it makes me burn: their inactivity ain't at all beautiful. They are fucking unhappy. What graces they have are traces only, of what was & of what, I'd guess, can be (to be a colored people today is something! yah?

      But the Negro in the States is way ahead of these 400 yr slept people! Honest! Sounds crazy? Hell, straight: yr Hyderabad drums, for ex: jesus, the only thing you hear here, any place, when they make music (which is little) is the *drum*. But stacked up against [the Negro *crossed out*] Baby Dodds[30] or who-ever, pigeon shit—*or, what is most important*, stacked abt [*i.e.* up] against these old Mayan drums I've worked out on—five, so far, cut out of trees—you wld hear them, lad, hear 'em

           And the sounds they put into the feet & bottoms of their *pots*, those people, to make noises, when you placed them, or moved them, on the *table*! . . .

Point (2), above, was VIOLENCE—killing, the heart, out, etc: those sons of bitches, those "scholars"—how they've cut that story out, to make the Mayan palatable to their fucking selves, foundations, & tourists!

                 [Littleton, N.H.]
             Thursday [1 March 1951]

Dear Chas/

      Good, but goddamn well sad, also : to have yr letter. Meaning, I feel the same goddamn way—as tho I were moving, call it, away from whatever I gave a damn abt. But can, or wd try, to figure it as, a usual distance; hence, have made it before. And cd continue to.

I wanted to note: that Slater, this summer, had told us of this—he took a set of the little pictures of the Quetzacoatl (what he had from the divers texts he'd got hold of) to a man he knew, a naturalist (who did, a point, not know of any of this, nor saw, as it happened, anything more than these "pictures"), & said: what is it? And this man answers, straight off:

SEA HORSE. Well, the thing, or what Slater sd: he had traced, or noted, several re-occurring details in ALL of the drawings he had seen, & it was, precisely, these details, which the man, in explanation, used to make his point—that is, he sd, sure, stylized, etc., but these details make it clear enough, whoever drew these things, was working from the base figure: sea horse.

         Now, certain enough, I don't know a damn thing more. Slater had sd: was sure enough, that no one else had figured this god, as related to the sea. I.e., I had remembered that Lawrence relates the tradition, concerning him, to a lake,[31] & I had lazily supposed, this was it, i.e., figuring 'lake,' you can let it rest—being, that no major thing cd be very deeply hung in on the lake, what cd be figured by means of, it, itself.

         BUT: as SEA/ as you say/ as this now makes it? Have to start over. Because wd be so, because of some convenience of form? I.e., we saw him on the beach, this form, so used him? I couldn't believe it. Or not so simply; & more—being such, of the sea, so in the hierarchy: makes it stronger, all round, this SEA biz?

         Tell me what you think. (I don't myself figure Slater to be off, on this; i.e., he is a very careful man. Not, then, like man he wrote me of—who, devising alphabet for Mayan language (which did not exist as such, etc.) he proceeded to translate this "book," to find, after, not only his error on the alphabet biz, but that had such existed, he, nonetheless, had translated the book backwards.)

At least/ a wreath? For Slater & yrself?

Well, what's up/ —just that we still plod thru goddamn details on trying to get out of here. Endless fucking shit, & can't say that we move fast, or at all. Have placed a few of the animals, in fact, most of them. But when it comes to passports, etc. : get nowhere.

But this thing. Last night, Ira [Grant] drove up with abt 30 chickens he was to deliver to a man living out on a farm, in this town. Because the roads were so bad, & his car, a wreck (& useless for me, or him, to call it otherwise), we figured the truck wd be the thing. So he, myself & Dave started off abt dusk, for this farm.

Wd note, that Lisbon itself, the town, sits between 2 ridges. The west ridge is just beyond a river that runs thru the town, & up on it, over it, many farms, tho all, usually, well separated by woods, etc. (They give these distant-sounding names to such places, as the woods across the river from us, that land there, is called Egypt, & another tract, to the north of it: Oregon.) Anyhow, people up there—very cut off, solitary, by themselves.

The roads were shit. Goddamn ice & when there wasn't ice, mud ruts/ where it had frozen. And goddamn narrow, & these steep rises, with the road sloping off, a drop-off of sometimes 2 or 300 feet. And neither one of us knew where the hell we were going. Just had it in 1st, on these hills, & kept going, slurring all over hell & the damn motor grinding & roaring. Etc. Dave, altogether delighted, & Ira sitting, with a bag, a goose in it, held between his legs.

It was abt 8 miles of these dirt roads. We stopped twice, to ask, & after all these goddamn turns & hills, pulled up in front of this long low house; set back, dark but for one light, & cd see, right off, from the look of it, was one man living in it. Ira went up, got him, & then I took the truck around to where the hen houses were.

Right off: fact everything was so goddamn neat. Houses, fresh white-wash, & on the outside, he had used what you call a roofing paper, that you wd lay under shingles, etc., but, because this tears, in a wind, he had used big round 'washers' on the roofing nails, so they wdn't tear round the nails.

He had every goddamn kind of bird. He sd: even got doves. . . fantails, swallows, & rollers.

Neat, himself. They say, for example, sloppy farmer, which I am, always has his pant-legs falling down over his boots—him, neat, stocking folded, just so, equal length of it, over the boot, at the top. Cap on; but everything real worn.

Damn it: this was it. Impossible, here, if you never have talked with such a man, to get it over clear, i.e., man who may talk a couple of times a week, & because most of them here, won't talk but to those they know well—maybe says half a dozen sentences. Because in the hen-houses, Ira was going full

blast on the birds, the barring of same, the other, said little anyhow. But
after, we went into the house; as you did, that way of it, the outside,
becoming, in stages, the inside, as an entry, & from its having no door,
water in it, which had frozen, on the floor; & going along, narrow, get
to the door, which opened into another small passage, & then, opening
that, 2 of them, storm door & inner, into the kitchen.

Well, stove. Two
kettles on it/ with a crust on them, must have been half an inch, of black/
soot. Table: this one light, over, & there was this book, turned down, I
wd say, printed abt 50 yrs ago (large & bright colored picture/ grotesque), open : Life And Adventures Among the American Indians.

And on the table, game of solitaire. (Seeing, so/ the goddamn cards:
there—that sickness, from how, always, in movies, just so—too/ lonely
man.)

Fuck it/ VOICE: speaking, he wd switch, a little, try this & that, as one
wd, talking, before a mirror, or trying it out, this & that word, & a little
laugh. A little high, in pitch. He asked us, if we cdn't stay, for awhile,
which we did, as long as we cd, because, to talk, so—comes to final, no
matter the damned words. IS: communication. His mother, who had
lived with him, had left, getting married again; he had this little Black
Cocker, in the kitchen, blind, which he sd: cdn't last too much longer.
Big fire/ long stove. Had copies of old Pratt live-stock prints: chickens,
cows, horses, on the walls, & this real big desk, all sorts of stuff all over
it, to one side. The floor had worn to where it went with the spacing of
the joists, & where they were, you cd see the outline.

I don't know.
Coming out, back, as it was: back—figure, sure, as it is, sentimentally :
where is the gain, over, over: this man? Or what, seeing him, & with
him: how, different?
Damn words, stripped, down to, almost, patting
the dogs (he had abt 7 or 8 in all) or talking to the chickens. Or to
himself, always, to himself, as you cd tell it, even cd see him, hearing
his own words.
Some fucking thing sd, he sd it: everything here a man
wants, every damn thing. The woods, at the back, a pasture, stretched

out to: woods. And that goddamn road.

I damn well do NOT know: being, precise, that being the fix of it, of me, in Boston, or you, in Boston, or anyone: in Boston?

Like this: Ainsworths got a new refrigerator, a refrigerator, for which, they paid, not knowing & not being able to come to ask, $80 extra for a deep-freeze unit, because at the bottom: there was a tray marked: Meat Storage, & they thot: you froze the meat, 1st, in this deep-freeze place, & then, frozen, put it into the Meat Storage. It isn't so, etc. GOD-DAMN/ NOT so.

Their kid, Evelyn, takes bottle, thermos, to school filled with, I think it was, grape juice, with ice cubes in it. This was today—is abt 15 above.

Tear & fucking slip of it—constant. Damn shoddy, fucking cheat.

Being so/ that I'm neither here nor there/: exist, as witness. No good. Hence, move? Shit. Move, to move. One yr/ back.

Well, simply, that I feel my own cheapness tonight. Any goddamn night. Cheap fucking cheap.

Cid writing today/ seems happy. The woman, who has apparently, or so it had seemed, been on the verge of backing him for the past 5 months—now asks him, or did, IS what yr doing, of any moment, of anything above what one might see, anytime, anywhere? What the fuck he said—was: "My angel, teasing me for data on the lay of the land, etc., asked me whether I think I am doing anything unusual in ORIGIN and if I honestly believe I can keep the level of the contents high over a substantial period. . ."

I don't know—this from a woman, who, supposing her to have any of the loot Cid says she has, allows him to issue it on the variatype format—is shit, pure & simple.

About it/ at the moment. Dull cold weather again, & hope to christ it gets back to where it was. Mess, trying to get much done, with moving of chickens, or furniture, in this weather. So/ write & will do same myself, soon.

(Slater wrote, today, saying: wd want to make it with us, or wd not want to go—which is his politeness. A damn shame.)

Yr lad/ & all our love to you both:

Bob

Also to note, back to Quetz/ biz: as Ann says: Slater figured it as him, the center/ the others, back then, call it, as what was washed up on the beach—but him, as center, being: big, being: Sea Horse, being IN/ the sea, just so, of it.

Also to emphasize, that NONE of the details, noted prec [*added:* v!]iously, exist in relation to any other possible figure, i.e., are such, clearly, that they must make it: sea horse—& fact that they were immediately taken to be such, by aforenoted man, gives weight to this point. I.e., are in clearly recognizable form, even, as stylized.

(Man, taking figure of sea-horse, picture, as such wd represent the actual one, in short (fucking devious this eve): A picture of A sea-horse as it DOES exist, etc., pointed out to Slater the correspondent detail, that convinced him of the sameness, of root.)

[*Added in pencil:*]
Before taking much of this in—let me write & check with Slater, i.e., want to make sure of names etc.

Mar 1 [1951]

bob:

    no letter fr you in days, frazzles me.

What I write to tell you, is, that I am mailing off, now, the final DO on GATE & CENTER—and that it is back almost precisely to, the form you gave it! And with, I think, that tough spot that threw me, the 1st rewrite, so badly, with that spot SOLVED—and quick, just by a twist, pretty much that para, on, what those 700 yrs, were, what, those people offered, anyone else

                ((it is, by god, just that one para
                in length *more* than you had it!))

Cid asked me to remove "arse" and "fuck," and i have, without, I take it, loss: I have discovered that, all you do is what any skillful pornographer does! You just drop the offensive word, leaving the construction as it was. And bang! You have it, eewalaymente,[32] as they keep saying, here

For which—you took me by the hand so exactly—I thank you. Yr notes of objection, and analysis, were so exact, and worked, that all I had to do, actually, was to hew to them. It is as fine a critique as I have had the experience of being offered, my friend. And I owe this piece entirely to yr pertinacity, twice.

But it was a hell of a struggle to pitch myself back into that mood & tone, and I am all tied [*i.e.* tired?] out, and spent. Must go over to Campeche now, and have a beer (as well as have this machine repaired again: the bastard did something to its timing which makes it most irritating to work; as well as find out what our two landlords have arrived at, it being the 1st of the month, and they, during this month, having got into a tangle, from which I stand a chance to get the place for this coming month at the old rent, of 80 pesos, or, 10 bucks).

Please write, soon, when you can, whatever: miss it, very much.

Love fr us both,
Charles

[*Added in ink:*] I think this G & C squares me away with Corman, so far as he is concerned. (So far as I'm concerned—if I can bear to look at it—I should like to make yr corrections on ADAMO ME—which he tells me he will use.)

[Lerma, Campeche
5 March 1951]

monday   mars   (Or, as I figure it comes out, on the Maya calendar:
CEH, day AKBAL
(Ceh meaning the New Fire Ceremony, Instituted by
Kukulkan, 1159 AD or c.[33]

rob't:what shld interest Ann, is, that, her pix, with kids,[34] was so craved by boy Ramon (whom Constancia cannot keep her arms off of around, but who is already a severe male, and takes it, with such pleasure, he objects, draws
away: age 8)
that he made every sort of bargain he could, offering, etc., to possess same: ANN,
& pix of ACANCEH, town we shot to first day Merida (for facade, there)

(also her best bracelet, Oaxacan, present fr Riboud, & so too prized, too) yesterday was a bitch, & beautiful: we took 7 AM bus down coast, to a glyph, then set off up the road back, walking some 8 kilometers to a place on coast called Sihoplaya, which same beach is only equaled by Oregon coast: we stripped, and washed each other with the sand (not sand, but minute fragments of shells) and crawled around that whiteness and green, out into a submarine garden.

But the sun is already beyond taking, at midday, and of course, like mad dogs, we get caught out: we ended, under a small bridge over the only tidal river between here & the next large town, Champoton. At which place the bus caught me in as I was born, in, that thing which is like beginning, for me (tagged by the Annisquam[35]), a tidal, same! So much slugged today, too much to rise to, in the mails, (1) Tozzer's Maya Grammar (by air mail thru Corman) and (2) MAP of sites hereabout fr Tulane[36] (plus egregious letter fr one Vinc Ferrini

So I write you, to cheer me up! And for the hell of it, let me send you a leetla thing, for the throw, for what it is, notes, for a beginning

> The fish is speech. Or see
> what, cut
> in stone,
> starts. For
>
> when the sea breaks, watch
> watch, it is the
> tongue, and
>
> he who introduces the words (the
> interlocutor), the
> beginner of the word, he
>
> you will find, he
> has scales, he
> gives off motion as
>
> in the sun the wind the light, the fish
> moves

END. Is it or is it, a veritable, conjunction?
Say, lad.   CLOSE this note, for, 25 centavos.
                Do write.
                            & blessings,
                            the trip. O

_____

                                        lerma   march 8 [1951]

lad!
        Yr letter! How it spotted itself. This way: (1) arrived precise to
eclipse of sun (½); (2) arrived, at climax of long gab with Con, in which,
after a go again on how to get nominative out of substances in order to
allow such substances to be free forms, I had made this proposition: that
Kukulkan vs the Chichimec was the true contest, not the Spanish, and
that I proposed to pick up again, now here, on the life of this very great
man, saying to Con, that, with so much registration of him in codices,
frescoes, stone cutting, stucco, it should be as possible, or more, to
recreate him as, that Barlow, from mss., sought to do same by Moctezuma:[37]
                had just sd, "I forgot, to tell you, that, at Champoton, after
you took the bus last Sunday, I got into conversation with a bar boy,
there, and, talking abt the Isla Cuyo (the remnant now standing in the
sea of the pyramid K had erected for himself, there, on departing Tula-
ward, he having done his work, here), it was my notion, that, that he
had the imagination to build *in the sea*, was another sign of how unique
he was" (asking myself, the relation of same act to (1) the fact that the
Maya hereabouts put their cities (in contrast to all since) on the hill over
the sea ("Senor gusta monte," sd the lady, fr whom, bananas, on the
road in, one day), (2) the Island of Jaina, just above us here, abt as far
north of us as Champoton is south, and not yet visited because it *has* to

be *reached by sea* [*added:* had most beautiful workings in clay], and (3), that, on the east coast, the big beautiful place is TULUM, and, the *Island of* Cozumel (by map in yesterday fr Tulane, the sites on Cozumel are thick ((propose to go there, if possible swing it: three days by sailing vessel from Progreso))

when LETTER-LIGHT, comes, in the midst of a context undupli-catable—(1) the stir outside with all, *all,* kids & grown-ups, watching, the eclipsa, excited (contrast to States, abt 1930, when, a total eclipse, and only me and the birds, apparently, aware, until it was suddenly dark)[38] here, with no real shrinkage of light, yet, everyone, these, descendants of, astronomers, than whom none more effective than one Kukulkan, apparently ((the month CEH, as, I believe, in last letter, I, identified as HIS new fire ceremony—Spinden dates its institution as 1168 with a Day 1 Knife, when, K started a year count as Year 1 Knife, and in Year 2 Reed, 1194-5, he declared the Fire Ceremony to be celeb-rated at intervals of 52 years))[39] all of them, with smoked glass and old film and rolled up newspapers, anything, looking, upward

(2) the con-versation, me still beating around, these things

&

(3) CARLOS WALKS IN WITH YR NEWS, YR NEWS, BRO, OF K & a sea-horse (for same thing, a sea-horse, is also precise: using as fetish to hold down yr letters in the wind which sweeps through this room, what do I have, have had since third day after arrival, as present from a boy I have never seen since? and same thing I have thought again & again, it's light, and I should like to send it to Creeley & Ann & kids as SIGN, but haven't, because, to box something, seems, beyond huge, for to get a letter off, a money order say, is already proved murder: one for book fr Merida lost already!

And now it is too late. For you have it, already. And have made me the present! Beautiful. And tell Slater, for me, he's HOT. Or so I'd guess, round abt now, with, what is, in hand:

Let me go back.

I: why I still beat up against this biz of, getting rid of nomination, so that historical material, is free for forms now, is

> Ez's epic solves problem by his ego: his single emotion breaks all down to his equals or inferiors (so far as I can see only two, possibly, are admitted, by him, to be his betters—Confucius, & Dante. Which assumption, that there are intelligent men whom he can outtalk, is beautiful beacause it destroys historical time, and

> thus creates the methodology of the Cantos, viz, a space-field where, by inversion, though the material is all time material, he has driven through it so sharply by the beak of his ego, that, he has turned time into what we must now have, space & its live air

>> ((secondary contrast is Joyce, who, it comes to me now, did not improve on Duns Scotus Erigenus, or the Irish of the time the Irish were the culture-bosses, what was it, 7th–9th century, or something: he tried to get at the problem by running one language into another so as to create a universal language of the unconscious. Which is, finally, mush & shit, that is, now. Not so, then, DSE or Irishers, for, then, Europe was, both, in language & dream, of that order
>>> ((further thot: Joyce, the Commercial Traveler: the worship of IARichards[40]—by the same people, accurately enough, who mug Joyce—is more honest: that is, that this internationalizing of language is more relevant to commerce, now, than it is to the aesthetic problem.
>>> ((((all
>> this a better way to say, he, ENDER)

the primary contrast, for our purpose is, BILL: his Pat is exact opposite of Ez's, that is, Bill HAS an emotional system which is capable of extensions & comprehensions the ego-system (the Old Deal, Ez as Cento Man, here dates) is not. Yet

by making his substance historical of one city (the Joyce deal), Bill completely licks himself, lets time roll him under as Ez does not, and thus, so far as what is the more important, methodology, contributes nothing, in fact, delays, deters, and hampers, by, not having busted through, the very problem which, Ez, has, so brilliantly faced, & beat

Which ought—if my mouth had words in it, this morning—bring you to see why i hammer, on, nomination, thus:
                              each of the above jobs are
HALVES, that is, I take it (1) that the EGO AS BEAK is bent and busted
                    but (2) whatever it is that we can call its replace-
                              ment (Bill, very much a little of it)
HAS, SO FAR, not been able to bring any time so abreast of us that we are in this present air, going straight out, of ourselves, into it

You see, Creeley, I followed you, a bit back, when, in responding on Tarot & Maya, you sd, sure, & it's whatever you or anyone makes hot, is hot. Of course.

& two: that, we already have both (1) the ego as responsible to more than itself and (2) absolute clarity, that, time, is done, as effect of work in hand

Perhaps, as I sd before, I am only arguing with myself, that is, I am trying (you will recall yr bye on a previous try of mine at it, the *bigmans* throw) to see how to throw the materials I am interested in so that they take, with all impact of a correct methodology AND WITH THE AL-TERNATIVE TO the EGO-POSITION

I keep thinking, it comes to this: culture displacing the state. Which is my guess as to why Ez sounds so flat, when, he is just talking, when, he is outside the Cantos, say, that, walker of his than which there is, yet, no better
          (so much of Ez, is, the 19th century stance: PRO-
          TEST (Dahlberg is the funny man, of this same
                    biz: they both wld love to have been,
                    who was it, Lousie 14th, "l'etat, c'est moi"?[41]

     what burns me, is, they never speak, in their slash at the State or the Economy, basically, for anyone but themselves. And thus, it is Bohemianism

and much too late, just abt as late as before Fourier, Marx, &
Nietzsche, not to mention the real guys, then, Riemann or any of
the geometers, who were really cutting ahead

Tho, again, here, one has to give Ez his due: that he did write KULCH

Which ought to get us to II, or, Kukulkan. This way:
                                                    why the problem
is tougher than Ez's throw, or Bill's, failure, is, that, the shift is SUB-
STANTIVE (it delights me, to recognize, that, the word has that other
                    meaning, of "noun"!)
                                        that is, another reason why i don't
think Ez's toucan works after 1917 is, that, after that date, the materials
of history which he has found useful are not at all of use (nor are Bill's,
despite the more apparent homogeneity: date 1917, not only did Yurrup
(West, Cento, Renaissance) go, but such blueberry America[42] as Bill
presents (Jersey dump-smoke covering same) also WENT (that is, Bill,
with all respect, don't know fr nothing abt what a city *is*)
                                                            the which
says this: that the substances of history now useful lie outside, under,
right here, anywhere but in the direct continuum of society as we have
had it (of the State, same, of the Economy, same, of the Politicks: Ez is
traitor as Dante was, to Florence: the difference of F to USA is not
difference at all, other than, the passage of time & time's dreary accumu-
lations by repetition
                    (((something of this must have been what Ratzl meant,
                    when he sd, HISTORY IS UNIVERSAL
                    MONOTONY)))[43]

(*Note:* I note that I assume history is prime, even now. I assume it is. I
        assume this one thing—man's curiosity abt what his brother
        zopalotes[44] have been about—comes through to us straight from
        that previous civilization, and is the one thread we better damn
        well hang on to. And the only one.

Perhaps because it is as much a prime, as, an eclipse?

The substance has changed. Period. BUT: we are confronted, as men
forever are, by the LAG. Our fellow cits are, I take it, quite easily
thrown off by any noun which contains Z's and X's. (Not, again, that,
thus superficially, it matters a good god damn: bust them over the
heads. Right. Only, what i am saying is, that, to use X's and Z's
makes for difficulties John Adams, or Kung Fu Sze, or even Omeros,
don't. ((Or is this just a little bit argumentative, & petulant, as one is,
when, the work, is not done, and one is talking abt it instead.))
                    (((Doesn't matter. For, as you'd guess, the op-
                    eration is otherwise, is, actually, the other
                    edge: how *was* this Kukulkan, how are you,
                    Mister Creeley)))

How can I pick up these injuns—that is, as Stephens, Prescott, Parkman
did not so pick them up 100 yr agone, that, at the same moment of time
as one H. Melville, they made them stick as he did, Pacifica? What's
wrong—or, likewise, Sumeria. Or mao. Or usa, today.

NO. Erase above. Somewhere I've been dragged off the methodological,
here, by my own mention of the substantive. And am sucked into a
substantive argument. Which is not what we're here for. Let me try it
another way. For it's still this man Kukulkan we are talking abt.

Shots:
   (1) is not the Maya the most important characters in the whole
       panorama (diorama was the word contemporary to above fine 4
          workers)
       simply because the TOP CLASS in their society, the bosses,
       were a class whose daily business was KNOWLEDGE, & its
       OFFSHOOT, culture?
                 that thus a man of K's temper & interest
                 could become Big Boss, & then, God?

and
that any such society goes down easily before a gun? or bows &
arrows, when Chichemecs come along with same? ((The absolute quote here, is, one prime devil, Goebbels, who sd: "When
I hear the word 'kultur' I reach for my gun."[44a]))

(2) that such a society is precisely the contrary (really the contrary,
not the opposite, to use Blake's careful discrimination,[45] and,
by so doing, show up the collective or communist deal for what
it is, only, an opposite) of what the West was, has been, is, and
will continue to be as long as the rest of the world wants what
America has had

Comes up, out of the sea, a sea
horse (my question is, where
here
do the rains
come from, is the serpent
who shall fight the jaguar[46]
another norther, of
another season, is
weather, here, as on the earth because
the earth turns eastward, is
all movements, as was the people's coming, is it from
the west?

they say,
he was the wind, they say
also rain, anyway
he was water, not
sun fire not this heat which makes the day less
than the night

he wore a hat, a sort of silly hat, had
short breeches, a tortoise back with mirror on it, and
a tail: he died
just as the heat was at its worst, just

on the day the fields were burnt, just that day the morning star rose
anew
    his eyes, she sd,
    were like a caracol. [47] And when he left us,
    he walked straight out into the sea, west
                            he was also
                            a bachelor
                                    but what
seemed most important, he
was just, was
a child
of water, they figured it, was
precisely what
they needed, was
the image of
(Well! To hell with that. Pardon me. Get up off my face, olson.)
themselves

It is a beautiful thing, what Slater found. You are right, of course: it
bears right in on what I have been turning over. I figure, now, that why
(as I think I told you) I abandoned him, in the two throws of The K's,
and The P's, was, that, it is this thing, the sea, which, one finds out
here. And nobody told me. And which sea is the addition to him as
Venus, which, makes up a package.
        A favor, if you have an encyclopedia at hand, or any source,
        could you write me what this damned star Venus does with
        itself in a year? That is, is there a coincidence of its brightest
        brightness with April 12th, or thereabouts?

We await, e.g., that day, or c., because, they tell us, on that date the
farmers burn their fields, and, for a month, it is here, as tho there were
an eclipse—or as it was, there, last fall, when, the Canadian woods, were
burning down[48]
        FORGET IT. I guess the time has come for me to dig
this biz. And it's large. And better be done whole (all I was after, I'll tell
you, another day [in a minute crossed out]. But 1st:

what cools me, is, a sentence, like this, fr Spinden:

"Date I: 11- 8-14- 3-16, 10 Cib 4 Yax, May 5, 1136 [*note added by Creeley, perhaps to Slater Brown:* which must be his fixing of the "transit" date, which comes by my calculation, i.e., working from that bit noted in *June* of *1139?* or *1131?*]

This phenomenon took place before the Toltecs had conquered Chichen Itza but easily enough it may represent data upon which Quetzalcoatl worked and which possibly he presented in his Sacred Book."

or

"In the Vienna Codex the Venus staff" (which Quetz is chief bearer [*added:* of: olson note] "is stuck in a valley between two hills beside a trumpet shell" (which trumpet shell Con & I find plenty of—even found one at K's Isla—and is, of course, our sea-shell, or, here, the CARACOL (the astronomers' house at Chichen, is, a snail!)[49] [*added in margin by Olson:* drawing of same, next page: IS PERFECT PIX OF CORRECTION I PROPOSE]

It's the damndest thing, what a cat I got by the tail. For, you see, here is this supposed land-maize people who use
(1) for the house which brought them culture, the astronomy house, a SEA-SHELL
(2) for the man who appears to have made the language of this people for time in the universe available to all neighboring peoples, a SEA-HORSE!

AND—and this had broke in on me before I got yr letter with Slater's shot, yesterday—THE EVIDENCES Spinden here above is referring to, are not Maya, but MIXTEC, in other words, of the Central Valley of Mexico, not Yucatan. SO THAT, the whole picture has shifted wider & out, west: in fact, what i ought to be, am, proposing, is, THE SEA IN MAYA & MEXICAN CULTURES & ECONOMIES.

AND AND,
somewhere in this mixing of the two geographies is the key to why there is KUKULKAN here, & QUETZ there: same man, same imagery (the

serpent with fuzz) (SEA-SERPENT?)

What the astronomy establishes, is, that the complex is WATER: that is, Venus-sign (Q & K Venus-God, April 13, 1208 thereafter) is "Nine WIND."[50] Is also RAIN (the seasonal need). Is also, somehow, SERPENT (contrary of sun, which is, Jaguar). Is—shall we allow, for the present—SEA-H. In other words, see what I mean: snails, for noise, water, for maize, and a man, fr the west, where (does it) the wind (yes, northers) & the rain (also?) comes from

Crazy. And much too early to say. But, is, don't you think, HOT?

Please shoot me anything else you have or that, without him losing anything, Slater cares to: for he shld be warned, that, I look on this stuff as verse, and will, in any case, use, use use. And I respect another man's work too much not to warn him, that, if he has special uses of his own, well, maybe, he would rather, let me do the work myself.

(O, yes, as of wind: the drawing of K o Q most like an s..h...., is, actually, not of him in himself but of the wind, God K of the Codices, who is, to be sure, by reasoning from a like union in Mexican mythology, seen as K:

let me send back that drawing, for, Ann's to me:

Christ, I better
quit this, laboring
you, when, it is,
perhaps—hell,
no, definitely yr
biz, too: for,
to take it all the
way back, it's

that the time has come when, a bunch of men (ex., this case, you, Ann,
Slater, me)
are already disposed, by bias of attention born in them, away from ego
but without loss of cutting edge, to themselves & others as, fresh critters
going about daily business with some certain difference from the way
immediate predecessors have gone about any business, including ART

love,
[*carbon copy unsigned*]

[Littleton, N.H.]
March 9 [1951]

Dear Chas/
A letter in, today, from Slater: which I'll copy out for you.

"At any rate those drawings you saw of mine were mostly from the
Borgian Codex and therefore Aztec and not Mayan. But it is not impossible that the Aztec version of their Gods was perhaps based on an
extremely early Mayan form. Both, of course have a Plumed Serpent
though in Mayan he's called Kulkulcan (as you had told me/ C.). Q- was
often represented as a wind God—wind, air and therefore Life—and you

will see a little picture of him among the day signs in Valliant's book.[51] The head is the day sign of wind.

"It was the stalked eyes on some of the Borgian pictures that made me think he was really a sea-monster or sea horse, for stalked eyes or ones on stilts are, I imagine, only common to sea creatures. As Q-, but not K-whose sign I don't know, is usually represented as a sea horse he was certainly Fish. Moreover, he is supposed to have come out of the East where the Mayan sea, at least, was and he was also supposed to return from the east which he did, the poor Mexicans thought, when Cortes arrived.

"In the Borgian codex Q- is paired with the God of death, in a two-headed monster with the sea horse head on one side and a skull on the other. It was quite evidently a representation of Life and Death. It's an amazing and terrifying thing and in the Kingsborough edition of the Codex, all faithfully hand colored, it is quite beautiful to look at.[52] I think it's in the fifth volume if you ever want to take a look at it in the NY Public Library.

"But I wish I knew more of what Olson has to say about the great Mayan migration that baffles everyone. Morley thinks that they exhausted the land and had to move, but I doubt it.[53] (Ann, here, makes the note, that perhaps there's a parallel between this biz, & that in India, antient, i.e., that the natives were unable to break up the soil enough to prevent crops from becoming root-bound, with the divers implements they had to use, etc. Cd be, etc.) The Mayans were far too intelligent a race to exhaust their soil. They were a highly spiritual race besides and highly spiritual races always regard their soil as something sacred (or vice versa? C.), as of course it is. . .

"If I were in Mexico I would certainly take a look at the stars and I hope Olson does while he's there. And if ever I get to Mexico City I shall want to take a look at Venus for I once came across a passage in Sahagun, a priest in Mexico at the time of Cortes, in which he says "they (the mexicans) say that Venus shines with a light like the moon," a remark which everyone has thought to mean that they were saying "as bright as the moon" though it is quite obvious to me that the bright-eyed Mexicans were trying to tell the old priest who couldn't have understood the remark anyway before Galileo, that Venus had phases like the moon. . .

"(a footnote) Of course one thing that troubled me was where did the Aztecs have a chance to see a sea horse? They lived on a lake and presumably came inland from the north. . ."

He began it: "I was enormously interested in what Olson had to say but I'm sorry his typewriter broke down just at his most interesting point. But he was talking about the archeologists and they would make any-one's typewriter collapse, the Mexican ones in particular. They've all lost their eyes."

That, & one comment abt the Mayans having been astronomers, as well as astrologists—& that fact, no effort is made to figure out their constellations or the signs for them, ends it.

Have you seen any pictures of Kulkulcan? I.e., how does that biz of the stalked eyes tie in? Jesus, wd be SOMETHING. Figure, one can reverse Slater, on this biz of the spirituality, or make it: that sense of land, wd be the sign, or even, better, the beginning of such.

Write as soon as you can get to it: gets HOT

Cid wrote: "Tell you? Charles has revised GATE & CENTER for me. Whot a difference! Really something now. Fine! Youll get a kick out of it. Shorter, but cleaner. I mean that it moves with his voice and says (without pushing too many parentheses around) what he wants to say. In that wonnerful stimulating vein of his."

Well. . . wonder if you SHOULD change it around again; or his 'ap-proval,' very often more insufferable than his dislike, etc. Even so, IF it hits him, IT HITS. Ok.

I am angry, anyhow, with him, etc. I mean, had sent him three poems by Paul Blackburn,[54] that the latter had sent on to me, for possible use with Gerhardt. I enclose one—I won't put my last dollar on the stuff;

very damn little I wd, etc. BUT fucking decent writing, AND a hell of a lot beyond what Cid does shove in there, some of it (Emerson, Eberhart, Hatson, Ferrini, Hoskins, for a start). SHIT: it was his very damn vague comment, fucked me—'too loose' or something, etc. I mean, he snapped it back, quick. And I do damn well believe, at least the poem enclosed, worth printing. Well, to hell with it.

I damn well don't know—of course, & most certainly, ONLY my petulance, at not being able to railroad this item thru. But where he put down, the bulk of the German stuff, I figured, sure, i.e., NO kick, etc. But this—seems not the damn same thing, & it was: he figured me, immediately, to be taking his side, &, of course, I damn well don't, in this instance. So, to hell with it.

We move considerably better on this biz of getting out of here. And the papers begin to come in; also, weather improves, & that is damn cheering. Yesterday, Dave & myself drove over to Danville, Vt., to deliver a rooster, etc., and very fine : all these hills, way up, in the air, & fine bright sky, & clouds. Well, damn well fine.

Otherwise, tired—it goes with these damn pressures, & will be very damn fine, to be clear.

Write soon—once getting this sourness out, will be back to it; idiotic to be bugged by this biz abt Blackburn, but, being, as it is, an edge, etc., it does bug me.

All love to you both/

Bob

[*Added at top of letter:*] Kids rolling thru this room/ PHEW.

lerma   march 9   (friday) [1951]

robert: (picking up, on, yesterday's stuff, on K and abt) —tho i shld tell
you, 1st, that "archeology" is not good for the lungs. Or, maybe,
Lerma, the people here, have, so much, "catahrro," as they seem to say
it, maybe that's it. But yesterday, after i finished, to you, & posted same
(which, here, is always a pleasure, for, there is no box, one seeks out one
Carlos and together we weigh it, he or i gums the stamp, we talk, I look
at his shells, or his new Brownie just acquired for the pilgrimage, the
Sunday of Holy Week, to a shrine CHUINAH somewhere beyond
Champoton (thinking of making that one, we are), and I dole out the
centavos. It is post office as I, ex-letter carrier, believe in playing it:
much human businesses abt same, gab, etc: the maids on my route
always found my mouth ready for their cake or, for talk. As well as
anyone else. Result: one day I came out to my truck—after an hour of
coffee & gab with a painter named Sacha Moldovan (never heard of
since) and a Jap store keeper named Susumu Hirota (a much better
painter than Moldovan, whom M had taught to paint)—and thar be John
Drohan, Foreman of Carriers, standing, with his watch out, and never,
for the rest of that morning's run—he stayed with me that day—saying
a word. [55] (Those peculiar ways the "people" have of getting things
over!)

    Anyhow, yesterday, by god, Con and I hit our secret ruin here.
And hit pay dirt: only, such dirt, the dry spill of it, and the resulting
clouds of white lime, knock me out: all week I have suffered from the big
operation last Sunday at Pueblo Nuevo (nothing, the result). But yesterday, in 10 minutes of it, I pay today—tho, we came away, with one pot
piece which, if my ignorance is right, is, Tzakhol, or even possibly,
earlier, maybe Chicanel (which wld mean sometime before, possibly, the
Christ). And more of a piece of hand I found a few days ago, in hard
stucco. And Con landed another piece of a headdress (in same) I dragged
home a while back.

        We also, yesterday, for the 1st time, met the
farmer on whose land this "cuyo" is. And his wife, who offered Con
limes. You see, to give you the picture: sd ruin is just abt 5 mins fr the
house. I spotted it, the very 1st day I walked out (sign, surely). But I was
asked, what the hell you doing here (or so I thought the tone was, not

knowing, of course, the woids. I have tried, since, to meet the farmer,
and ask, permissions. But, until yesterday, no luck. (Each time, of
course, that there was no one there, I scratched.)

Now the other advan-
tage to sd ruin, is, that this farmer is having a man take it apart, for the
faced stone and foundation stone which he is using in town to build a
house!

If it were just another ruin, there wld, of course, be no need
for the diplomacy with which I am trying to set an operation there. BUT,
by god, if this CUYO isn't HOT, and precisely for the reasons of SEA &
INJUNS, I am missing gears in the cabeza. [56] You gather (1) if it's 5 mins
fr here, it's less than 5 mins fr the sea. (2) every piece I've found,
including my owl, is finely made. (3) by the ceramic evidences, the cuyo
is old (establishing early importance of sea in Maya needs: did I throw
the idea out to you that it just may be a reason why the Maya came
north, that, they needed the protein & fats that the hunting and fishing
of this peninsula alone could supply in sufficient quantity to start the
building of a large people?

I did tell you, but, then, I did not know abt
THE MERMAID! By god, yes, that, too!

1st, it was Azar. But he's got
Ez's disease, and if he says he saw one, one, says, my name is Columbus. But then it was Martinez, fisherman, and no fool, at all: he says,
manatee. Still, the word is such, I think: well. But of course there is such
a creature, it does look as tho it has breasts like a woman, and, as
mammal, it does moan and fold its arms over its young when same
young are harpooned. The same were, once, thick along this coast.
And—here it is, the package—in the Vienna Dictionary, [57] by god, it
says, the ancient Maya did so harpoon sd mermaid for FAT.

So, the CUYO. Now, I want, before shooting the knowledge of
same, to anyone, to scratch it, to watch Vasquez's man dig (each time he
heaves a crowbar, a new "face" of the stratigraphy shows, of course), to
carry all pieces here, wash, match, gum, or live with, until, I have, the
feel of same, the directness of it, fr start (the finding) to boredom.

Anyhow, yesterday, we four talked in V's fruit farm, just over the fence fr, the cuyo. The round was his, that is, I did ask his permission, but, the Spanish comes so fast, and he has such eyes, I cldn't tell you now, whether he sd, yes, or no. And I am hung with anxiousness! But one great gain was made: tomorrow morning at 7, I pick him up at his house, and he and I walk off into the serrania[58] in order that I may show him (pay that one!) 4 dry cenotes we found not too far from him for him to use same, if there is, as I would imagine, water to be got to in them. (It turned out he is being licked, for irrigation, by the sea! It cost him 1000 pesos two years ago to drive a well, and, tho the water was fresh at 1st, now, it is salt! Which, he tells me, has happened to all the other wells between him and the sea.

It was beautiful, really, to come right up against a live technical problem, just at the moment my pockets were bulging with potsherds and the hand-piece, and Con's crown piece—and me feeling like a kid who had stole the farmer's apples! And the wonderful bearing down of Vasquez on his water problem, that beautiful thing, of a tough hardworking man, and a man who had the drive to pick himself up ten years ago, buy that land, and, moving off fr maize, take to making an orchard! (His pride I first felt thru his son, and their worker, Juan Pablo, each of whom did what he and his wife did yesterday, walk us all over that thar farm, showing us each of the trees, telling us the names ((you will know fruit here, is, many and very good, very much better than the over-irrigated Californias and the refrigerator ripened Florida (still, New England has the advantage of his compactness of market, in this 20th century))

The damn thing is, I am going on—to take a flyer at solving his problem—precisely my assumption that, if the Maya built as solidly as they obviously did right on his farm and along this road I am taking him to tomorrow, then, there must have been water. In fact I already know the remains of these 4 cenotes.
BUT

(1) I am wholly ignorant of geology, and of the ways of water

& (2) if Vasquez's well sours now, maybe the exact same thing happened then (?)

Apparently—and this is what is really bewildering (tho of course it ain't)—here is a Mayan farmer so broken fr his tradition that—as he was

straight enough to say, yesterday, he nor anyone knows anything abt
the cuyo, or, abt the Maya who once lived there—"study" was his
verb—

        instead of going around testing the cenotes (which I may be
wholly wrong abt, of course, that is, both that there may be water and,
that an old cenote is ever usable again), he, like any gringo, went and
hired "experts" (Vasquez is that funny kind of a "modern"—his drive is
more American, than, the fishermen, here, say, who go in the old
tracks—obviously, if he threw up maize and went for a big fruit farm, he
is, different, too, fr the campesinos[59])

                        & these fucking experts appear to
have done what they always do, sunk a well which has soured

        So, Robt, tomorrow, up there, kill a chicken and pour its blood over
an altar stone, for, this lad, who, tomorrow, takes a hell of a practical
risk with his damned imagination: I even go so far as to predict which of
the 4 cenotes is the one which will bring it in! It is the nearest one to
Vasquez, by god. And I'm betting on it, simply because, instead of its
being on the same altitude off the sea as his farm (the other three are,
but much farther inland), it is—o, say, 50 feet higher.

                                But I love it.
For, here I am fighting for the permission to work his cuyo by exchang-
ing for it something—a well—I never before in my life had to do with!
And same well, I am proposing to find, simply because I take up from
where *his* ancestors, left off!

                        The CUYO, by the way, does not even
have a name. I figure the reason it has gone unnoticed is, that, like a
neighboring one in a marsh nearby V's farm, it has no noticeable height
at all. And, until, say, the past year, when, after 10 yrs of fruit, V has
made enough money to build himself a finer house in town than the
Maya hut he has lived, and raised his family in, the slight mound that it
is was never cut into. But once cut into, it shows to be about ten feet
above the neighboring plateau. (I can't figure what it was, other than, a
run of houses, but I sense, fr the quality of the work there, plus the
astonishing range of the ceramica, that, it was, possibly, the working
town (port? or pot-center? or sea-outpost?) for the much larger cities
which existed on the hills around it (same towns no more than a half
mile, to a mile, away). Maybe it was the coast road stop. This is the best

guess of all. For it lies where the two roads from the back country converge, as well as where, if there was a coast road—as I think, from other evidence, there was—such same road wld about come in.

Well, it has us dazy. If I had the dough to spill—and V's *permission*—I could kill this one, with a handful of workers. But right now our only curiosity is, to hit it every day abt 4 (the heat is already impossible between 10 and 4) and pick at it, alone, the two of us, just watching hard, for, things: yesterday, e.g., I picked this beautiful piece of plumbate ware[60]—thin, black (with polished lip, black), and with design in white—out by just seeing its edge (all white with lime) sticking out, no more than a match stick from the face of the rubble, rather, the fill

(the joker is, of course, that we are learning archeology, without instruction, or tools!)

[*Large space; letter begins again halfway down a new page:*]
To get back, to what is, finally, more interesting (perhaps). Is time. Is how, it's grabbed hold of. Is, so grabbed, how, it can be pushed, this instance, so hard, it is turned into, space. Is—or so I take it—one precise conceit for defining, what, is usually left as, life, or, what's this all about. That is: that each of us is, this, operation: break time back, breaks its back, break through it, make it, do what is also us, disposition in space: the weight of the ship is the amount of water it DISPLACES. Which latter, be it human, is, the recognition of, earth as larger & previous demonstration of same action (thus, relationship, GEA or GEO-graphy, the graph-act the declaration of functioning as displacement (same conceit to be seen as much more than mere geography, including, as it does, the raising of potatoes or the catching of fish or the punking of what is as image of what has or is, happening)

what remains more important than knowledge of how to reach the corner of 17th & Leroy Place, is—still—(because it is bigger brother's business moving around the larger city): how come, last night, moon set ahead of evening star? Why, of course! Because, day before yesterday, at 4:30, same thing moon, not seen, was able, to blot out a good third of third member of family which governs so much of nerve ends of this animal or any animal still prowling same threshing floor called earth, the sun

all of

which stays time in the very fishy sense (slippery & squamous) as it has
been as straight line forward since Greeks (equals progress or progression NOT CONJUNCTION) *unless* same pieces are seen as pesos or
weights, as counters which move by their own motion as much as
you-me move by our controlled volitions, same volitions now to be seen
as also obedient to some certain primes not sufficiently allowed in speculations *or actions* since a certain date (in that "line," at least) round and
about, say, olson's cliche: 1200 BC

The which difference, it strikes me, may be the reason why these Maya
remain interesting. (I am coming back to what I promised, yesterday,
abt astronomy   abt astronomy, abt what we call "Venus" (which reminds me of a come-uppance, a like beaut to what you tell me Slater tells
abt the dope who figured he had the Mayan language & translated a book
he found out afterwards, if he had had the language, he'd, translated it
backwards: the fact that the boys, for yrs, calculated Egyptian astronomy records on their assumption same records were of Venus when,
god damn them, it turned out all the time they had been interested in the
Dog-Star! (Or v-v)

I know nothing, here. In fact, instead of trying to find out, I am writing
you speculations instead. But just to go along, I am turning over this:
how come, if I remain interested in this people, do I, if their astronomy
was, what the books say it was, a time-triumph? given my hate of that
dirty thing when it is allowed to run around without its mama?

I keep going back to this (drawing, here:
[*Olson's carbon copy lacks drawing, has only the following note added
in pencil, referring perhaps to Sylvanus Griswold Morley's* The Inscriptions at Copan *(Washington, 1920) or his* The Ancient Maya *(Stanford,
1947):* Morley, of Copan, & Apr 12, Stela 10 & 12.]

CONJUNCTION & DISPLACEMENT, the sense of, C & D, D & C, etc
etc. Is verse.
          Is quite another thing than time.
                              Is buildings. Is
des ign.
          Is—for our trade—

THE DISJUNCT, language
in order to occupy space, *be* object (it being so hugely as intervals TIME)
has to be thrown around, re-assembled, in order that it speak, the man
whose interstices it is the re-make of

> ((Is the other side: of Kukulkan
>   perhaps?:

VIOLENCE

I remain wholly fascinated that K's reputation was not the invention of
maize, calculations of Venus, or the hieroglyphic system (which, wld
seem, any one of them, to be sufficient reason for the arising of a
humanistic god-figure (was such, apparently, fr Pelasgos, or, earlier, by
Waddell's LISTS[61])

> O THESE MAYA WERE COOL, WERE NOT SO
HUMANISTIC

K's reputation (he comes late, as 1st HUMAN god) was something else:
WRITER, actually—or so the hints seem to be, that, he made Maya
language & astronomy available to *others*

> Look, RCr, this begins to get
out of mind. Let me ride it, some more. Just shoot this along—o,
for—say—the pictures!

> Love, and when you can

> olson

[Littleton, N.H.]
Monday [12 March 1951]
Chas/

VENUZ:

". . . the time it takes Venus to complete a revolution in its orbit is 225 days, but its synodic period, or the period of its phases is 584 days. At its maximum elongations it recedes about 47° or 48° from the sun, so that in middle latitudes it can set or rise over 3 hours after or before the sun. . ."

". . . Its greatest brightness is attained at about 36 days on either side of inferior conjunction (I take that: when it is closest the earth, i.e., it notes that it is "26,000,000 miles from the earth (at inferior conjunction), at superior conjunction it is 160,000,000 miles. . ."), its elongation from the sun then being 39°, and its phase similar to that of a 5 days old moon. When suitably situated the planet is easily visible at noonday with the naked eye, and after dark readily casts a shadow. . ."

Here was something, since that tells you, still, little of when those times might be (there being 2, etc.):

Sometimes Venus 'transits' the sun's face, & is there projected as a 'small black disc. . .'; it says, were the planet's orbit plane coincident with that of the earth—you'd get such at each inferior conjunction. But since it isn't, you get such a 'transit' 4 times in every 243 years, & the intervals between these 'transits' are as follows:
8, 121½, 8, 105½, 8, 121½, etc.

The first date they give, i.e., list here, is 1518, June 2nd. Going back/ at 243 yr stretches: (but it seems better to go back, yr by yr):

```
1518.6   (& the next length is 8, the next 105½ etc.)
 121.6
1496.0   [sic]
   8.0          Well, I was hoping that it wd hit those dates you had
1488.0   noted, but now having this table, etc., you might check to
 105.6   see what might coincide with these years
1382.6                                              (Perhaps his
   8.0   birth? wd make him either 69 or 77?)    They must have
1374.6   taken such, that projection occurring TWICE in that time, as
 121.6   a sign certainly. (I wish I cd check the possible other eclipses,
1253.0   or such, in that same time-span. Will see what I can do,
   8.0   etc.).
1245.0          But note, that the 36 days on the fore side of the dates
 105.6   given, notably the June, land you in April—well, just the
1139.6   June. I haven't any way, or understanding, to check when
   8.0   was the inferior conjunction of sd planet in sd year:—I tell
1131.6   you what, will write the University here & bluff them into
         giving me, the date of sd conjunction in sd yr; will also, ask
         them to note possible other phenomena, astronomy/ wise,
         that same yr.
                          More, this eve.
```

[Littleton, N.H.]
Monday [12 March 1951]

Dear Chas/

      Ann had rushed me on that other, i.e., the biz of Venus, & had for one thing: not had time to look back thru yr letter—where one thing, that quote on the ''phenomenon,'' off from my own placing of the time of this occurrence of transit, by one year & one month [*both* one year *and* one month *circled, with the following added in the margin:* my damn *error*—i.e.—remember my two dates are: 1131 & 1139. But still believe it must relate to one or the other? (In one case is 3 yrs 1 month off—in the other 5 yrs. 1 month, etc. What "phenomenon" precisely is he referring to? Does he know?]; I should suspect, human agency, like they say—these planets being, of stable stuff. Anyhow, I suspect the May—being that the 6 month break, so established, wd have it fall either in the first week of June, or in an equivalent period of December. But they must be the same phenomenon? I should think so. Does he note, then, that there was a similar phenomenon, 8 years previous? There was. And both supposedly having fallen in June. Well, only what I had already found, etc. But I should very much like to get an independent placing of that transit by the boys at the Uni/ if they rise to the bait, etc. I mean, a note on all possible phenomena occurring in 1208—also, of those two earlier transits—I perhaps the one is off, etc.

But the thing: I mean, what counts—the apparent rarity of these transits, or must have been apparent to sd people, i.e., as the fact is: 4 times every 243 yrs, & that coincidence, then, of two showing up in an 8 yr space, & then over a 100 yrs passing, and having passed before, before their reoccurrence

These transits: straight eclipse, i.e., the planet projected on the face of the sun, so crossing, etc.

So much for that for the moment, will wait & see what Slater & those written to, may say.

The whole goddamn letter knocks me out, I mean, just that—damn well wish it were possible to join you, or something; jesus, it is HOT. Very damn much so.

And amazement, blank, that no one had made these connections, you do—cannot believe, finally, that men can be so goddamn abysmally STUPID.

(But that is usual, or their blankness, is usual, & no surprise, to any of it.)

Well, it is TOO MUCH: the whole works, how it opens, & it is a fucking whopper, you have hooked on to: like pulling up the whole damn SEA. Which IT IS. CRAZY.

(The things, that open up: as Ann says, just a minute ago, thinking, of Prescott, wherein he notes, of that people, Thalaxans,[62] who were friendly to Cortes, etc., & then notes their need, of salt, how they had no provision, for same, & that conjecture (hers): wd an inland people, or one, so used to such, the in, be so caught???)

I wished to hell that Slater still had his notebooks, but lost: & hopeless to hope they'll be sent back, etc. I mean, would be all the damn notes, etc., wd sure help now—to get to it, quick. Certain that he wd do anything he cd, etc. Have sent him these new notes, of yrs: he will FLIP.

Goddamn well, PLEASE keep this coming, to us: not a damn thing has hit, like this, since yr notes on the Sumer—& it is, I believe, of a piece, but that you shift, have shifted, to what's directly under the hand:

YR

fish.

Anyhow, don't for christ sake, do anything BUT labor us; this dullness, of waiting, even of this miserably dead season, how it takes 4 months to produce: a bud. . ., deadens us, & damn well ONLY yrself, to be of such, that damn taste.

(On yr Ez & Bill: not this eve, I mean, here it is too noisy & I am too hungry, but it is the damn REAL thing: &, again, yr fantastic precision. (Thinking, of reading CALL ME ISHMAEL, as it was, then, still wondering (not abt yr 'merit'—god forbid) but abt how far, how fucking deep, can he carry it??? And, jesus, was fantastic, & IS : this is, the fucking same sureness: ok.) Anyhow, or this evening, I lack all the damn 'terms' & too tired, to make them up: but it is, anyhow, this damned: ego/

what the fuck IS it, for, but to—sustain, the fineness, to gain the weights of, relation?

And that wd be, right off: NO 'I'/ NO : "it's mine. . ."

(I fucking well wonder, at that, how much Ez had dug

into Williams, to throw him into this, possession, of a "city," he damn well can't: possess. It won't be THERE/ never was/ & certainly: ISN'T.)

To ride this other fucking river: being that force, even, as river, underground, can thrust up: be IN light—what the hell else? Any-"time" ANY DAMN TIME.

            Write soon/

                    All our love to you both/

                               Bob

                                       [Lerma, Campeche]

thursday march 15 [1951]

my dear robert: crazy, not to have written you. not doing a hell of a lot: not well, either of us, or, for that matter much of anyone around lerma—peculiar weather, either too hot or, the last three days a wild and beautiful norther, the wind blowing the hell out a new moon. One day, the 1st, it was like any small Maine fishing village in storm: not even the muchachas out in the streets, every house barred, and severe, and if a man about, wrapped (like pictures of Mexicans) to his teeth in his cotton blanket (no such handsome things as zarapes, here, just cheap cotton blankets—& the choicest hat is a fucking chauffeur's cap!)

                                        i can't quite figure, what's wrong with me, but never knew a better law than, if the body lags, it's somewhere else the lag is. Figure it's a huge shell-hole i'm in, from, recent firing. And me just lying there, figuring, where i was hit, or, better, what bore & raise of gun got me.

                                       ·Anyhow, nothing raises me. And I waste time reading, murders (which all seem written by those filthies, newspapermen). (((A library of 'em, here, fr the wreck of a shrimper, American, beached on the farm of San Lorenzo, 10 kms down the road. Never read em before, much.)))

Went off by myself, the grey day, down the rd to sd farm, just for the motion. And by god picked myself off another ruin: right the hell on top of a little mt right the hell up over the sea! These Maya shure went for vistas.

But this proving of my case—how many Maya did live here by the sea—palls on me. Proved, it's a bore. Or at least I don't see putting any more of my time & money into it. (Thought this morning, how curious it is, that, there comes a time, and it comes quick, when one is interested in knowledge such as this, exterior, to a large extent, to one's own usage of same, when the interest cannot maintain itself unless one is being paid, or, at least, supported for same. Right now, e.g., I could be had, that is, I'd like, for the returns in verse it would give me, to putter this coast, to go a little more into this location of sites, determination, fr ceramica, of dates, etc. Yet, by god, it just ain't thriving enough to go on with without a jeep, a job, and immediate publication of results. Which means Carnegie or something like. And even that I want to fall in my lap, don't want to push around for.)

That is, I'm prepared, now, to make any conclusions in that area of culture-morphology, which is my essential interest. The rest wld be proving, which is not, finally, my business (I'd do it, just now, because I am on an off-swing, and would like, merely the movement of it, into the woods, or, if I had a launch, along this sea.)

But it's hieroglyphs, which are the real pay-off, the inside stuff, for me. And that's not in situ, that is, you can't *see* them—why Sanchez is so very much the value, for me, here (he came to dinner Monday night, and by god if he doesn't come in with the whole set of little books published in Campeche with his drawings of same,[63] damnest sweetest present, and, too much, as Creeley'd say, too much. Beautiful stuff (I've already suggested to Cid, that, he raise some dough to use a couple of these things, for a future issue: it would be so much more pertinent, now, than, what he seems to have been offered, thru Achilles Fang,[64] a job on Chinese characters, for nothing the cost

:it cld be a live graphic job, to present these glyphs, without comment, in such a way that their clarities & the width of their comment on human face & gesture, all animal and abstract nature, should sock any

reader
     i'm working on the problem, now, and have secured Sanchez's permission to use his work: I'm tearing out, for you & Ann, one small page fr the books he brought me, just for you to see

What wilds me, is, that here, in these things, is the intimate art (as against the mass & space of the buildings (god-stuff), and the corn-god, woman-temple, sacrifice-stone (the social-purpose))
                            Or Jaina! Jesus, what work, there: the only trouble is, they know, and it's guarded, & for me to dig, no go: have to be official, have to be, what I was talking abt, above: just one thing, in Museo, Campeche, two clay things, abt a hand-span tall, of the calix of a flower with a human being rising, right where the pistil would be! Incredible delicacy, & sureness: as in the glyphs, only, the glyphs already one stage formal, one stage set: the same glyphs, with variations, fr north to south! (What a bunch of live, working men, in this business, there were, wherever, there was a site: ex., down the rd, Sunday before last, a place called Pueblo Nuevo, the site no more than 75 feet over-all, and spang, there still, a stone-glyph!)

* * * * * * * * * * *

Don't know that this little place is healthy, or maybe it's the bad season. Much catarrho, mucho grippa. What we need is to make a trip, which we will do, any day, to Uxmal, then, for a couple of days, with hamackas, fr Uxmal to Kabah, Sayil, Labna, and maybe take in one of these caves, thereabouts, which, say all, are terrific (have never, myself, been, in a cave)

Still going along on Venus, or, as they called her, *Noh ek* (the great star)
                          or, *xux ek* (the wasp star—
         which sounds, this way: shoosh ek)

& the story seems to be, her attraction, beside her brightness, there for all to see, is: she's the asymmetrical one, of the Big Three, she's the one who is off the count, and does not put in regular appearance: works on a round of 584 days, but, is a real witch, in that she is two, that is, for eight months is morning star, then disappears completely for three

months, to reappear as evening star for eight months, after which time
she takes a dive for 14 days, to begin again, to be born, out of the eastern
sea, from the balls of, father, the sun[65]

I like her, and like that they called her—why—the wasp. why

****

And hope all goes well, now, with yr plans, for, France: i did not answer
you on, whether, we'll be back, before, just because I don't now know.
Haven't yet come up for such a look-around. Present mood is, pull up,
get moving around Mex, get back. But to what? Can't set out for Wash
with much will. Don't, for some reason, want, that, back, yet. Yet don't
have dough to just go along—or, for that matter, can't tolerate not
getting on with work. Dread Washington, at the moment. Am fucked
up.

   And know cause: my dreams are telling me. (Was thinking, this
morning, of Rimbaud, his decision: one understands; the human whatever, is such a snarl & wilder, what goes on, inside, what is. One falls
back, even in the advance, before it, the more so, the more, as he,
the—"what's on the other side of, despair," was it not?[66]

                                                              Why, finally,
I like him more than the apocalypts, DH, & Blake, say, is, that, I can't
see that he'd buy the idea, let me rest my elbows out, on nature. Strikes
me he was that stubborn deal, it's gotta be me, this substance, without
reference outward, or, no dice. And that substance, sd he, is, requires,
some such extra biz, for the other side of

                                    It's probably that, like he, I
like a formality better than I do, a guess, or, a symbol, which, I take it, is
all that human conversion can do to that which it rests on, if it is
anything other than itself:

                                    why Homer, or Melville, when he's tough,
I pair with R, as opposite, or, rather, as same as he Menelik[67] without
subtraction of his own act, the making of, words:

                                    for Homer, or Ovid,
without letting go what R had a hold of, grant & work with formaliza-
tions, rather than symbols (what R turned to, in mother, the Church, &
gun-running)

That is, for this tribe (and I count Keats in, despite), the struggle, due to *negative capability* (i dare say you know that biz, of K's, n.c. over against, contra to, the Egotistic Sublime)[68] is peculiar, is, neither, allows neither solution, Lawrence's or Homer's. Or did not, then.

I guess I'm saying, that, today, given similar tribal marks, the discovery of the formalization *has to be done*, that they did not do it, that, of another neighboring tribe one Melville came the closest (I am never comfortable linking him to Homer, yet, in his penetration of a formalization *beneath* both the human *and* nature, he, without Homer's advantages of a society, did a job most necessary then, & now).

Yes, it is this thing, *beneath*. That is, I take it DHL rode in by will alone, knowing, despair, yet, by way of woman (as he she-male as well as she as male), pushing nature back into human shape (as act of *magic*, surely, no?), yet, of importance for any tribe, because, he was *in* to a prime, the, androgyne

Blake (whom I do not know—for that matter, I do not know Rimbaud any more, for that matter, but whom, both, I take as such kin I have permission) Blake was *intellect* only second to R's, but, as 2nd, something less than R for the job in hand, Blake all intellect, and going, by that keel, from childhood straight through to, what?, without intervention of, despair, without the necessity of same: I picture him as a combination of clear physicality & mind (the kind of physicality Burns, I take it, was—maybe Anglo-Saxonish? for Shakespeare, certainly, was the finest of this sort of thing, the very clearest, no problems, of liver, kidneys or lungs). Anyhow, however, Blake's perceptions were of the order of stars, were, of the spheres, of that sort of prime—and not very close to the human except as he stayed, non-adult, stayed, child, was fanciful (I never take him as close, as DHL, is, as R is, as Melville is not, as Homer is not)

I come back to an old feeling, that Rimbaud saw there was nothing more to be done, *then*, that, still, he outranks us *now*, that, not one of us has matched, now, what he is capable of, granting him the century sleep I think he took—with his eyes, open. He'd not buy Christ (what Blake, and Lawrence too, did, when, the going, was roughest). That was that. He took the Church, &, mama, as preferable. Which, to me, makes sense: Christ was, contra, *down:* was, UP, pure levitation, and powerfully attractive to, a brain somewhat less than, the very best (that is, as of DHL, take, what has also to be taken, that shit, of Escaped Cock 2:[69] he is so close to that shit Yeats, in that part, giving up, surrendering, as Yeats did, clearly, no?, the struggle of his own sexual ball of twine, and substituting, some confusion of Christ & Woman, a FILTHY TRICK much practiced in kulch west)

                                        No dice, sd, that harle-
quin, that dead serious no-clown, Rimbaud.
                                   The proposition is: that we
are permitted, because of a huge "fault," to take horns in hand for
another broach of, what still can be called, I suppose, reality. Tho I abhor
such an abstraction. Let me repeat what stands, in my mind, as, necessary formalization)somehow forcing that word to be completely other
than symbol(

what lies beneath both the human *and* nature is, the cause. And which
same is, today, due to the fault, discoverable
                                   that is, I do not take it as
yrs, or mine, or Gerhardt's requirement, that, we rustle crusts in Paris
ashcans. Or pick up a poisoned leg, and lose it, anywhere.
                                                      I keep
throwing Homer in, because, he strikes me as, peg: his "reality" is
wholly formal without loss of intimate spaces, with the ball still snarled,
yet, with a light (and not stars) and a heat (not androgyne) which
declares, the persistence of both organism *and* will (human)

                         Towards which, just now, I am
                         fallen back

Love to you, & Ann, & the kids. Miss you very much. Yet you see, you
are here. And thanks. Thanks. Please write.
                         Love,
                              Charles

sat march 17 [1951]

christamiexcited. getting that load off my heart, to you, thursday, did a
trick. for i pulled out, that afternoon, down the road AND BROKE
THRU—

> hit a real spot, which had spotted fr bus, and which same,
> apparently, untouched: Con & I came back with bags of sherds
> & little heads & feet—all lovely things

> then, yesterday, alone, hit further south, and smash, dug out
> my 1st hierogyphyic stone! plus two possible stela (tho, no
> crowbar, so no proof)

> and today i want to hit again, while the run's on: and the joy,
> that everything, I can get to, in an hour (necessary, however,
> to risk getting a ride back, bumming: which, last night, took
> until 10:30, with Con, here, shure, fr a conversation of warn-
> ing fr a friend the night before, scaring the shit out of both of
> us, that snakes will get you! she saw me in the wilds with no
> one to suck the wound, and this morning, the zopalotes eating
> me, with the rising sun!) To tell the truth, I was scared, yes-
> terday, where I was, for the 1st half hour. Then, the excite-
> ment, the loveliness, the hell with it

will let you know more. right now wanted to tell you how good it was to
have four letters fr you yesterday (three: the Venus, note, for which
much thanks, the help; the letter including Slater's quote; and yr long
one, abt self, etc.)

let me give you back more on Q & K soon. my plot, this morning, is to
go into Campeche and see if I can get that horse's arse Raul Pavon Abrue
(Director, Museum) up off his ass, and go and determine for me (he does
know glyph reading) the date on (1) the stone I found yesterday and (2)
another stone, Pueblo Nuevo, he may or may not know. then I want to
go back to my 1st little baby this afternoon, and work till dark.

[*Page torn; possible to add from* Mayan Letters: Had started to reply. . . But] my nerves are so bunched toward these ruins, I better go, and get back to these things later, if you will understand, please. For I am wild for it.

Example: the big baby I spotted yesterday means CHUN-CAN means TRUNK OF THE SKY—and by god, the pyramid is so sharp and high it is just that, and most beautiful, high over the sea and the land (more like a watch-tower than anything templish[70]

Love to you all

        Charles

                                [Lerma, Campeche
                                18 March 1951]

sunday   (si, Palm Sunday! which must be why, yesterday, i suc-
cumbed to the sun & bought me a sombrero, for 4 pesos, of
palma de guano: very handsome, tho, how it looks on me, is a
question i can't answer. See! no mirrors, friend.)

by god creeley it's good to have two poems of yrs in hand again, by damn good. And thanks, for surely HELAS is most most beautiful, most pure, very grabbing (it was wonderful to watch Con, when I read it to her late last night: it came then, crazy, yesterday, three mails—and, this will kill you, A BIRD in each mail—#1, Blackburn's, fr you; #2 (after-noon), fr K.O. Hanson,[71] his 1st to me in over 3 yrs, and what is it, BOID (also gull); and yr, HAWK—which, of all, makes me, makes me go, to work. For you I ride, the others, well, what the hell are they but (too late, tou

tu-late, the
bird birded)
poetick

What HELAS does, is teach, how, now, what Arnaud cried, *trobar clus*,[73] is done. And so i hope you will follow me, in closing up, your lines. That is what its musick is, and, so, I'd, if you have any influence with one Corman, get him to print it thus:

Helas! Or Christus fails.
The day is the indefinite. The shapes of light
have surrounded the senses,
but will not take them to hand (as would an axe-edge
take to its stone. . .)

It is not a simple bitterness that comes between.
Worn by these simplicities, the head
revolves, turns in the wind but lacks
its delight.

What, now, more than sight
or sound could compel it, drive, new,
these mechanics for compulsion (nothing else but
to bite home! there, where
the head could take hold. . .)

                    which are vague,
in the wind,
take no edge from the wind, no edge
Or delight?

(note purposeful cap on Or. Also, I think I'd even close it up further, that is, make no break at all, all the way to "which are vague." YES. For what you've now got is just what all these arses keep chewing their mouths abt (including Hemerson the Hit), HOW TO DO NOW WHAT USED TO BE CALLED a SONNET. Let me make it, the way, I'd, set it:

& excuse, please, but it is such a delight I like copying it (it is very close, o, so nice & CLOSE, the feeling & the motion—it's a beauty, Rob't. And the more conventional it looks, the more, its explosion, strikes me:

> By the way, is it, now, to stand by itself—or, to be 1st part of the whole POOR SEASON? Anyhow, I'm setting it, here, as tho it was by itself, and was called, say, HELAS

HELAS

Robert Creeley

Helas! Or Christus fails.
The day is the indefinite. The shapes of light
have surrounded the senses,
but will not take them to hand (as would an axe-edge
take to its stone. . .)
It is not a simple bitterness that comes between.
Worn by these simplicities, the head
revolves, turns in the wind but lacks
its delight.
What, now, more than sight
or sound could compel it, drive, new,
these mechanics for compulsion
                              (nothing else but
to bite home! there, where
the head could take hold. . .)

                              which are vague,
in the wind,
take no edge from the wind, no edge
or delight

That seems abt it. Anyhow, I offer it. Very quiet and tough. Love it very much. (Wld make 1st break, as here, at (dropping one line, the "nothing," as you had it; then, dropping (again, as you had it) the "which are vague"; and leaving the last line as you had it, except, for, dropping, "the"?

It's a beauty. Because, all in you, in, yr process—out of it, straight, all of it, the sounds, the image, the feeling of the most dry nouns. O it's a pleasure, and you, can be, proud.

I'm not sure, myself, but, my favorite line, isn't:

It is not a simple bitterness that comes between

As a matter of fact, now that I look back, the stanzaing, or the running straight on, is, a matter of, not much import, that is, I think either of these two versions I send back to you, declare the formal organization that hides, & so reveals, the closeness of, the musick. Whichever seems best to you, I'd say: only, in both cases dropping, "nothing else." [*Added:*] (like best, rereading, #1, with drops, added)

(Item, to prove, another language does, have clues: last night, Martinez here, and we talking of how poor the fishing is (he earned 40 pesos this whole week, and him with five kids: 5 bucks) he was giving out, on the bank (it is called ANCLAR, BANCO ANCLAR (anchor), and on what reaches it takes to get their cayucos home. At which point he uses the verb *bordar*, to tack. And suddenly, for the 1st time, I have an answer to, the origin of a word, which same word has bugged me one long time. For to tack, is, of course, to embroider. Yet you'd never guess that from the confusion of meaning of tack, in English, no?)

[*Page or pages possibly missing.*]

                                                              [Lerma, Campeche]
tuesday, march 20 [1951]

bob: picking up, going back, over: (1), Ann, was shooting good, on the agronomy of same: only it's a little different, and, another measure, of—a damn good measure of—what machines, in their laziness, lead to: viz—unlike India, the soil, here, is most shallow, a few inches, & only occasionally, in drift pockets, 6 inches or more. So the struggle of the roots is intense. But a long time ago the boys beat it this way. It's grass that is the big enemy of maize, the only real one, for they burn off the bush, before they plant. But grass keeps coming in. And in the old days, they were able to stand it off—for as long as seven years (the maximum life of a milpa)—by weeding out the grass by *hand*. [74] But then came the machete. And with it, the victory of grass in *two* years. For ever since that iron, the natives cut the grass, and thus, without having thought about, *spread* the weed-seed, so that the whole milpa is choked, quickly choked, and gone, forever, for use for, maize (grass is so tough it doesn't even let bush or forest grow again!)

One curious corollary, that, the Communist future of this peninsula will have to reckon with: that, the ground is such, and its topography so humped & rocked, that, still, the ancient method of planting—with a pointed stick, and sowing, with the hands—is far superior to any tractor or planter or whatever.

So I wonder very much abt Slater's pass, that the Maya were far too intelligent a race to exhaust their soil, not to speak, as you are right to question, of his observation, that they were a highly spiritual race and such races always regard their soil as sacred:

for example, what i can't find anything out about, is WATER. Judging from the bizness here now (that deal, a week ago, I wrote you of, say)—and adding it to the *apparent* fact that the Maya depended, for water, upon these accidents of nature, where the upper limestone crust collapsed, and created these huge cenotes, near which they built their cities—I'd guess that this people had a very ancient way of *not improving on nature*, that is, that it is not a question of either intelligence or spirituality, but another thing, something Americans have a hard time getting their minds around, a form or bias of attention which does not include *improvements*

AND (by that law of the toilet, beds, etc., I wrote you about, once, from Washington)[75] I'm not one myself to say they were *backward, are* backward (my god, talk about the stars here: I ought to get off to you about the *flesh* here! Jesus, to ride a bus with these people, of a Sunday, down the coast, the stopping, the variation of quality between, say, Seybaplaya (allegre) and La Jolla (a sugar cane plant there, and a bottom, all, creatures, most of them, garage proletariat[76]—to steal, an accurate, phrase)

BUT, the way the bulk of them still (the "unimproved") wear their flesh! It is something I never had the occasion to guess, except in small pieces, isolated moments like, say, an Eyetalian family, or some splinter, not making itself clear enough to take over my assurances. For this is very much the result, I'd take it, as, the agriculture, the water problem: the flesh is worn as a daily thing, like the sun, is—& only in this sense—a common, carried as thethings are, for use. And not at all exclusively sexual, as, it strikes me, the flesh is hardened, and like wires, focused ("foco" is the name for an electric light bulb, here) in the industrial states.

The result (and this is what I think is actually the way to put what Slater makes spiritual or sacred) is, that the individual peering out from that flesh is precisely himself, is, a curious wandering animal (it is so very beautiful, how animal the eyes are, when the flesh is not worn so close it chokes, how human and individuated the look comes out: jeesus, when you are rocked, by the roads, against any of them—kids, women, men—it's so very gentle, so granted, the feel, of touch—none of that pull, away, which, in the States caused me, for so many years, the deepest sort of questions about my own structure, the complex of my own organism, I felt so very much this admission these people now give me[77]

This is not easy to state, I guess. BUT OF EXTREME IMPOR- TANCE. For I come on, here, what seems to me to be the real, live clue to the results of what I keep gabbing about, *another* humanism. For it is so much a matter of resistance—like I tried to say, about, *leaving* the difficulties, not removing them, by *buying* the improvement so readily available at the corner. You buy something all right, but what gets forgotten is, that you sell, in that moment of buying—you sell a whole disposition of self which very soon plunders you just where you are not looking. Or so, it seems.

The trouble is, with this imagery, of industrialism. I distrust it, as (1) too easy (2) too modern and (3) too much, not contrary, but merely opposition. For the shift, which took away (is taking away, so rapidly, that I shall soon not be able to get into Campeche, it is such an ugly ("feo," is their word) demonstration of what happens when COMMERCE comes in)—how do you get at what happened? when did some contrary principle of man get in business? why? what urge

well, that's not hard, I know—i figure it always was, only, once (or still, here, at Seybaplaya—and a bit back, Lerma, before electricity) these big-eared, small-eyed, scared-flesh characters stayed as the minority, were not let out of, their holes. Because there was a concept at work, not surely "sacred," just, a disposition to keep the attention poised in such a way that there was time to (1) be interested in expression & gesture of all creatures including at least three large planets enough to create a system of record which we now call hieroglyphs; (2) to mass stone with sufficient proportion to decorate a near hill and turn it into a firetower, or an observatory, or as one post of an enclosure in which people, favored by its shadows, might swap commotes for shoes; (3) to fire clay, not just to sift and thus make cool water, or, to stew iguana, or fish, but to fire it so that its handsomeness put ceremoney where it also belongs, in the most elementary human acts. And when a people are so disposed, it should come as no surprise that, long before any of these accomplishments, the same people did an improvement, if one likes, of nature—the domestication of maize—which is still talked of as one of the world's wonders!

It is all such a delicate juggling of weights, this culture business—exactly like, I'd guess, what is the juggling of any one of us with the given insides. Which is why generalization is, a g.s. [78]

Christ, these hieroglyphs. Here is the most abstract and formal deal of all the things this people dealt out—and yet, to my taste, it is precisely as intimate as verse is. Is, in fact, verse. Is their verse. And comes into existence, obeys the same laws that, the coming into existence, the persisting of verse, does.

Which leads me to use again Ruth Benedict's excellent proposition (to counter the notion that, the Maya, having done so much, need also have developed an agronomy which would not have exhausted their soil and a system of rain-gathering which would also have licked the thirst problem): says Benedict,

> . . . .techniques of cultural change which are limited only by the *unimaginativeness of the human mind*[79]

Or which, perhaps, is just a little bit the bitterness of an old-maid-almost-Communist before she died. It seems to me now, she over-loads, by using "imagination," even negatively—a little bit too much modern Hamletism (I am thinking of Hamlet to Horatio (is it) on what a glory man is, the top creature, what nature was working towards, etc).[80] Benedict is the reverse of same. One needs to be quieter—but still not miss the point: that, in a given lifetime a man, or, in a given expression, a culture, cannot get any more done than it can get done: that time, & our life-machine, are not infinitely extensible. Which dream—the Renaissance, & all ecstatic propositions—is well dead. We'll know and do more if the limits—there'll be more reaches, etc.

My point is, what more do we have the privilege to ask of the Maya than same Maya offered

> Will get this off, & go in to Campeche to see if I can get Pavon off his arse, and go with me to read the glyph-stone at Chun-can (you know, it only has slowly dawned on me, that, Friday, I made myself the sort of discovery I was hankering for! By god, I did dig out a glyph! And if the other two stones turn out to be stelae, I'll have myself one of those coups these characters live their fucking lives on. Only, I still want only one thing: I want to *see* the stone and have Pavon tell me what the glyphs mean, the bastard! And turn those two stones over, to see, if, on their face down in the earth (which should preserve them) they are also worked.

CHUN-CAN, by the way, which I told you was TRUNK OF THE SKY, is—says Martinez—not that (which is what the Seybanos told me) but TRUNK OF THE SERPENT. He says, to be the 1st, it would have to be CHUN-CAAN (which of course it may have been).

Lerma   March 22   51

My dear CR: It is Holy Week in this Spanish nation, so I imagine the reason we have not had any mail since the weekend is, that the airplanes are blessing themselves, and doing other services over the middle of the Gulf. It irritates me, as do all Sundays, holidays and such: tho, yesterday, I shall say it was pleasant, sitting in a Coney Island stand (the best cafe Campeche can offer, on a sidewalk—o, for Vera Cruz, on such a day), eating turkey tacos, & drinking mineral water! (We had had to go in, at 10 am, to settle an argument over the rent of this house—which we lost, I am afraid: the two owners got into a snarl a month ago, and I was hoping we could take advantage of it to force the rent back to what we expected to pay when we came. But I guess not: it was fun, trying—and much worth while, for 5 bucks difference, here, is a good week's food.

In any case, the whole uproar brings on the problem of what I ought to do, running out, as I am, so fast, of funds. It burns my arse, to be put to it—and just when I begin to pick up, feel freshened, toughened, and hoisted forward. It is that old problem, how a man, whose goods are not bought, whose daily drive turns out to be non-economic (Corman tells me we are all dollar-an-issue men) eats, sleeps, gets on, with his work.

I keep turning over, where, to strike out, for a stake. It is so stupid, that, if I want to stay here (as I do), I should not be able to raise up some birds who could use the results of my labors—the joke of the pack is, that I think the best chance of all, to seek a job (ACTUALLY, a job), on the reconstruction of Mayapan (now on), might be the most likely—but would, after a few days, be more hindrance to me, than help. For I long ago learned that I range, or I go dead. So what I am doing, have been doing, for the past month and a half, is what I should ideally get staked to continue to do. But that means some claim on somebody for something other than verse—and, by the same economic law as above stated, same does not exist.

So far as I can see it, my only hope would be to convince one of these professional Maya outfits in the States that what I am doing would pay-off, to them, in some form or other. Which, it still strikes me, is small chance, they are so backward in admitting culture-morphology as a discipline (my premise being, of course, that only a poet, now, can be said to possess the tools to practice culture-morphology at its best [added: & its, highest heat]). But who'll buy that posy, except thee & me?

So I crawl forward, on that one. I have feinted toward it, twice—one jab at Tulane, where, by accident (by ordering a map) I came in touch with a "boss": Robert Wauchope, "expert" on Maya domestic architecture; and one roundhouse at Samuel K. Lothrop, whom Crosby had sd, write to, before I left (he is a fine scholar in this Maya business, his major work, a three volume study on Tulum, the ruin on the other coast—this work, so far as I now know, seems the only substantial one in that area I am curious about, the coast, etc. [81] ((one issue of yesterday, was, I found out how to get a boat fr the island of Cozumel to Tulum for something like 20 pesos—which is guarantee I can now make that trip, if I can stay here: before, all information was, it would take 200 pesos! A guy came up, a friend of a friend, and he, for 20 yrs, had been a chicle buyer at Cozumel. It's these events, which delight one, in this unorganized country!))

Of course, as you pointed out, my ace, is Sauer. But one plays an ace, careful, no? For my problem is, always, that, there is no end to this economic pattern, that is, that, one has to figure it will happen again, and again. So one has to weigh all moves now against necessary moves three–five yrs ahead. And I hold back on Sauer, always, until I have something solid to offer, I respect him so much: I have kept on, will have to keep on, right up to the last extremity, before hitting him, in hopes I can lay the most on the line, from work done here. In fact, just because he is, in a sense, the best backer I could turn to in such work as this, the most open, one wants to offer the most, eh?

The only hitch is, the extremity fast approaches, god damn it. Which interrupts my mind. And deters, deters!!

But not much. Have been digging the old Maya chronicles,[82] the last couple of days, and come up with interesting stuff on Quetz-Kukul—and the question of, sea origins. Will be folding it yr-way, I suspect, soon. One curious thing is, that the place of origin (in the legends) keeps coming up as TULE (also Tula, Tullan, Tulapan). And it is sd to be the place where he, "the great father-priest," was—where, in fact, according to a Quiche-Maya tale, he gave the first captain who set out for Guatemala-Yucatan, a present called *"Giron Gagal."* (What in Christ that is, nobody knows.)

But this TULE is curious in other ways (not to mention the fact that, in one people's version it is on the other side of the ocean to the east, & in another, to the west): the wildest of all, is, what you will remember, that, *ultima Thule*, was the outermost reach of the world to the ancients, was, to the Greeks, Thoulē, or Thylē. In the light of Waddell, I should like to know (or Berard, as well as Waddell, for that matter) if that word goes back behind the Greeks to the Phoenicians, Cretans, Sumerians.

I say this, for another reason—which goes very deep, into the whole question these Maya raise (and it's treacherous ground, where all that I have seen try to walk on it, have fallen for the most dangerous Nordicism there is). But it is this evidence (you see it all around you here, and clearly, not from Spanish mixture) that there was an Armenoid-Caucasian physical type just as clearly as there was a Mongoloid type among the ancient Maya. (Hippolito, for ex., was telling Con and me—with considerable excitement—about a Lacandon Indian who was his & Stromsvik's guide when they were at Bonampak three yrs ago (these Lacandones are an isolated tribe in Chiapas, near the Guatemala border, who have stayed in a state of arrestment apparently equal to the period of the Maya *before* the cultivation of maize—which goes back, maybe, 3 millennium before Christ, or, into that area of time which coincides with the opening out of the Persian and Mediterranean world by the Sumerians). Hippolito was struck by this man's whiteness, his scimitar of a nose, and the whole caucasianism of his mind & behavior.

The funny thing is, I have come on one Maya "expert" who is pushing an argument—strangely enough—which is most close to Waddell's (tho this bird Jakeman obviously doesn't know Waddell at all).[83] It is this: that the Itzas (who, he declares, were the priest-tribe of the Maya, the inventors of glyphs, astronomy, & the building) were the Caucasians, and can be distinguished precisely from the Mongoloids, who were the subject people, the farmers, the workers, etc. And of course his most telling argument (though he does not use it [added: maybe he does: not sure, yet]) is that business of Quetzal-Kukul, as *white, bearded*, and from beyond the eastern sea.

Of course I balk at same, or at least resist, simply because I take it, racism has to be kept at the end of a stick. Or put it this way: until we have completely cleaned ourselves of the biases of westernism, of greekism, until we have squared away at historical time in such a manner that we are able to see Sumer as a point from which *all* "races" (speaking of them culturally, not, biologically) egressed, we do not have permission to weight the scale one way or another (for example, Jakeman, leaves, so far as I have read him, the invention of maize to the Mongoloids, as well as the arts of ceramica, weaving, and baskets! And, *contra* (contra all these prejudiced Nordics, among whom I include Hooton, who has sd, from skull-measurements, that it is true, there were Caucasians here),[84] there remains China, ancient and modern China. Until the lads can verify that the Chinese, as well as the people of India, came off from the Tigris-Euphrates complex, they better lie low with their jumps to conclude that only the Caucasian type was the civilizing type of man). ((As you know, this whole modern intellectual demarche, has, at its roots, a negative impulse, deeper, even, than the anti-Asia colonialism of Europe: at root, the search is, to unload, to disburden themselves, of Judaism, of Semitism))

What excites me, is, a whole series of scholarly deductions which widen out the rear of the Maya sufficiently for me to pick up confirmations to my imaginative thesis of the sea, that is, of migration. (I had much joy this morning showing Martinez how the peoples of the Pacific made maps—I was using match-sticks to stand for those extraordinary charts of sticks and twine by which the Polynesians & others made the voyages from the Malay Peninsula out across that space.[85] And trying, in this

still struggling Spanish—"practico," as they tell me, I still resist studying books of same—to describe to him those huge out-riggers the Pacific
peoples used!)

Well, as you say, there is so much here—so very much—I am a fool to
think I can amass it fast enough to stake myself, now, to go ahead. If my
nervous system was not so completely place-committed, I'd get back
under the lee of Washington, and continue mastering the material there.
But of course you'd know, beyond any man, how false such sense is, for
me. In fact, it occurs to me, that, precisely in this business, I have struck
the organic next phase to what I had exhausted, in Washington. (You
smelled, first, the relationship of all this to that shot out from the States,
I made, last summer, on Sumeria.) I should be quite content to go on
now, for some time (years?), right here in this triangle, of Yucatan,
southern Mexico, Guatemala, & Honduras, exhausting this problem.

For example, GLYPHS. I begin to bear in. What I wrote to you, abt the
glyphs as verse, seems more and more true. As a matter of fact, perhaps
more important (for me) than the study of Maya, living Maya, is this
other thing, the study of the glyphs. For here—beyond everything—is
the real increment, the exact same raise, for me, as those "poems" on
the clay tablets of Sumeria. And of such an even more important order
of language (again, for me). Here is ideogram in a state much more
available than Chinese. Here it is, as it was, in this geography (ours).
And by god if no one—no one—has seen the glyphs as what they are!
They have all been so blinded by not knowing their "meanings" that
they have missed the real point, that, in themselves as *images*, they tell,
tell, tell!

Well, it's all one package—the two of us scratching these cuyos, hereabouts; the tease of these pieces of ceramics we pick up (to know more
abt those styles, and their chronology); the sounds of the Maya speech
back off this main street; the hunger to get the hell off to Palenque (a
train ride away, by god!), to have the dough to fly to Copan, or Uaxactun, even to stir ourselves enough to backtrail by bus towards Merida
and see Uxmal, Kabah, Labna, Sayil; the glyphs; and this other door,
which leads in, in, & back, the sea & its life, on all these other things.

A

big order, requiring the smallest of change! And (I am scared), maybe, all beyond my grasp! Christ.

And thanks again, for being there, to talk to. Will get back to our various other businesses, as soon as I win a little, or lose all, in this push, to stay, and master, what I've got so hot in my hands!

Love to Ann, and the kids,

charles

lerma   saturday   march 24 [1951]   (yr two letters in—always, saturdays, it seems—& same answering me, as of two weeks ago: the spread)

CR: which, makes, another point landing! for, yr dope on switches, for water, is, precisely what i need this very day, by god! how abt that: you see, Vasquez (the fruit farmer) came, *yesterday* evening, for the 1st time—and, with interpreter this time—the 1st time we have talked over the trip to the wells, two weeks ago today! Also (my purpose) was to settle just how far he will permit Con & I to go tearing up the ruin which adjoins his farm. The upshot was, he invites us to do anything we want, take away anything we find! And then, adds he, use the shade of my farm anytime—and if you can locate water there, all to the good! SO: sez I, I'LL have to use a stick—laughing—and by god, NOW, you, yr pertinence, by GOD I SHALL! And today, this Holy Saturday, by god, by god, by god............

Such thanks. And for Slater's kind maps, ditto, the which are exactly (as you knew), to hand (one crazy thing I can't figure out—why is SB's map *and* the published map made exactly contrary to both the skies and to normal NESW (clockwise)? that is, did you notice, both maps read with E to the *left* of N? Most great mystery.

As of E Baron, and the ART of the GRIMACE: if that goddamned Cagli ever wrote a letter (it is near two years, and no further communication), I'd have the answer on Italy, anyway (will try him right now again, but little hope, for answer). But in France, right off the bat, EB's answer is EASY: and it shld damn well insure confidence in her sponsors, as well as satisfy your (and my) demand of MIME: she shld manage to get permission to study—or at least say she goes to study with—whatever his name is, anyway, the guy who played the Pierrot in LES ENFANTS DU PARADIS:[86] jesus, than whom, in the known theatre now, there is no more fine than (he who is finer, CHARLES chaplin—but whom you are absolutely correct abt, is out, as, senile &, very damned busy, impossible to get to, even, his friends)

And my memory is, that SAME FRENCHMAN does have a school or group or discipline which EB should be (as American, shouldn't, where mime is his base, have trouble) should be able to enter.

Course, as you'd know, I don't believe one who was really going to make it, would do this at all; but your reasoning on EB's case, that, only this way can she get the dough, is, absolutely sound. If, however, the deal falls through before next february, or whenever, please let me know, and we'll go in, with her, to a discipline here in the States which (ought to) do a job for her, now, that, would, in the end, given her drive, make it (the body, on, fr the heels, literally the heels, on up: speech (like you say) LAST

(i guess this biz waz why—now that it's behind me—I found black mt/ ground, that, there, i was able to work out that discipline   And had one girl & one boy who (EB must know them, soon) had themselves enough to learn & teach me: the boy is still there, & did, for me, in Wash, in Dec., a dance (did i tell you?) which. . . and is now in SCarolina doing another (Cernovich, the name[87]); the girl (Diyulio[88]) I fought with, & kicked out (sex, mixed) & is now in NYC going it, on her own, or something, but is the most gifted of all (she it was taught me the heels, to a piece of Bartok's, taking me that bone, further: beautiful thing)

O, yes: if EB could swing it, my impression is, there is no better
base worker than Katherine Litz (is it? YMHA, NY), a modest lady, sets
up as dance teacher. Or Merce Cunningham, perhaps, for EB, simply
because, my impression was, Litz had most effect on men (not to say
either of these are major, but, that they'd got a toe hold on something
beyond what is, a little something, at least, the old respect for, movement as, to be played on, no other instrument than, the skeleton, these
"bones"

Which brings up the dismal absence of, same, in this people,
here (& in MEX, as far as I touched it)—I thind I sd, only, a drum. The
rest, is, filthy Spanish, ecstasy shit, mambo/ no go (but i guess i sd, the
Negro, THERE. . .)

[Added:] (1) EB cld do what some of mimes have done—get lessons fr
        Litz or Merce, for a week, two weeks, in NY & then keep
        at it, at Brandeis
What I meant, on Litz, was, for EB, between now, & next Feb, say.
Well, I'll also write to KAGG, and if I think of anything else, will let you
know. But surely, that guy, that Frog, is, her man.

[Added:] (2) Or 2nd idea, this summer, go where either of them (like
        Litz, last summer, at Black Mt) go
((As of SIMP, & such (Rowen, Rainier, or, whatever[89]), this, fr girl[90] in
Washington whose boy, has our house:

"Ran into large segments of
EP's crew (including Mrs. EP) at the Segovia concert a while back. Mr.
4-pages, EP economists, all the beards in town plus the diplomatic
set."
        which tells the whole story, yes?))

OH, ya: right near EB, is a crazy girl, who, before she left husband (the
Williams I sent Corman to), I told not to, told, instead, to do, there,
Cambridge-Boston, what she wants to do, become, a professional clown,
which, delights me, sounds, right, and, leads anywhere. Name's Vera
W—and (her husband writes) returns home July. Vera is dizzy, & gift-
ed, and very good. We ought to put EB and her in touch, when. . .

Hope yr landlord has a stroke (like I'm hoping ours, here, does, before
Monday, when I have to cough up, the 20 bucks, for March!). God damn

nuisance for you. can see, tho, figure, you'll take care of him. yes, hope he konks out.

Let this be it. Anyway, it was, to get the board done, between us. To leave it open for. . . for what yr other letter is, on snap-the-whip, very, exact, very, has me, is, what the hell can one say when, a man is, putting his hand in, exactly where he is. Anyhow, thank you.

Will come back, with, as, under hand, anything, comes out (one good biz in fr corman, this morning, that, he can use "line" drawings of glyphs by Sanchez, wd like same, for future issues—even (which is what one can like abt the boy) proposes to try to get space in Boston gallery for display of sd drawings! Shall see Sanchez, and wrap this up: it shld be good, picking out, the glyphs, eh? by god: am started! and where i take it, is, really, the biz (as I sd, this week, to you). (And Slater, by the way, is on the ball, when, he sez, the Germans [*Added:* A guy named Herman Beyer[91] very good—& in English, tho, German push]—and that, any joining of stars to glyphs ought to, give up what, Rosetta Stones, won't ((even here, still, the same goddamned business, that, the analogies, of western procedures, BLOCK)

                love to you all   charles

lerma, campeche, mex. march 25 [*i.e.* 26, 1951] (monday)   rob't:

you are, of course, most right abt sam morse—fr this one poem he comes over as clean & gentle & sharp a man as (whatever is a good simile, the whiches he uses too many of—but that, is, is it not, implicit in the iambic pentameter, is, a device of language much used when a man (or a time) are consonant to the life local to them ((this seems to me

to be capable of considerable extension, as much extension, for that
matter, as the Elizabethans gave it, who, I take it, were "comfortable"
with their queen & ships, with/mercantilism

((& this also is a way to answer the glib urban objection to
"localism," which is almost always an objection to non-
urbanism:

tho it is forever bearing in on me that there be nothing more
local than city-writers (& the attention they've been given no
more than a sign of the attraction of the largest city extant:
dahlberg, say, who, to me is, the best of the americancity-
productions, but is, that, is, 8th St Viaduct, Kansas City,
inside-aswellas-out, merely, another kind of Bronx (as "Awake
& Sing" was, whoever it was, wrote it)[92]

that is, that, a localism is a thing men fall back into when, they
have given up—or can't make—the pitch: the thing that
makes the Elizabethans exciting is, that so many of them, and not just S
and Jonson, kept going—not necessarily *out* (truth is, they had plenty of
out, fr Drake, etc., as did Melville have, who made it count, too), but on
the ground (lunnon town, or whatever: stratford)

i mean, morse makes what is his count, right now, and he carries up
from it, by accuracy & personal commitment, freshness—& a deliver-
ance from, mere observation or "capturing." Of course it's in his line,
that he tells, and that keeps me

(contrast is, at the moment, Bronk,
who—I suppose because he has not yet settled on a line—cannot maintain me that long—though Bronk's roughness of person is attractive,
however vulgar he seems beside Morse

BUT I SHOULD SHUT UP,
until I see more, of both!

(((the thing that strikes me, tho, is, how both proceed from bases which i
would call prose-base rather than of verse. But these are my own
dogmatisms, perhaps. Or rather, I am prepared now to give up that
distinction as not good enough (you have satisfied me that narration is

forward, and that it is not at all to do with any other instrument than
the man under hand

—what I imagine I am quietly objecting to in
"Creatures like Chameleons" is a sort of narrative method I don't
think has much life in it; and in "The Mind's Landscape,"[93] a similar
speculative method, ditto

and the reasons both use same is,
themselves, that is what they have decided (Morse, by decision, Bronk,
not so) to dispose themselves toward

Which brings me back to "consonance" (as it has been on my mind as
contrast to other dispositions which I think are done for, however much
they did, & might, now, produce—

that is, it occurs to me that if i am
right to bracket so (dante to pound), then it is time we saw the most
intense productions of the west (the work of those two) as constituting a
kind of literature which can be called *infernoesque* & same as precisely
the opposite of the *apocalyptic* (which can be sd to include the
"romantics"—again, Hamlet to Horatio, on man, the crowning...—

lerma march 27 [1951]   R Cr: Over the house, last night, 3 am, the
SOUTHERN CROSS! please tell Slater, that, & that, with a flashlight, I
confirmed it with, his map: tell him, the SC, here, is, at that hour, much
like, & a gentler, say, feminine counterpart to, earlier, in the west,
ORION: tell him, another thanks, for his drawings & note, on the
SeaHorse (which came in yesterday, along with yr other testimonial)

tell him this: that, it is quite quite true, that, here, the life of a night sky
is very thick & close—and that same fact i have not seen anywhere
admitted as good & sufficient reason for the Maya exploitation of same,
that, in fact, in contrast to the day, which is so goddamned strong it is

whited out, is, so pervasive as to make it necessary that one either blind oneself to it or hide, the night is delicious, & the sky so swift in the passage of the constellations, in the play of their colors, that it is impossible to leave

(one good & sufficient reason why there was, here, a class of men who mastered this other life is, I just bet, that, if you could choose, if you did not have to work fields, or whatever, by the light of, the sun, then, by god, you'd do what I've always sd any civilized man wld do, arrange it, that, you lived in the night not, the day!)

sure, the Mayans, too, hid from THE WASP, as they called her, that STAR: she gives you the jimmies right now, the other night, settling down, in the west, and throwing such a fit of light & color, you'd swear she was going to blow right up in yr face then & there SHOOSH ECK

at which point i transfer to you how the Maya took it the other two citizens behaved:94

moon is girl, living with grandfather, weaving. sun is not yet sun, is young man full of himself, who wants this girl, & poses as great hunter, to win her first looking. to come closer he borrows the nature of hummingbird, but, while drinking honey out of the tobacco flowers near her house, grandpa pings him with a clay shot fr blowgun. moon picks sun-bird to bosom, then to room, then sun to consciousness, then sun to human shape, and business! he persuades her to elope. but g-pop gets rain to toss bolts at pair fleeing in canoe: sun converts to turtle & escapes, but moon, trying on crab shell, is not protected enough & is killed

dragonflies collect moon's flesh & blood in 13 hollow logs. after 13 days sun uncovers logs, finds 1st 12 to contain all known noxious insects & snakes, which, released, spread all over the world. log 13 reveals moon, restored, to life

only, moon has no cunt, ah. deer, however, remedies same defect, &

sun & moon do it, the first persons to have such/pleasure ((some passage
of   time))

enter sun's older brother, creating triangle of sky, for elder bro. is,
venus, who comes to live with sun & moon. sun begins to suspect there
is something going on between moon & big star, they are so much
together. by a trick he exposes them, & moon, dispirited, is sitting alone
by river-water when a vulture persuades her to go with him to the house
of king vulture. Which she does, becoming his wife.

sun (the dope) seeking her, borrows the skin of a small deer, hides
under it, & when vultures come to eat what they think is the carcass of
same, sun snatches one, gets on his back, & rides off to king vulture's
house, where he recovers moon, who is somewhat reluctant to return.

at which stage, for reasons of cause or not, sun & moon go up into the
sky to assume their celestial duties. but sun finds there is one last
thing he must do to this dame before all's right with the orb: the
people on earth complain that because moon is so goddamned bright
they can't sleep & it is always the same as day. so sun, to dim his
dame's brightness, knocks out one of her eyes

the tale has this superior gimmick, for its ending: eclipse, sd the old
ones, were nothing more nor less than fights between sun & moon,
presumably because sun can't forget moon's promiscuity, though the
Quiche have it that moon, anyway, is erratic, very much a liar (is
constantly telling sun tales about the way the people on the earth
misbehave, drink too much, etc.), and as difficult to understand as any
bitch is.

I'mp tellink you, Robert, yure right, i got a horn by its tail! and fr the
way it looks today (i mean precisely today, things keep shifting so, as i
cut away at my ignorance), that introductory glyph (of the fish) which
led me in, was sign of where i am intended to go:[95]
and i sure back off!
for it is straight forward into GLYPHS (like you probably smelled, the
last few communications). and that's one pisser of a task (& the bitch of

it is, is no way to raise dough to continue here, any smart guy saying,
such study is years, & in lieu of any immediate addition to "knowledge," how can you justify staying there, instead of here, to make same
study?

    which, of course, is cockeyed, for, it is by being here where that
life was that i pick up on same, including glyphs, and would best continue, but (again) who knows that but thee & who:

it is a joker, straight: this way, that, these Maya are worth remember-
ing because they were hot for the world they lived in & hot to get it
down by way of a language which is loaded to the gills of the FIRST
GLYPH with that kind of imagination which the kerekters have a way
of calling creative

yet i have yet to find *one* man among all who have worked this street
in the last century who is, himself, confident of his taste, is even
possessed of that kind of taste, or drive towards a hot world, which is
called creative power!

and the result, of course, is, that the discrepancy between what the
maya did and what these birds are finding out about it is just another
of those gaps which confirm the old man in his shot, that, it was not
original sin, good bro. possum, which was the fall of man, but
o-riginal, in-nate, stu-pidity![96]

ex., glyphs: give you or me the "alphabet," just the rudiments of the
first meanings, plus a Maya dictionary, and as full a knowledge as
possible of tales (such as above), and by god if we wouldn't walk all
over them as to what the rest of the story is! i swear (adding as long a
time as possible just being here to observe, not so much contemporary
maya (another of the wise boys' phoney smartnesses) but the *geography* in which the old maya lived

excuse me, there's no use beating you with sticks i ought to be getting
the chance to beat some others with. and anyway, what i want to get to,
with you, is, at the nature of this *language*, of which the glyphs are the
most beautiful expression (much more beautiful, by the way, than the
codices, which are late & Mexican (pictographic, not, as were the Maya,
both ideographic & phonetic) and much more beautiful (due to the limits

The Olsons' house at Lerma, with a zopilote on roof. Photographed in 1949 by Diana Woelffer.

The Olsons' house at Lerma (1949). Photograph by Diana Woelffer.

The beach in front of the Olsons' house at Lerma, with a Spanish cannon in the surf (1949). Photograph by Diana Woelffer.

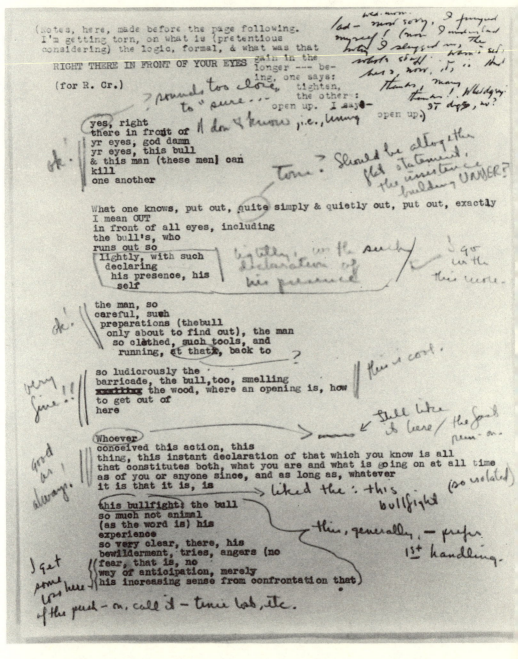

Early version of Olson's poem "This" returned with Creeley's 16 April 1951 letter, with notes (both typed and written in pencil) added by Creeley. The note dated "wed. morn." (i.e. April 11) in the upper right corner is by Olson (above and over). Charles Olson Collection. Literary Archives, University of Connecticut Library.

he is
involved

the thing: can you afford same after drift in the explanation of / fear? So the room it takes.

cow-like) (the fourth bull was a doe-like creature who backed off

((the legs of a bull in the ring are not
what they are in a field, are)
colt, or
calf))

← I don't know — doesn't pull much, for me.

the men (the man)
so much more
animal, so
aware, their
courage (fear) so
most clear, so very much the reason why
we too are
involved, why
we,
here,   *? I mean, do you need it?*
are:

((the man, down in that dirt, so much
a scampering, so much (advancing) a   *← this detail, I
sort of picked bantam))   go with.*

                              YET

those horns

that voice repeating "toro"   "toro"   "toro"

those words, ~~saying~~ing

that head, the plain danger of same

you know you have

been

asked

*It's a fucking
fine thing, anyhow.
Mainly — the RUSH, the
CROWD of, perceptions —
can you keep same*

                    END

*moving as — simul-
taneous? That's
where the longer one had gained,
in spite of the looseness of same.*

Ann Creeley with sons David and Thomas, Littleton, N.H., 1951.
Charles Olson Collection. Literary Archives, University of
Connecticut Library.

of stone plus the limits of language) than the sculpture or, for that matter, the architecture

> ((my god, what i've *got* to see,
> before leaving her[e], *is:* a
> STANDING STELA—jay-hoo!))

anyway, i'm started, in getting this same attitude moved forward, even if it ain't solving my own problem: yesterday i talked to sanchez—who, by the way, is a sort of exception to the wholesale no one, above, tho, he is, a draftsman, and is it because he is young, as well as maya, that, he makes it? And sanchez accepts the idea of both a show in boston plus my or corman's use of repros. The hitch is, his boss, Raul Pavon Abreu, who is one of these "calendar"-glyph birds, and is also a politician, & is also without taste. Fortunately he is in Mexico this week, and Sanchez and I can work out the whole deal, picking the glyphs etc, before he returns. And I thought up one thing which make [*i.e.* may] hook him: to double the show corman suggests—get some museum in Washington to agree to take it after Boston, and that way, because the Peabody gang can see it in Boston and the Carnegie gang see it in Washington, hope to christ Pavon will agree to let Sanchez ship the stuff (you see these drawings took one year to do, and are the only ones in existence—I must say for Pavon that his idea to do this book (it was contracted for with the Guatemala govt, at 1000 copies, cost, $10,000 American), to do *all* the glyphs at one site (Copan), the only time this will have been done (if it gets done, the hitch, that a dictator threw out the G Govt., and the contract is no longer alive), is a damned good one ((also went whirring off with the notion, try to get the Bollingen people to publish it, in the States))

it's a good gambit, i figure, the best at hand, at the moment—and i'll push it, will use every tease i can think of to get Pavon (who plays all things like a Mexican politician, and, is doomed) to agree.

look, orb't (!), excuse me i spend all the time in these letters on what i am doing. but the push is now on. i've got to break thru fast, or get the hell out. haven't yet made any move money-wards. can't see the play.

so, the next few days are crucial. so, excuse, please, the wildness.

                                                                    and
keep writing: it is the same, here: yr letters give us both touch. touch
                                    love to ann & you   charles

lerma   wednesday   march 28 [1951]   robert: just may have hit on
the play, the right plunge, to get 'em all pushing—dreamed up this idea:
a book to be called THE GLYPHS OF COPAN, to be based on Sanchez's
drawings, to include (necessarily) Pavon's readings of the glyphs, and to
give me the chance to compose the book (to organize the visual presentation, so that—perhaps for the first time—the glyphs are seen as LAN-
GUAGE by way of DESIGN: which same would also be the subject of
the introduction, an essay on language & on the kind of culture which
produced this language

that's easy, to block out the idea, but what pleases me is the proposition
by which it gets published: i wait until monday, Pavon's return, to cut
him in & to get him to agree (not easy!); then, if so, i write to the
Bollingen gang (who have the dough, & who have, so far as i can see,
been biased toward just such combinations of scholarship & presentation), laying out the deal, proposing those who know my own work, &
listing Pavon's & Sanchez's claims

at the same time plugging, that ORIGIN will publish preliminary round,
& that there will be two exhibitions in the coming year (sd he), Boston &
Washington

what d'ya think, laddie? it would give me one hot chance to continue
work started—get me to Copan!—etc. etc. AND it's concentrated just
where I'd wish to be, on these wondrous things, GLYPHS!

but let's don't let ann think, she, & los animales, marine especially, are being left behind. for all this started fr a fish (the INTRODUCTORY GLYPH), and it will come flying home, fins & all: yesterday, for example, I found further evidence (& right spang out of Sanchez's drawings) that the big boy of it all (J. Eric S. Thompson) must be wrong, when he sees the fish as a rebus of a mythological monster more like a crocodile than an actual fish (the land-bias, of the mayistas).

> Ex.: "The fish and the Imix prefix to this god's glyph (God L, Dresden, p. 46) are probably clues to his identification (he wears fish in his headdress, twice) ((Imix, sez T, is water-lily)), for both symbols are primarily those of the earth crocodile, and secondary attributes of all deities of the soil and the underworld."[97]

It is as underworld figure, or passenger, that T sees Quezal-Kukan, throughout his book:[98] that is, he is both Venus & the sun because they go down into the underworld. And so fish, water-lilies, & conch shell, become, by way of ponds, I guess, plus geologic deposits in the limestone, perhaps!, associated with his disappearance, &, reappearance! (come here, leo, fro, benius!)

And you can tell Slater that Thompson hasn't even guessed at sea-horse! (He's a respectable worker, this T, but, I very much surmise he's playing with things he ain't bought the rights to. But it will take us a little time to find out!)

As a fact the beauty of Copan is, one small beauty is, that it is precisely in the glyphs there (& they are the best there are, on all counts, both calendar & art) that the fish gets drawn most accurately.

I can't resist setting down one shot I made this morning, talking with Con, which, I think, opens out in several directions. I was complaining, that I have not been able to find, that any of these birds start with the simplest of a proposition when they are going on about the question, whether the glyphs were a language or not. I was saying, if they agree that the chronicles (The Books of Chilam Balam) rest on records previous to themselves (as do the codices, definitely), then, why don't they tell us—or just ask—what kind of an alphabet was it that preceded the

Spanish letters in which Maya has been written since the Conquest (it is in our alphabet that the Books of Chilam Balam are written). The question answers itself: it was in hieroglyphs (the codices supplying that answer). So all that's left to answer is, was the invention of a written use of glyphs contemporary, or later than, the use of same on stone? And by god if Thompson doesn't let the whole thing fall into place, without knowing it, so far as I can see now, when he tells this beautiful tale:

(preface: the codices are books, the paper was the wild fig beaten thin, and then coated with a wash of lime on which the colors and figures were "written"—and a book was as y & x was originally designed, that is, one continuous sheet of this paper (the longest known being the Codex Madrid, about 20 feet!), folded as was y & x, the text running left to right on "pages" abt 5 inches tall & 2½ to 3 inches wide and the same left to right on the back, the book completing itself on the back of page 1: many of the pages are simply in red and black on the white lime, but in some places the details or backgrounds are in blue-green, light & dark yellow, brown, red, pink, black, all of several tones).[99] ok.

Very destructible. Only three survived. However, sometimes codices were buried with the so-called "priests," or the learned men, which, still, I'd prefer to call 'em, until I know what this was they talk abt as "religion." anyhow.

At this point T writes: "This information—that the codices were buried with 'em—has been confirmed by the discovery of heaps of thin flakes of lime with painting on them in tombs of Uaxactun and San Agustin Acasaguastlan. These surely represent the sizing of pages after the vegetal backings had disintegrated. A tomb at Nebaj yielded a codex in a slightly better stage of presentation."[100]

The point is, Uaxactun (I can't find where the other two were). But Uaxactun is the oldest, or twin-oldest, of all the cities, and was apparently not lived in after 889 AD (the date of its last stela).[101]

Well, said, it doesn't seem to say much. But i smell it as important, tho, just yet, i can't demonstrate (it opens up, the fluency of, the glyphs, for me: which is what i have felt in them since that first day i saw them through Sanchez's drawings. and leads straight in to the heart of their meaning & design as language, not, as astrological pictographs

the distinction is, that it is necessary to separate the glyphs from the use they were put to, that is, no argument, that the major use was, to record in stone the investigations by the learned of time & planets, but— because the stone has stayed, while another use—for books, painted or written with a brush—has mostly disappeared, is no reason not to come in quite fresh from the other end, and see the whole business of glyphs as, 1st, language, and, afterwards, uses of same

and it is the fact that the glyphs were the alphabet of the books that puts the whole thing back to the spoken language. Or so it seems to me, this morning.

and with that established, it would seem that the Maya language as we have had it since it got the Spanish alphabet should be, by way of its sounds, the clue to the meaning of that two-thirds of the glyphs which are still wholly unknown

I worked out, yesterday, this, as the method I'd like to follow:

the glyphs
(their design & rhythms, in addition to what denotation the scholars have found)

the present Maya lan-guage (for its sounds & mean-ings, not its orthography)	*all surviving tales, records, "poems," songs etc: the "liter-ature"* (Books of Chilam Balam, plus Codices, plus)

and that means as much Mexican Indian as Mayan (or, for that matter, North American Indian, for you undoubtedly tasted an old flavor in that tale of the moon i sent you yesterday, eh?) [*Added:*] ((I still prefer what Sumerians incised on clay!))

But all this is too fucking bearing down to bother you with. Let me shut up, and, instead, shoot you, quick, other impressions which have been coming in:

(1) that these Maya were a damned nice uncertain, uneasy, nervous, fragile bunch of humans with eyes wide open, and jumpy, like a bird or animal, in the midst of, themselves as creatures and the seasons & the stars—(ex., the way the sun, moon, venus come out, in that story; and all over the place the way they never set anything symmetrical, even, the sun (don't know, but just wonder if, those peoples who plug the sun aren't always, warriors, cutthroats, like the late Mexicans (aztecs, or, even earlier, the chichemecs)

   ((another: at Copan only *one* glyph with the head of a snake split open, and the design made as the Alaskans did it, by the symmetry of, such, a paper cut-out—in other words the danger, the stereotype, of the very formalism of which the maya were masters

   on the other hand, the way, the glyphs never got out of hand (out of media) as did the architecture & the pots, running, to naturalism, say, the danger of the other side, the openness, the intimate)) the way they kept the abstract alert

& (2) time: Copan D answers, for me, the whole contradiction I had felt, fr the fact that Morley & the rest keep blowing bubbles, abt, ah, the mayah, and time–ah! shit, sd i: no people i'm committed to could be devoted to time as these loose-heads say they were. but i knew no answer, and, surely they did spend a hell of a lot of time on time, surely

   but the 1st chance i get, and can get a copy of Copan D to send you, will, so that you can see, that time, in their minds, was *mass & weight!* and they even doubled the onus, making, in Copan D, as well as generally, making the *number* of the given time unit (20, say, of 20 days) the carrier of the burden of, the unit itself! that is, Copan D is a date 9 baktuns (400 yrs)

    15 katuns (20 yrs)

      5 tuns (year of 360)

 3905 yrs total   0 uninal (month of 20 days)

          0 kin (day)[102]

it is pictured thus:

    man 9 carrying baktun (a huge zopalote) on
    his back (as the woodsmen still carry their
    baskets, by the band across their forehead)

man 15 wrestling with katun (same vulture, only, clawing)

    man 5 somewhat pleased with himself
    for now carrying a dead vulture over
    his shoulder

etc.

well, lad, i'll quit, go for a swim, eat and shove off again for campeche
for another session with Sanchez over his drawings: we get a solid two
hrs in, working them over, together—and it's good, damned good

    this is not a letter but a report—will make up for it,
    another time

      love, o

[Lerma, Campeche
28 March 1951]

bob: just beamed one to corman,[103] pushing him, on the SHOW! & i
wanted you to have the picture, for there is more in it, than just, this
one arrow

the idea is, now (though it isn't all sd, yet, to cid), to make it

THE GLYPHS OF COPAN

open it, Boston, as an "ORIGIN" show (which is what c.c. wants, eh?),
at the Mus of Contempt Art—with stela fr Peabody standing there, in
that room, and *all* Sanchez's drawings, interspersed with photos I found
out abt yesterday (by Pavon, by god) of same glyphs (could be blown up,
are very fine, and wld serve as constant reminder, that, it is stone, one is
looking at, not, line drawings, stone)   and maybe, if they'll throw a
catalogue, i might write something, say, like this: THE ART OF THE
LANGUAGE OF MAYAN GLYPHS, and Pavon (this is bait) making
new words abt importance of sd glyphs at copan fr their point of view:
ex., due to Sanchez screwing himself around back of a glyph and making
full drawing Pavon was able to show that this particular stela (I, eye) was
a record of an eclipse of the sun, which date the Wash. Observatory
confirmed, thus confirming the Goodman-Martinez-Thompson correla-
tion system (to AD & BC): big business for same (which reminds me, to
tell you I had found out the Spinden dates were cockeyed, and was to
have writ you so the very day you came in here with Slater's blast at you
for having fallen for same: please tell Slater your ignorance was my
ignorance, that, I hadn't yet caught up with such fine points, and that i
misled you, that, i'm the one he should have jumped, and that, anyway,
when was it not true, anyway, that any man who goes in as we do is
bound to catch up with such businessess eventually, but what the hell
can they ever, the others catch up, when, they start with the warning,
never, make an imaginative error? And one thing more—that my reason
for going along a little while with Spinden was due to the peculiar
corroboration of Spinden's dates on Q-K by none other than, that most
respectable of all Maya gents., one Alfred Tozzer,[104] of (you know
where, as does Slater, graduate, of same)!

aw, to hell with the rest of the show stuff (ideas for presentation, where to take it after Boston—Washington (and, not to cid, ideas abt NY, & Philly), anyway, that, sed i to sed, you got a big baby, one which ought, done right, be, to today, what Armory was to 1913, & Frobenius's CAVE SHOW (Mus Mud Art, NY) 1928:[105]

for it strikes me, the principle behind all this is: *language as, root, graphic:* sound, not as time, but as object in space, as mass, to be pushed around, to be heard as things are eaten, as, in process, of the organism not the "mind" or "taste" or "aesthetics"

which brings me to another biz, which, one day, i'd like to mount: a double barreled show, say, LANGUAGE AS STONE & CLAY (something better, surely), a show, somewhere, of MAYA & SUMER together! the two of em, sitting there, on walls, on floor, with drawings, picx, plus: the tablets (with Kramer's readings & expostulations), the glyphs (with Pavon's); with photos (blown up to size) of stones, there & here; also casts, standing, or pegged to walls; plus mss: of translations, then transpositions, of the SUMER poets, of, same, of, MAYA, tho, this, that they were poems, to begin with, not yet established, or, better, that, just because this is another kind of language & use of same (local to this continent, eh?) sd poems do not resemble what the West (cheap child, half prick, of sumer) takes as poems (1st exs of which were, the city & hell verses of those birds back there, 3500—and good); jesus, creeley, what do you say we go see a queer business I saw the anouncement of, a show of SUMER & MAYA, what the hell is that, let's go, and after, we'll have, a beer lerma   saturday   march 31   51:

what a downthrow the week had
yesterday, what with me fucking the day up, and then, in the evening,
yr three letters—which, crazily enough, i seem to have opened in reverse order, so that outsailed the half-century *before* i knew the evil
news, the gugmemora had choked itself again in its own shit, like any
dog! And we two figuring, only day before, that, it was so late, maybe,
it meant, you waz in. And I telling Con, but, if Creeley wins, he'll sure
send a wire. And so, when I returned last night, there she was, on pins,
to have me open, the mail, figuring, this must be it—and i dismal,
thinking if it is, it's not good. Which, for christ's sake it was.

well, lad,
it's a goddamned shame. those fucking fools had themselves a chance to
wear a feather—and again, they beat themselves. it's a fucking nuisance,
and is more proof nothing advances: it's another one of those misdeeds,
which, they have, so far as the real men go, have repeated & repeated. I
was hoping, this time, we could unseat whoever it is that sits unknown
behind the grants in this bizness—who? edmund wilson? (was him,
once, which is, measure). Did figure, as I sd, that maybe, by now, Bill
wld have come home, there

only, berating, we give them too much—
they're just a trough, and please don't turn, in bitterness, fr future use
of same. They are not medicis—who did things themselves. Nor, as you
advised me, personal and vicarious in their throws, as old Simon
Guggenheim himself might have been. They're middle men, with somebody's moneys. So they play it safe. Probably dumped you, in the final
decision, because you were "new," young—always, that gag.

Which,
of course, was just what we wanted them to ride over—and by god Bill &
Slater & I certainly had the right, given you, to hope to christ, this once,
they'd ride. God damn them.

It knocked me out: went right to bed, and
am just up, after 15 solid hrs of lousy sleep, with a nightmare of Three
Jacks (by god) I have known, troubling the piss out of me—and I waking
to the overwhelming smell of a dead body, which, joined to the dream,
was so unendurable I woke Con to ask her if she smelled the same smell.
And she did, which I hunted for, with a flashlight, at 2 AM, and found

nothing. Had to open all windows, and sleep, frozen, the rest of the night (a norther, the day before).

Well, turning away—and ahead. 1st, thanks, to you both, for the throw: crazy, that the 1st extra push for me shld come fr you, crazy wonderful, that you, who are, inevitably, in the same pitch of dough, shld be throwing, to me! My only concern is, that, with yr departure & all that, you are not putting any cramp on yrselves, with house troubles, the kids, etc.? But I take it this way, that, a yr from now, when our positions are reversed, I shall have to have given up the daily bizness I have managed for, now, six good years, and will have salary, and can, with you pushing out, do a like save—am going to have to, it looks like, manage some other way: (have hoped that some such goof-business like you say, of some dame or Texan, might be brought forward to stake me. But can't see that such appears, or, that I am of the order of temperament to pull such. On the contrary: I am taken as self-sufficient, for some fucking reason—probably because I don't look right, and, besides, am arrogant, hard, just here where I hide.

(And, with the exception of Ezra, I have taken the economics of all such dependents as intolerable.

((Anyway, my pitch on this problem is—I am the fool of—my belief, the heave has to come on the whole front, not for this one or that. But you know this, where, I sit.))

The point is, you give us a flip, a freeing. And we run with it: Con, this morning, knowing how, after this week, I am wild to go to Copan, sez, won't this, make it? And so, by god, we figure my fare, train, bus, etc., to Copan, to see! It was beautiful

But the sound NewEnglander in me knows, what it gives, is, better than a couple of weeks to drive on what is here in hand—and maybe, that margin, what will insure, the afterwards! It's a save, lad, a straight save, and that it's you is goddamned special, that's what I got to say, that's, what I say, that's what's okay, what's, okay.

What I meant—that I'd fucked yesterday up—was, as per usual, driving,
i drove too hard: broke my own schedule, got up early, went in there to
work the whole day on the rest of the Copan drawings, to finish them.
And found Sanchez committed to some other job, some goddamned
engineer's blueprint, or something, and me bitter, that he was, and thus
unable to go ahead together, so, going on my own, grinding, pushed for
time, etc., and, of course, these Mayan guys who did the work, paying.

But, checking last night, back here, turned out, my edge was not as
broken as it seemed—that is, had spotted the pieces which mattered, and
had pegged them, in the movement of the quality of the cutting there,
at, Copan.
          It's this that I'd like to get across to you, what a distance in I
find I am. Very exciting. It comes to this, that, due to Sanchez, and that
these drawings are a complete take of all monuments on the site which
carried glyphs, that I am now, after this week, able to spot style, be
pin-point on date any given stela was done, and see the whole organism
of the place as it unfolded Stela 7 (615 AD, c.) straight through to Altar
T (783). [106] Very surprised, & delighted, how the grip came up all by
itself, with no hints, straight out of the things themselves, out of differences in the cutting of these men who were certainly not (like the idiots
have all believe[d]) mere tools ("stone-cutters") of the priests, certainly
were "sculptors" in another sense than, but necessarily of the same
power & purpose as, what we are used to calling such.
                              And beautiful
workers they were! I have pulled out 6 major pieces, and have a dozen
more I'd go to bat for, and—with only a visit to Copan to see the actual
stones themselves—I am ready, at this moment, to set down to doing a
examination, a declaration, and, in some respects, an annunciation in
prose of this "art" as it expressed itself at this one place. Which is—isn't
it—a damn big jump? It seems so. I never wld have guessed I'd be, this
soon, that confident.
                    And what gives me further pleasure is, that, with
one site in hand I'd like very much to do likewise by others. The only
hitch is, no such job as Sanchez has done exists, for any other site, alas.
But I had one important gauge thrown to me by him right in the middle
of the week. And I think it was that made the whole biz shape up. He

pulled out of his work sheets a copy by him (from photographs) of the "tablet" they call it which was unearthed last year at Palenque (I had heard of this fr three characters who came in on us here a month ago, fr Merida on way Mexico, and who had all been to Palenque and seen it: white, and clear, they sd, and very beautiful.)[107] ((And there's a story of archeological politics abt it I'd spin for you if we were chewing the fat. But to hell with that.)) Point is, suddenly, I saw—fr its beauty and yet my preference for, the style of Copan—how wide & different this art of glyphs can be seen, and shown, to be. As a matter of possibility, it would be most revealing to toss Palenque directly in contrast to, Copan. For I have a notion, fr this "tablet"—evidence on the design of the stone— that Palenque rested itself on quite another sense of life & "religion" than Copan. It is this: that Palenque (it may have been the center, from its "priestliness") were Opium-Eaters (in this case probably the peyote plant), religiants by intoxication, or, better, by states of vision so in-duced. (It's a wide, swaying guess, but, something gives em this other core, this horizontal & "feminine" line, this sloping composition by limbs, say, instead of as (in Copan) the hands alone.)

And I'd reinforce my own preference for Copan by marking what was their stem, contra Palenque: it was, it appears, the center, Copan, of the so-called astronomy of the Mayans, a discipline, I dare say, which one could take as of more use than that other vision. Or at least you and I might, eh? (I am thinking of yr exact remarks abt Crane, Duncan, Rexroth, which I run with, to the end; and contra Anderson; and that we stand in, here, stay, for the count.)

((A break, hereabouts, for a meal, and another short snap at Vasquez's cuyo—fr which I brought back a good haul of pots plus ear-flowers (stucco), several animal-shaped pot feet, and a couple of more parts of the bead of a frieze which once ran along some part of a building thar. And now I am writing under two wine bottles with candles stuck in em where corks once were. And want to say this, thinking as I was, that, in what—about two more letters, say—it'll be the break, you'll be off, too, and this big year will shift, which has been something, with you coming in, and three others going out (my mother, Ed (thru my purposeful default on his book), and another, which, to my bewilderment, had to be

gone by),[108] and now you and Ann and the kids are the closest things I
have, and it makes me happy, god damn it, that it is so, that it is this
good between us, as it is, never seen, each of us (and i don't much figure
I'll be back, or ought to, before you leave, despite, what—I'd not say the
curiosity—what, just that it will happen, and now, is as good as any, eh?
but it won't, and that don't matter, for it is, what is this business, is, and
fine it is, and goddamn good

                    (and which brings up what you yrself, sd,
that, it is true those letters Corman publishes are, I'm sure, reasonable,
and was so goddamned surprised, when, finally, I learned they were not
letters to you, were, instead, all, to ferrini,[109] so surprised, and caught, i
figured, the hell with it, i won't even ask to look at them because i know
they can't be what I would want, are not what corman might have had,
fr you:
          i'm fucking sure i'll look on my face with em, but, hoping, the
rest, will carry it, i sd no word, it was so late, and it was so painful for
me to contemplate (the whole business of letters, out of yr hands, gives
me the jumps, anyway, the whole concept of a mag scored that way, i'd
not trust to any taste but yrs. And there he was, taking it over. And it
did seem (does) that, as it is it is a push, and that, by keeping our hand in
we ought to be able to salt something away, there, tho, he is so slack, i
don't know for how long it will be possible (letter fr him yesterday
announcing, he has an epigraph for his mag![110] (god help us, at this
stage, an epigraph, and me hoping, this once, it could be avoided, and
that, by another issue, i'd have him some fine glyph as sign, as signa-
ture, as unspeaking spoken graphic). And by god, the idiot, he tells me,
to tell me he has got it fr a lead of mine! that he has gone to my sources,
the Sumerians, for it! takes it fr Kramer, fr a hymn, Genesis, no less,
and it is—well, you'll see, and die, right on the spot:
                              christ, imagine,
fucking it up before it's even out, the Sumer push, making it sound just
like that gd old deal, and imagine—the very business I am trying to
clear. And in the same issue as G & C, showing, how wholly uncom-
prehending he is

But don't breathe a word. I tell ya why. We have to pay, for the fact that
(as you did on Blackburn's poem) that this is a small guy, this corman,

who is jealous as all shit that you and i go beating along the path. He can't stand to have anything which he hasn't fooled himself is somehow, just a little bit, his own (is, a movie title, just fit): he maneuvered, until he got you and I leaving out just such intervals as he, if he were a man, needed to make his mag a thing; he passed you back Blackburn, just to put on an act, that, he has independent taste; he chose the ferrini letters, just, to not choose yrs (as well the fact, I'm sure, that yr style, or mine, between us, is not, as easy, for him to misunderstand, shall we say). aw christ, it is sad, and will be, i very much fear, not long good, however not good it now is. the only thing, is, that, we have something to show, haven't we—and that's more than we have fr emerson, that superior personality, eh?

My own feeling is this: let's work corman (who does work, I'll allow), as far as that next issue, with you centered. To do that let's keep along with him, as we are going, me keeping out of personals with him, giving him every lead I get, you doing what seems best with you (I think you have much more open ground, just because he owes all to you, and, in the end, has to allow it, in his private nights).

And I see this as straight, that is, I do give him every lead, and just read his letters fast, once, and forget em, or, if i didn't, I'd raise my hair and stick my words right up his arse, good, he is so horrible, his rhythms are so deadly, so unborn, so stupid, really, he is so stupid, it hurts.

I've been passing all this by, simply because other things matter more. And because, frankly, I'm scared: don't trust his choice of my stuff at all, any of it, and in the future will only see he sees anything *after* you have seen it: the one gd thing I am set on, that he is using, on [*i.e.* of] my own, is I, MAX, which, for me, is some kind of a fetish I'd see published anywhere, and not give a fuck; and GATE & CENTER, simply, because, here, you and I are eye to eye. The rest? well, just as registration of things done, say, in the past year. And if that sonofabitch Emerson had PRAISES out, I wouldn't mind so much, for then, anyone interested, could put the ORIGIN stuff into a proper frame. But with that Emerson not having sd a fucking word to me since a telephone conversation before I left Washington—not a word—LOOK: I'm telling you, if that prick throws the book down now, I'll stay after him the rest of my goddamn life, and no matter how highly I may think of his goddamn verse, I'll

beat him and beat him and beat him whenever and wherever I get a
chance. In fact, I'll go out of my way to hit him—ask for reviews, or
whatever. And go after him. (The bastard, he wanted me to write to the
Guggenheim for him: I tell ya, I will, I'll say I will. And in the dark I'll
give him the knife. But sure. I never in my life wanted a guy as much as
I want him for this whole year of cheap business he's given me. And I go
back to my hunch it was all worked out just like a goddamned lousy
small plot.

Jesus, do I burn to get at him. And remember, I have the
advantage of having had my eyes on him—and he's a kind of placid
bumptious fat flesh I could take the knot to, anyhow. Fat arse, as well.
Not a lean thing abt him. And the head—missing. Jesus. But cheap.
cheap, the bastard.

Aw, well, I wrote him this week, a one sentence
note, saying, please (mind you) have the courtesy to write me what
goes, with, THE PRAISES. (Your word, that he is abt to issue a brief, to
his authors—he must have been a navy lieutenant, I just bet—makes me
figure, I'm done for, that son of a bitch, at this date, that stringing shit
house son a bitch. Jesus.

What the hell else, is there, on this literary stuff, I have avoided ruining
my days and drive, about? Well, to hell with whatever, I can't think of.
(By the way, any late word fr Gerhardt? Any sign of fragmente #1? or
anything? I must say, it's my own fault, for I fucked up, by losing my
German dictionary, taken with me, specially, for Gerhardt; left on boat,
I guess. And me helpless, without it. Couldn't translate his BRIEF to
you and me. And so, no way of acknowledging. Helpless.)

All of which piss breaks me off from what I wanted to say to you. But let
me pick it up again. This, to tell you how damned grateful I am, and how
sore, that, you couldn't also, be gladdened. Will get back to the other
things, next mail. Please keep em coming at me: most most fine, to hear,
all of it, and special thanks for the Blackburn poem on as the sand, when
the wind, is a turbine:[111] of course he has the very hand you say, and it
is fine, and who the hell am I to say the guy can't add head and heart to
it, get off, that three inch stool? christ, sure, you see im, in NY. And if
he'd answered my reply to him (some months ago, on some bizness, of
an exchange of unpublished materials in a packet, passing around, like a

chain letter (I sd, sure), I'd be willing to keep after him. For he does have stuff. (Which brings up another thing I want to have it, over the fence, with you, on: how many of that bunch take that old Buzzard's[112] advice altogether too wrongly—example, also, Ringer, who wrote me, as you sd, and whom I answered. You see, Creeley, you've spoiled me, by clearing, yrself: I expect these others to do same, to have done, same! And am impatient. Oh, well, no importa, no

love,

olson

[Lerma Campeche]

sunday   april 1 [1951]   here   (yesterday's, was, saturday's, so, mark this #2)

rob't: This idea—for french, on way, or there, get hold of VICTOR BERARD's translation of, ODYSSEY:[113] christ, yes, seaboard (get somebody, NY, go foreign bookstore, & have it ready for you, when sailing (Slater?). Wonderful/ you, Atlantic/ reading, Berard! Jesus, it jumps me. And will, you. The real thing (& french friends told me, it is the school version, there!)   The TRUE PERIPLUM, he, checked the coasts, & translates, fr the ground (the look—it was good, in the house of the Bennesvet Brovig, going over charts, & reading—"remarkable white house," or, etc. (And in France, keep eye out, stalls, for any & all Berard—many volumes, of which, "The Phoenicians & the Odyssey," or something, the first, and as good as, any:

what Berard did not seem to know (how could he? Sumer not known, actually, until, was it 1920?) was, how right he was that, the Phoenicians, were themselves only transmitters fr, sailors behind them (as, of course, were the Greeks, same, after:

it is one of those things to shake you, a chart of coasts, & soundings, when you read, say, above, or, "wreck reported here, 1873," that, to this advanced day all sea charts are an accumulation—and some, still, carrying the oldest sort of reporting-in—of all previous charts reaching back (the Mediterranean, or the Persian Gulf, sure) to the earliest quick eyes which took in those coasts (ex., Berard, that, a passage I have now forgot, Odyssey, could not refer to Etna, or something, because, despite its prominence on land, cannot, fr sea level (ship-level) be seen at all! Love that, accuracy)[114]

and that still, a coast is, a necessity as, it was ALL, when, men went alone by COASTS, and their shapes, or, remarkable features: EZ right to hammer PERIPLOI,[115] only, he is all wrong that (must be some defeat of his own) that Homer did not know his, sea. Or—wait—maybe he ain't so wrong. As a matter of fact, it has to be put a little different: what Berard seems to me to prove is, that Homer was writing his poem on the base of another poem, a Phoenician predecessor, and that the accuracies are sailor's accuracies (or his predecessor's) not, his. Only, again, it ain't that simple, for, what is the most wonderful thing of all abt Berard's work, is, the way it argues that Homer's inventions of his incidents & personages rest entirely on an animation of geographical features which sailors after sailors had noticed until the names of "remarkable" rocks, headlands, etc. had got fixed as nouns characterizing sd shapes. And that what Homer did (or maybe, the Phoenician before him, or, maybe, some guy of Lagash) anyway, what he did was to spin a tale riding out fr these nouns! That is, Circe-Kirke means nothing in Greek but, in Phoenician periploi, the name for the island precisely in her spot on the coast of Italy just north(?) of Cumae (which seems to have been a Phoenician point of call before it was the 1st Greek settlement in Italy) translates as SHE-HAWK (as I remember it). Which leads on, in Homer's hands, to the presentation of, her nature, etc. etc.[116] There are better examples—the rock, CORFU, which was the stone-froze bark of the Phaeacians, after they had done wrong by Poseidon in returning Odysseus to Ithaca, was, in all ancient sea time, known, that rock, was as, THE VESSEL (just like, here, I think I told you the tale, fr Martinez, of the rock, down the coast a piece, which, because it is shaped like a ray, has got attached to it the story of the fisherman who went against god and tried to fish on Good Friday; he got a fish all right, but it was the devil who towed him all that day & night until the crow of the cock Holy Saturday morning, when, right before his eyes, sd devil in shape of sd ray turned to stone!)

I figure this swims up, now, this business of noun as graphic 1st, allowing for narration afterwards, the double function, man makes noun then makes verb, because, such movement, such transposition, is, at root, I figure, as process, to what constitutes glyphs:

are "rocks," of 2nd stage

What continues to hold me, is, the tremendous levy on all objects as they present themselves to human sense, in this glyph-world. And the proportion, the distribution of weight given same parts of all, seems, exceptionally, distributed & accurate, that is, that

sun

    moon

        venus

            other constellations & zodiac

snakes

    ticks

        vultures

jaguar

    owl

        frog

feathers

    peyote

        water-lily

not to speak of
fish

    caracol

        tortoise

&, above all,
human eyes

hands   (PLUS EXCEEDINGLY CAREFUL
      limbs   OBSERVATION OF ALL POSSIBLE
              INTERVALS OF SAME, as well as
              ALL ABOVE (to precise dimension of
              eclipses, say, & time of, same etc.
              etc.)

And the weights of same, each to the other, is, immaculate (as well as, full)

That is, the gate to the center was, here, as accurate as what you & i have been (all along) talking about—viz., man as object in field of forces declaring self as force because is force in exactly such relation & can accomplish expression of self as force by conjecture, & displacement in a context best, now, seen as a space more than a time such;
                                              which, I take
it, is precise contrary to, what we have had, as "humanism," with, man, out of all proportion of, relations, thus, so mis-centered, becomes, dependent on, only, a whole series of "human" references which, so made make only anthropomorphism, and thus, make mush of, *any* reality, conspicuously, his own, not to speak of, how all other forces (ticks, water-lilies, or snails) become only descriptive objects in what used to go with antimacassars, those, planetariums (ancestor of gold-fish bowls) etc.

[*Final page of original lacking; supplied here from* Mayan Letters, *pp. 64-66:*]
This gate got to, gone in by, 2nd stage, follows, that is, *invention* produces narration & verse also of a contrary order (the last example of which, which comes down to us, being, ODYSSEY
                                              which, for my
dough, is not good enough (ditto only modern example i know, one melville), simply because humanism is (homer) coming in, and (melville) going out
                      and i take it, a Sumer poem or Maya glyph is more
pertinent to our purposes than anything else, because each of these people & their workers had forms which unfolded directly from content

(sd content itself a disposition toward reality which understood man as only force in field of force containing multiple other expressions

one

delightful fact, just picked up: that *all* Mayan jobs (sez Tatiana Proskouriakoff) are built around *a single human figure*, in all reliefs, etc.[117]

which is, of course, that ego which you, me, Mayan X were (are), he who is interested enough to, seeing it all, get something down

What has to be battered down, completely, is, that this has anything to do with stage of development. Au contraire. The capacity for (1) the observation & (2) the invention has no more to do with brick or no wheels or metal or stone than you and i are different from, sd peoples: we are like. Therefore, there is no "history." (I still keep going back to, the notion, this is (we are) merely, the *second time* (that's as much history as I'll permit in, which ain't history at all: seems so, only, because we have been all dragooned into a notion that, what came between was, better. Which is eatable shit, for the likes of those who like, same.

Animation of what presents itself, fr the thing on outwards: rock as vessel, vessel as tale, creating, men & women, because narrator and/or poet happen to be man or woman, thus, human figure as part of universe of things

(Other things, of same, the provocations, say:

the *eye*, in Mayan (other Indian as well) & Sumerian fixes (jesus, in these glyphs, how, or stones, how, with *any* kind of device, the eye takes up life (contra Greek, Rome, even, Byzantine): ex.,

Museo, Campeche, a wonderful little "monster" with eyes made so

and the hands (fingers):

             this is peculiarly brilliant at Copan (as I sd), where, if any dancer now living had sense, he'd be, finding out, how, to exploit this part of his, instrument

          not to speak of how the face is, the other dominant glyph in addition to the abstracts of all other natural forms, is, the human or animal *heads* . . .

———————————————————

[Littleton, N.H.
5 April 1951]

Thursday/
         I passed out, somewhere back there, & looking back, like they say, will let it go anyhow.

         On Cid, again: I may very well be off, but I don't think so. In any event, the one point is : he wd be altogether open to yr suggestions, et al, & as far as I can see—this, for a long, long time.

One thing more—was that [Peter] Viereck wrote back. I don't know why this biz, with him, goes on, i.e., why I get into it.

         One echo: "We who have perhaps nothing to lose?" I was thinking of that, & I can't keep away, etc. A useless thing, most certainly, but even that chance to argue: more or less welcome, at the moment.

I had gone at him, 1) on the Pound & 2) on this humanism (& also, a little on this biz of reference). Altogether foolish to suppose I cd get thru.

Even so, I wd have, still, to say same, etc. And, especially, now, i.e., with this sentence of yrs, in my head:

". . . a Sumer poem or Maya glyph is more pertinent to our purposes than anything else, because each of these people & their workers had forms which unfolded directly from content (sd content itself a disposition toward reality which understood man as only force in field of force containing multiple other expressions. . ."

(Here was a funny thing: in writing him, I got out this sentence, the irony of which I expect he'll never damn well see. Anyhow: ". . . I take it, your more specific concerns come to this matter of a humanistic logos & the re-instatement of a non-obscurantist verse & criticism. . ." Ha/ ha.)

As of reference: ". . . he can talk of love (which everybody knows, etc.) but hen, he can talk of his own love (which no one knows) & somewhere, between, the balance is to be maintained. . ."

As of humanism: ". . . the only fear I have of humanism, & I by no means let it worry me very much : is that it tends, in divers hands, to run to the general, & also the loss of relation. It may sound very odd, to be saying that—but I was thinking of two things: one being, Whitehead's comment: "We seem to be ourselves elements of this world in the same sense as are the other things which we perceive ('. . . such as stones, trees, and human bodies. . .')"; and the other, from a letter, from a friend now in Yucatan, doing work there on the Maya: "(the above statement, of yr own)"

"I believe the loss, in humanism, is apt to fall somewhere there, in this kind of attitude (as each of the above note it), or in what this kind of attitude, toward reality, gains over the usual humanism. I, myself, figure as clear an evidence of this loss (as I can think of) as might be, comes in the split between Lawrence's two books of THE MAN WHO DIED, because The Escaped Cock, is the above, is that way of it—& the other, I believe to be a somewhat sloppy humanism. Well, for the first way, this quote from the 1st book:

". . . I will wander among the stirring of the phenomenal world, for it is the stirring of all things among themselves which leaves me purely alone. . ."

A useless biz; but no matter.

Also, one thing: that I was able to ride thru Cid, on the Blackburn, & so, that evidence of his flexibility. That is, I argued it, with him, at least that one poem, THE BIRDS, & got thru. Whether or not Blackburn is not now soured, on the gig, I don't yet know—& leave it up to Cid. now, anyhow. But, you see, it can be worked, etc., if the cause be just, like they say. Agh.

Very great that you do get, as you say, so damn sure, i.e., have the grip. I can't but think: even the whole damn way you came into this gig, was the best possible—i.e., the things cd be, so, open, & not the presuppositions, clouding yr eye, etc. (That wd be my fear, on Slater—he has read so fucking much, on same; he wd be checking on the illustrations, etc. But no—because he is the exception, like yrself, etc. But that danger, anyhow.)

Anyhow, this much : that yr notes are very damn fine, & reading them, am able to get some damn sense of these things, myself. Being both of us, certainly, i.e., Ann & myself.
                    The notes on: these weights. Very crazy, i.e., "the proportion, the distribution of weight given same parts of all, seems, exceptionally, distributed & accurate. . ." And then, yr balancings, there. Very damn great, & pulls in, real sense of same, for us.
        (I should have thrown, at Viereck, the statement at the bottom of this same page—but it wd have been waste. That is: " 'humanism,' with man, out of all proportion of, relations, thus, so mis-centered, becomes, dependent on, only, a whole series of 'human references' which, so

made make only anthropomorphism, and thus make mush of, *any* reality, conspicuously, his own. . .")

But altogether beyond, these matters of who, or what, call it: I cd throw these things at—that fact they come in, very damn precisely, to what I wd be calling, my own damn center. And for that fact: am very grateful.

The gain, of making it altogether clear, this language, as weight, as displacement, as, so, object—it wd seem, it does seem to me, that such a thing wd give us the reach over our own continuities & constructions, heretofore, call it, that wd then make possible—even a damn new, language, or language, our own, put to its work as prime, & no longer: what runs along side, etc.

Too, I begin to think of the incredible gain, it is, along all fronts. Well: 1) the death of, symbol—because symbol must be, false extension, even as, mask, & there can be no masks, with these weights; 2) the abstract, brought back to what it can be: the thing, in the hand (as, mind)—I thought, just now: how our current use of, the abstract, tends only to put a distance between ourselves & that original, that force, we wd have, wd so possess (so that, Love, is the denial, of, love, etc., etc.); 3) language, as the immediate, & because so, as the eternal (& I lack, at the moment, a better word, etc.).

Anyhow: it damn well shakes me, right the fuck down to my roots. You see, how much the gain over, even that strike of, ideogram : because there, still, it was too much, the usurping, too much, still, the figure for, etc.

But here: language as, again, damnit, this goddamn beautiful change, changing into, over, into: of force—that it can exist, so, as multiple, as anywhere, as in whatever, can hold!

It is a damn shaking thing!

Well, this for now, because Ann wants to mail same, etc., & I will miss the mail otherwise. Ok.

Will write soon again, & please, you do the same. I damn well don't want to miss any of this. It is, too much.

Again, very very grateful to you, for all the very great, & altogether
damn wonderful, trust.
>   Ok.

All love to you both/
>   Bob

>   [Lerma, Campeche]

friday april 6 [1951]   (it's 3 PM, at which hour I have just had breakfast,
which may be a gauge, the 15 hrs, of the toll of woods & ruins: two
days, & a day of preparation for same—Con not able to go along, so,
alone, whatever better than 200 kilometers is, away fr here. And the
craziest of it, being put up, the night before last in a jail! At Santa Elena,
the very town, it turned out afterwards, where Stephens based himself,
100 yrs agone, when he hit same sites [*added in ink:* (Nohcakab)]:

Uxmal & Kabah
>   (((found out, it's tick poisoning, which, I've had:
>   you shld not be me, this morning, with my
>   trunk wholly raised in sores, plus, fr the jail
>   water, tourista, viz, GIs: up at 6 this morning)))

[*written in ink:*]
look: jumped away, suddenly, fr this, with hunch, today was the day to
go to Campeche & settle the question of the use of Sanchez' drawings
with his boss, the shit Pavon. Walked in, & not a word did the fucking
coward say. So sat an hr reading Stephens, & feeling the air was fraught.
He & I walked out at 5, &, as we passed one piece a like of which I had
seen at Kabah, if the prick doesn't say—or so I confirmed he did say
shortly thereafter, thinking so, at the time—"I know all the pieces in all

the ruins of Yucatan," as much as to say, I'm not at all interested in yr ignorance & excitements, Olson—   (as you sd, these *innocences!*). But still not a word. And off he goes, the moment we get to the door. I leave him go, waiting, for Sanchez, to lock up. And still no word, tho, poor Sanchez, looks fucking dispirited. After a short while, it comes out: Pavon had told him today, NO—& not even use for Origin! That, sez the prick, the drawings are the property of the state of Campeche, and also of the govt of Honduras, & until contract with Honduras broken, no chance!

Anyway, this is a note to tell you I'm back, & will write you tomorrow—that yr two letters came in today, thank God—& will have much to say, mañana.

Love—
C.

[Lerma, Campeche]

saturday   april   7   51   —picking up / getting back

but 1st, on you on white-head: catch, only, for me, he is, like all of em, metaphysician (had dinner with him once,[118] house Beacon Hill, we the guests, and he was a distinguished man, small, odor of sanctity (decidedly priestly) BUT WHAT YOU SHALL WANT TO READ (it is not the physicists, but THE GEOMETERS of the 19th century, the real men, of whom whitehead is only a metaphysical totalizer: Riemann, Lubachevsky, Bolyai Farkas AND YOU CAN GO STRAIGHT TO EM by way of WHITEHEAD: read, in 11th ed of Enc Brit, the article by whitehead & russell, on, NON-EUCLIDEAN GEOMETRY:[119] it was these two lads' 1st major engagement together, and it's a beaut (And if, as I figure, it fires you, take it a step beyond them by looking into recent books by one COXETER, Canadian geometer[120]

FOR, it strikes me as crucial, it was not the physicists with their extraordinary analysis of the nature of the *substance* of matter, but the geometers who set out to figure the *disposition* of matter in space who opened up the kinetics we (& whitehead) are the inheritors of. Or perhaps it is better (these physicists were so valuable) to put it, that it was the initiative which was geometrical, that they were the lads who broke the whole thing open:

Riemann is beautiful, his 1st piece, forgot its title[121]

my memory is, they date abt 1840 or so, contemporary to, those americans, Melville & Parkman

& Bolyai Farkas, the story of, his 1st essay, & his father's remark,[122]

(Of the physicists, check the deBroglie brothers, a couple of Frenchmen, c. 1920, who seem more interesting to me than Planck, on the quantum phenomena)[123]

(It has kept striking me, that physics, as a discipline, restricts the person, even the best (the deBroglies, or Einstein), to an objectivism which keeps letting dirty time slip in. And contrariwise, geometry, by some breath of space, enlarges the temperaments involved until you are almost into the regions of the imaginative man, with a grab on object *because of* a comprehension of the mystery of, disposition, or, displacement

it broke, once, right in front of my own eyes, when I heard de Sitter lecture on the expanding universe[124] (by the way, take a gander at his book KOSMOS, some day when you get a chance: a wonderful high-faced, spade-bearded, nervous dutchman, an active descendent of Riemann, Bolyai & Lubache[v]sky (there is also a German mathematician-geometer whose name I can't remember at the moment who was the center of the movement forward fr these lads' work, Gauss, was it? something like)[125]

Or if you ever meet up with a diffident bird named Clarence Graham,[126] now, I understand, a full professor at Columbia, let him talk a while: he & I came out of Worcester together, & used to take girls out, & that sort of shit, but, let me tell you, that, sad apple though he is, his studies of the rods and cones in rabbits' & pigeons' eyes are written in a prose you and I would respect, than which I don't know the equal of from our so-called contemporary writers ((Graham & a guy named Selig

> Hecht,[127] now dead, & whom I im-
> agine Graham succeeded in post, both
> wrote a prose which taught me a good
> deal))

Anyway, it's only (like you say) to pick up the documentation. For the whole biz has moved off (again, like you say) into our business, or, say, such contemporary documentation as biologists, Frobenius, or a Malinowski[128] can give us culture-morphologists, or some other word than artists: call me klee!

> It's beautiful, that sentence, of white-hair:

> the only endurances are
> structures of
> activity[129]

(never could read him, and am especially grateful to have you spot him, for me, like that

> ((as of malinowski, can't say how readable he is—have picked
> up what i know of him from others' quotes, not, fr him,
> direct—never did like Trobriands, or any of the Pacific
> peoples anyway—am bored by their ways of life & their arts:
> all except their navigation, which completely rakes me

Or the geographers, biologists & geographers & anthropologists—the sciences which concern themselves with the in-story, the bizness of, man here, not, any longer, speculations (done) on universe & matter

And I figure (whether it was, like you say, by leaking into, anyway, that   ONE strzygowski[130]

> TWO frobenius

> THREE sauer

whether they know it or not are obedient to above clarification, that

the only endurances are structures of activity ((the last noun bothers me,
                                                is what i mean by, the
                                                metaphysical in, old wh:
1   WOOD   and fr such looseness has
        2   LANGUAGE   come a whole school of
                3   ICE   modern metaphysics
                                                (Suzanne Langer,[131] et al)
                                                which is very bad, very
                                                slack

but you sd that

Certainly, what keeps waddell or kramer (or any of these mayistas) fr
doing their jobs right, is, that they have not got hold of, same

LOOK; for god's sake, if the boat sinks, or you change yr minds, or any
wonderful calamity makes it possible, do change plans and come here!
Christ, it would be wonderful. Just take the wrong boat, get aboard the
Bennestvet Brovig, instead, of, the Wilhelmina Kronstadt, or whatever
it is, you are, alas, booked on to—make a slip & tell the taxi cab driver,
Brooklyn, Pier, Foot 53rd street! Please! Christ christ, despite the ticks,
we could really work this country over, my lad!

                        love
                            charles

[*Added on back of envelope:*] the only endurances are / structures of /
commitment [*with* motion *crossed out*].

sunday april 8 51   lerma

rob't:

am damned puzzled, hoy. figuring out. a new idea: to promote
myself a chicle plane ride to uaxactun (&, 6 hrs walking away, Tikal):
and with it, feeling, i got to make some decisions, fast. for ex., the
reason this pops up, is, that, by the end of this month, the rain, it
appears, makes such invasions of the Peten (the tough part of the Maya
parts) out, for this year.

at the same time, the two day jaunt to uxmal
& kabah flushed another project by proving to me that a man can make
distinctions of quality between two sites as handily as, say, among
glyphs

all of which, in its turn, breeds an anger which turns everything
sour, that, this whole Mayan business has been either blown up out of
its proportions OR, that all accents are false—i say sour, because, to
correct the picture is a job of huge scope, maybe, and, i ask myself, even
if i had the money, do i want to do it

for i am spending my nights &
days on this one thing, trying, to pack it in. And am getting pinched, fr,
the pressure

my impression, this morning, is, that maybe the best thing i can do is to
see as many sites as fast as possible (the rainy season & the money
problem both pressing in that direction, though, the money problem,
making the going to sites difficult)   the practicals being reinforced by the
size of the job, that is, that, in this go here, can i possibly accomplish any
more than, now, such seeing of sites (giving over, that is, the study of
glyphs & language & the literature, until i am back in the states with the
lib of cong & the carnegie at hand)

yet, this plan, irritates me, for some
reason, some vague sense of defeat & exasperation, which may simply
be my will, fr the size of the problem (the dispersal of the monuments,
the stupidities with which they have been presented & discussed, time,
& dough

or, more likely, that, the organic way to do this job is to do it
in one straight-out operation, on the ground, or at least, based, with air

flights anywhere (to the States, if necessary, & return)

on top of that con is getting damned bored with lerma & campeche, and
hankers for mexico proper, thinking, those people must be more allegre,
and, in oaxaca, or michoacan, there must be good live contemporary
pots, & mu-sick, mu-sick, real music, some present life (she, of course,
not riding, as i am, on this ancient thing)   can't say i blame her: the god
damned americanization has gone so far (i tell her, she'll have to hunt
anything else out in Mexico too), here along the coast that, it's enough
to piss me off (and i figured out some time since that the world wants
these fucking machines, and will have em, and that there's no use beating oneself to a frazzle over it, that, those of us who have had it, and
have figured it out, are ahead, and the only thing to do is to use our
position, not, put up with the boring repetition in every country of the
world

   but the vulgarization which accompanies same, reduces pleasure
eh? (and i figure another of Ez's true shots was, that, there are a few who
want to work, and then there is the rest, who want to be diverted. Or is
that olson? Anyhow, it's impatience, not stupidity alone, which fucks up
the raza humana—only, right now, it's the wrong kind: one is hungry
just for some impatience, of another sort, to get on with this filthy
passage thru the machine, and ahead to what has to come out the other
side, the raza humana is, so, impatient!

well, fuck that part of it—the only thing is, it's still only Sanchez who
gives either of us any real pleasure. And he leaves in a week for Carmen
(to do the mural in the museum there, a month, and a half) and, thereafter, to be gone three months to Kabah, for the reconstruction of same
now scheduled by the Mex. Gov't.

you see, what threw me forward was, the discovery that Uxmal, the
famous Uxmal, is altogether otherwise than you'd gather, from the
literature I have seen

   the two famous buildings, for example (the Gov-
ernor's Palace, and the Nun House), brilliant architecture & engineering
as they may be, are aesthetically dead it is clear to me that the period
during which they were built (c.1000-1200), at that time, the Maya had
become State-lovers, had lost all intimate & human preoccupations, and

thus, all perception of space (time)

yet, on the spot, are other buildings, much destroyed, which, actually, deserve much more attention than these two white elephants which happen to have stood up best (as State-history does, eh?)

for example, there are phalluses all over the place, huge stone realisms (it bugs me, that, this aspect of Maya life I can find no reports on, anywhere—except, by god (which proves how cheap the 20th century is), in good old John Stephens, 1841—who, by the way, though he was the 1st to call the world's attention to Uxmal, did have the taste to recognize that the ruins of Kabah (down the road a short piece, even tho it took me over night to get to them, travel, here, is such), that Kabah is richer & purer—Stephens, in his "Yucatan," has a Latin appendix on these stones he kept running into[132]

well, the whole situation, as Uxmal & Kabah reveal it, is close interval stuff (I'd guess that's the reason the work has been so careless; it's too tough). And makes me, of course, wholly suspicious of *all* ground observations (why, i say, i better try to get a look at all important sites). For the story shifts the moment you get yr eyes on any of these places I have so far seen (other example, Chichen: Kluckhohn, 10 yrs ago, sd, the Mayan archeologists are antiquarians & pigs wallowing in details;[133] the truth is more important than he was able to put it: Chichen, which they seem pleased to be able to blow up and at the same time dispose of as "Mexican" Mayan, contains one building, the Caracol, which is still the subtlest & lightest construction I have seen (and one of the loveliest buildings I know in Europe or the Americas)

i sd, a new project: an extension of the art of the language of the glyphs wld be a book straight on, on, the art of the maya, that is, just such distinctions as above, between the buildings, anywhere, among standing pieces (there are three at Kabah, and one of them, a head, with a tattooed face—African tattoo, with dirt put in, to raise the cicatrix—is a beauty: there is also, there, an archaic job, of a man struggling against a serpent wound round his neck, which has behind it a prime push so strong (there are other examples, one, here, in Campeche) as to lead me to guess that (like the Hopi) the Mayans had a snake fix long before the plumed serpent, and that that same fix was, perhaps, joined to a phallic biz in which each was a prime assertion of force in man as he takes it up from nature:

which is exact contrary to State[s], of course, but, where, anywhere, in the books available, can i find any more than (1) generalizations abt Maya culture & art as though it were all of one piece, and (2), if there are distinctions, they are merely low stupid classical european aestheticisms based entirely, not on taste, but on the dates of stela on the ground!

Please put up with these exasperations. But you'll figure they'd be damned irritating, on the ground, no? And I report them, only, because they are a gauge of more important things. The only thing is, to do what I'd like to do, only can't do it straight on, there is so much shit, to shovel away, first. I'm telling you, I can't think of anything more deeply offensive and harmful than, the Carnegie Institute of Washington, D.C., all, its works, just because sd works are blown up beyond what they so simply are: the exploration of sites. And what kills me even there is, that most of the sites they did not even discover, but went in only after *chicle* men had told em, there is, Uaxcatun, or Tikal, or whatever!

And besides, as you so accurately put it, they control this region, & my innocencies would die, fr their laughter—as well as i cld get no backing, in money, fr same!

I don't know. Maybe I better give it over. If I were a wealthy man, with State connections, maybe, it could be swung: one could come in here as Stephens did, a 100 yrs ago, and make a sweep. Then, with a little study, and the money for repros, do a book. But, as it is, I am discouraged. And wonder if I had not better spend my energies elsewise.

The balk I'm getting fr Pavon doesn't help any (proves, the Mexicans are as bad as the Carnegie). A further defeat: I have had no answer fr (1) Sam Lothrop, the Peabody big gun, to whom I wrote a month ago; (2), fr Robert Wauchope, the head of the Tulane operation; (3), fr the Mexican chief office (to whom I sent a buck for a book)!

Christ, in this biz, not even the courtesies are observed. I'm pissed off.

But to get back: I have the start of an answer to Slater on water. Do tell him that at Kabah there are holes in the ground opening into paved and cemented vaults which look for all the world like artificial storage cisterns. And that I find that Stephens, in "Yucatan," as well as his 1st book, "Central America," discusses the problem as he observed it at Uxmal: he says that the aguadas around Uxmal were artifical reservoirs, and reports that, his 2nd trip, he descended into four or five vaults (which sound very much like the ones I noticed at Kabah) and was convinced they were not, as the then owner of Uxmal sd they were, for grain, but were for water.[134]

And that (as of the Peten, the older part), I am beginning to get the impression that *rivers* were the answer (though, here, I can't be sure, not having seen the places and—by laws above, that is . . . .

Oh, Christ, Robert, there is so much, starting up. Another result of the trip this week, is, that (fr the close interval of difference in style between Uxmal (major) and Kabah (total), it becomes quite clear [that *crossed out; letter continues in ink:*]
Went off to see our *1ST BULLFIGHT*—it's after midnight—want you to have this— will pick up tomorrow. IS[?] BEAUTIFUL

Olson

lerma / april / 12: thursday [1951]

lad—still want to get back to that long & lovely letter of yourn, in which you sd such wild & true things abt (symbol & mask (abstract process (language

& was to set to it, today, only, at breakfast (because i had another dream abt one of my "competitors" when i was in school), Con and I have been sitting trying to get down the patterns (if any) of dreams (those i've told her) over the last few years. Still (as you know) believe, that if a man *had* such record, *made by himself & read by himself*, ((that absolute rightness, the Omaha, *you* keep it to yrself, don't go to medicine man, is, between you & the Makyr[135]

(the Amalgamated, Local #1, of The Sewers, the Finders, the Makers: meeting # 2, here, at this machine)

i shld imagine why, no one does keep such a record, is, it teases the mind out of itself, the complex is, so huge & so, close. Plus that it reveals, instantly (no?), what we are, that is, what we don't let thru fr, that rear—or what we didn't, at, those times of past which, now, are, say, also abt to be such, times, again, eh?

In any case my impression this morning is, that it was only about ten yrs ago that i began to get this bunching of ds. which, might make possible such, record & pattern (though one wld want to examine whether, it isn't simply that, abt 10 yrs ago, one got interested in, their occurrence: what still strikes me as strong, was, that the 1st bunching was, transposition of "the father" to State figures (date, the draft, 1940-41, winter of, same)

Well, to hell with such. And abt the bizness, of, what you say, there, last Wednesday, after, the go on, Kid Korman, which, as you know I, thank you for, believe, and was only (in my spleen) getting rid of what goes with, like you say, the back-up fr, his lack of, quite simply, rhythm. And that, by god, we ought to be able to ease him out of, if, we are worth, to him, anything. In fact, if you'll allow yrself to be just such a vent for my choking, as we go along with cid, it'll keep me fr lambasting him: which does not so much good as, the present go of, keeping throwing at him all ideas & materials I can think of. For he certainly does come up, ride ahead on, what I shoot him: not only did he himself take the Sanchez drawings that step further to a show (which, in its turn, threw me forward) but, in his last letter, he has the alertness to suggest (what I had thot of but sd no word abt) a whole issue of Origin (#6) devoted to Maya! Now that's moving, and tho I am sure a much better idea would be an issue on, say, Maya-Sumer-AND *that present people with graphic comprehension*, the Amuurikans, that triptych, yet, that, on his own, he works ahead so rapidly, is, to be thankful for, eh? (The contrast to all others, conspicuously, our dead-head fr Columbus, hemererer-sob,[136] is marked; on top of which I still stand in total respect to, the fact that, any day now, you and I shall hold in our hands, paper, & print, got there by same, called, a mag, origin (origo-dreme-imago)[137]

And I go ahead with you on, Blackburn, & ringer, Morse, & bronk, whoever keeps interesting you. ((I also had the pleasure, to find it possible to write a long letter, this week, to Vinc, the day I received his new gig, HEARTLAND[138]—for it offered me a disclosure, abt that problem of his, of society vs the personal, which I took the freedom (which is what, is, ok & very damn all right abt him, that, one does offer back, critique) to lay on the line, straight, to him.)) (Again, the contrast is, Columbus: how, his "discoveries," are stealings; if he didn't have the gall to send me that dirty little Bro. Aspirin Box—which angers me beyond containing, that, so soon, in less than a year, already, yr magnificent concept of form-ex.-concept [*i.e.* content], has been wholly vulgarized, misstated, and thus, that it is already dirtied and can, mislead. In other words, backwards, he goes, takes everything, because of his greed, ambition, and Cressidism ("slydinge o corage"[139]), backwards.

BUT, like I say, please hold yr fire, as I keep mine, until we know (the next month, or two as [*i.e.* at] the very most), whether or not he is enough expended on THE PRAISES, to make it impossible for him to draw back. For that is all, now, that I can see that he has left in, certainly, my relation with him (he is such a fool, how much he loses, by, his trickinesses. For I remain interested in one central quality of his verse—what I wld call a trick of dissolve, of a total dissolve of meaning in the ultimate Eliot of his verse's music (the word I use direct, in the sense of, the dead-end of "quartets": it totally fascinates my medieval & catholic mind (ha!) that, Emerson's present title for his long poem (the poem I am sure has dictated all his maneuverings the past months since August last, his ungovernable wish to put himself, he thinks, out ahead of you and me, in the van, to the rear of Bill's PAT and Ez's CANT) the title is THUNDER *SUITE* (he being the "Ohio Thunder," a noun, by the way, a laugh, I myself tossed to him, in total irony, as well as an assonance to, the way he called me, in the passage abt you & me, the "Wash. Wonder" (the shit).

And my interest in that curious one little thing, the dope has completely forfeited already, by, causing me such goddamn anxiety all these past months. (It occurred to me, writhing, reading the printed thing on verse (I had sworn to myself, in order to keep fr blowing the book up, I'll not look at it again until I have THE PRAISES in my hands!) that Emerson completely confuses the act of verse as technical, and the act of life as, shrewdness. And by those two errors he moves, backward.)

But, as I say, let me beef off to you without, just now, you letting the burn out, any more than I do. For this book, that you were the originator of, is still, despite the mess I'm sure he'll make of it, still, a part of the bizness which, made, will be of use. And I feel so sure I have become some Machiavel to him (the idiot), that, he is trying, somehow, to outwit me! And he has one stick: THE CONTRACT, for, the book. He damn well knows, he has me, a little, by the short hairs, just there. But, as I pointed out to him this week, he made an agreement with me in January (by phone, the bastard) that, if he was not ready to move ahead by March 15 to publication in May (with June as the outside) I was to be free to market the mss elsewhere. Now, with that silly nonsense, of everything made but the insides (how silly it is you 1st pointed out), he has led me along another little distance. Only, what he doesn't know (or does he? i shld never imagine myself a match to such constant going by shrewdness alone) is, that, I go along this little time more simply because, if I have to shift, the time is too late now to make publication before summer, and, if he tries to push it over until fall, I figure the time has come to call his game, take it off, and, hit (1) Giroux, at Harcourt—

small chance; & (2) Laughlin (similar delays, for another year!). So my present policy is to say nothing abt anything to this worm except one repeating & repeating thing: when. And he must already catch, that, if he wants anything fr me on his various mss., he better act on THE P'S.

Which, by the way, brings me to yr wonderful notion, of, ORIGIN EDITIONS. For, may we not, properly (& I do believe the Kid wld go along) think of doing yr stories and these verses, like any damn editors (much as I hate that fucking thing, nepotism, in these literary affairs)? ((I still like, in a sort of a way, that lad of ours, Vinc., because his good wife Peg types like mad, making up his own "books"! It is a thing I could never do, but, that he does it, is, such a piece with, his attack upon, this society &, its distribution—admitting, of course, the chagrin, the tries, anterior to it)

Anyhow, one day, I'd like to lay my whole corpus in yr hands, and say, lad, with the good eys [*sic*], please, make a book!

But this is to say, that, I wholly accept yr baby, this EDITIONS biz— and it shall stay alive in me, for what use, ahead, you see: it occurs to me as a wonderful fast way to register (like you say) going preoccupations. Say (fr my obsessions, just now):

(1) a fast double-take on SUMER-MAY[A], or, 2, one, transpositions of those poems, &, separately, a little job, with Sanchez if possible, analyzing, with drawings, the nature of that language &, its "writing" on the stones

(2) a reprint of, Douglas Fox's summary, of Frobenius' whole position—that series of articles I have fr THE NEW ENGLISH WEEKLY, back, abt, o, 1930[140]

(3) a go, by you, on, back there, the necessities of prose narration, now

& (4) say, pulls, fr altogether different disciplines, like, say, Sauer, on "Climate & Culture in the DeGlaciation"[141]

Well, over the fence, that's all. O, ya: one further thing, so long as, today, I seem to be catching up on, such affairs between us: I was bowled over, in that letter, in which you summarized what's coming up, in ORIGIN, to find, now, that you pulled back, you say, on "O & Bad Thing." That you say you always did. I tell you why: the damn fragile truth is, that I let it fly off to Corman because I had that note of yrs on the mss., so:

shit, can't lay my hands on the mss, fast, but, something like, one note, "diatribe, which, surely, narrative, must be"[142]

not at all to shift anything to you, but, simply, to register with you, that, i go a good deal on, how you take a thing, and (maybe because i am stupid here where such things are so fucking personal), if you do not ride, just spell that fact out—as, for that matter, I guess this is the *only* time you didn't, or, that I was asleep, or put asleep by, yr above notation!

knew, e.g., cold, how you sat on ADAMO—and, if it hadn't been for circumstances which have still not revealed themselves sufficiently to me to make it possible for me to stand the sight of that gd poem, I'd certainly, as you say, have reworked it—and precisely at those points where, in the mss, you bore in.

Well, hell. No importa. Just, that, want no flies in, this milk!

And i guess i mention it, jumped, when you sd it, because, that little job, the STORY, scares the shit out of, me! ((It's, generally, so god damn irritating, how few, there are, of what you do, that, you, inside, are, rock abt: must be wonderful to be, an egotist!

It's not the day, I guess, to pick up on, ur wonderful other things, in that letter. So I'll come back on it, as we seem to do, when, the thing is, has its, day. For that area, surely, we have our teeth in, eh? (It is still to me a beauty beyond dreaming up, how, you, fr yr own makings, grab, right

here—how, fr, going abt yr business, you, by precisely that biz., are
where we can swap, principles.

well, greetings, eh?

yrs

c

[Littleton, N.H.]
Saturday [14 April 1980]

Dear Chas/
            Yr letter in yesterday, & very great—many, many thanks
for the poem (& will note some comment, on same, further on). Also
here yesterday—a letter from Gerhardt (a real goofy one, which he had
glued together, so it almost reached the floor, etc.) & it seems he's
having some trouble with money and paper, but says he figures that
April 15th, will see the 1st issue out.
                                He asks (ha) if you are angry with
him, i.e., "Fand er beides so schlecht. . . ," meaning, like they say, did
you find both the things (the translation & his BRIEF) so bad? I had
written him, anyhow, noting yr loss of the dictionary, & so, he now
knows why he hasn't heard, etc.
                                But he sounded so crushed, I felt very
damn sorry for him. He is still going on yr book, i.e., "Olson's book is
as good as taken, but if no contract can be settled on, we have others,
still, to handle it. . ." It's the Claassen Verlag, Hamburg, who are on
same at the moment.
                                He had enclosed a long prose thing, a 'letter,'

which I take it, goes to Cid for possible use as a head for any selection of
new german poets, etc. It's ok—some slide in it, i.e., once they, he, get,
gets, on the 'abstract,' it's hard to pull them back, but there are some
very damn fine sections, to same, & so hope Cid can handle it.

Also a
letter from Cid in—will be seeing him this coming week, i.e., go down
to Boston on Tuesday, for a day or two. I have put the whole biz of this
house with a lawyer, i.e., fuck it—I can't get anywhere, & so my boy
begins by attaching for $10,000! How abt that! I mean, not the vaguest
relation to what I figure owed us—but I can't say I wd object to gaining
same. Well, apparently, this is the custom, to start some several
thousands higher than what you take it yr owed. At least—in New
Hampshire.

Very goofy poem, & very much like same. One thing: that I find myself
hanging with the longer version, i.e., what the shorter comes from. I
damn well don't know, but anyhow: figure this longer one has hits
beyond the small frame. Well, let me go thru same, here, to note, by
copying, what I take: is the thing—

[*Revisions made by Olson throughout, here in brackets:*]

mexico)
                          cld not
have guessed: wood, a
bowl of gray wood, of
an afternoon, already
shadowed (4
pm: very fast, high, sharp
rockets, a crazy trumpet of
a band, few
people, sloppy
cowboys picadors matadors bulls

                    but out there, on that dirt, in front, directly
                    before your eyes, more, yr existence:

death, the
possibility of same, the certitude
right there in front of yr
eyes, god damn yr
eyes
this bull and this man (these men) can
kill
one another

What one knows
put out, & quietly out, put out, right exactly I mean OUT
in front of all eyes, including
    the bull[,] who runs out so
        lightly, with such
           declarations of
              his presence

    the man, so
      careful, such
          preparations (the bull [*line break*] only
              about to find out), [the man] so clothed, such [tools, and]
                  [tools, & *crossed out*] running back [to]

                                so ludicrously [the]
[to the *crossed out*] barricade, the bull [,] too [,] smelling
its [the *substituted*] wood [,] where an opening is, how
to get out of

                Whoever
conceived this action, this
thing, this
instant declaration of that which you know is all
that constitutes both what you are and what is going on at all time
as of you or anyone since and as long as whatever
it is that it is, is

    this
        bullfight:

bull so much not
animal (as the word
is) his
experience so very clear, there, his
bewilderment, tries, angers (no
fear, or more than [*revisions not fully legible*]
he is
involved

the men (the man) so much more
animal, so
aware, their
courage (fear) so
very clear, so very much the reason why
we too are
involved, why
we, here,
are [*crossed out*]

   ((the man, down in that ring [dirt *substituted*], so much
     scampering, so much (advancing) a
     sort of [picked] bantam))

those horns

that voice repeating "to[-]ro" "to[-]ro" "to[-]ro"

those words, wooing

that head, the plain danger of

you [*line break*] have

been

asked

Both of us (Ann & yr lad) like it very damn much, & the above, finally
(or so I hope) no insult to yr own taking, i.e., what little I do, to indicate,
only, where I wd figure, there is some loss, due to the ride off (too much
of same) into the parallel, of how yr taking all this. The hit: that this
parallel holds, thru-out, but the balance—what's the tightrope. A couple
of things: I'm not, myself, sure, if the end, the last 3 lines, is too hard?
Meaning, flat, as: take it or leave it, but I wd be anyhow, for such
statement, so won't introduce sd bias here. I.e., I wd have written same,
so, but that don't prove much.

        Of the other changes: I don't know.
Where, for one, I cut out the 'here' in: "to get out of

                    here. . ." is that, I figure
the rush, there, some gain? I don't know. Certain that in reading, the
closer the 'Whoever. . .' section can get, to this fine detail, of sd bull—
the better. Strike while the iron is hot, etc., etc. Also, the logic for a
similar cut: "the plain danger of (same) . . ."

        I may damn well intro-
duce, by so doing, ambiguities a good ways beyond yr intentions. I wd
hold that the 2nd cut, keeps the logic, i.e., the danger is (& is no
'danger') of the voice, those words, "wooing that head. . ." & is also,
the logic in: "you have

        been

        asked. . ." (???) For me, it's that double. Well, I may
fuck that up—thinking of same now, I see where I can, etc. It's my own
head, etc., that wd make the confrontation, & the voice, share that fact:
or the coupling, of a 'danger. . .' Being, perhaps, my sense, that any
confrontation, & any act such as this, combine a 'danger. . . ,' tho the
only 'danger' worth knowing.

        Anyhow, I don't want to mis-read you.
And hope that I don't, here. The split, i.e., the break there, wd push the
1st meaning, i.e., plain danger of 'wooing etc.' anyhow? I think so.

And wd then allow, for the subsequent danger, as well. As it will be
'danger,' as it must be: to find oneself bare, etc.

        On the other hand, like
they say, the 1st can't be argued so blithely, i.e., it may seem, only, to a

reader, that the bull is trying to get out of "Whoever. . . ." Which ain't
the point, etc. Well, so much for same. The other changes being mini-
mal (or I hope to God they are).

But the thing: damn grateful for same,
& like it very damn much. Both of us.

Emerson: well, cool he makes some response. I wiggled out of the biz on
the poem to Schwartz, i.e., I took that chance to pull out a poem Emerson had planned to use himself, i.e., a sad little lyric, I'd wanted to get
out, anyhow, i.e., tear up, etc. So, now he prints these 3 in his #1, &
very damn cool, for my money, that they'll be there along with yr
chunk—I mean, precisely that company: GUIDO; LITTLETON, N.H;
& THE EPIC EXPANDS.

Only wish that HART CRANE (2) ("Answer:
how old," etc) were to be there, too; & HELAS—but same, & LE FOU,
are all I had for Cid's #2. So. That damn 1st one, i.e., Hart Crane (2), is
the one that stays close to my own ribs, like they say. It goddamn well
pleases me. And sure cuts the longer one, to pretty small shreds. However. All in a day's work, like they say.

So what I did: sent to Schwartz,
that little note on OBJECTIVITY,[143] which I'd worked over, just a bit—
trivial, but perhaps it will serve that purpose, i.e., of the gesture, etc.
Ok.

I like LA CHUTE (very certainly, & reading, hearing it so: it's real
crazy), but it's the one (no?) that cd most well go to S/. So, good that it
works out.

Keep me posted on the bk biz/ hope to christ he don't go
slack—not that he's fucking well ever been otherwise. Ok.

Also, cool on the Laughlin biz; jesus, I hope it makes out, i.e., that
Gerhardt can work it. Certain that it wd be a very great help to him. I
mean, that loot, so got, wd be a godsend. They are tightly fixed, I take
it—very damn tightly.

I was trying to get some word of the stories, with Laughlin, but I don't know what's gone wrong, with same. They were sent back in Jan/ (the 2nd, I think), & when I came to write, re Gerhardt, I had asked then abt the stories—but no answer. Jack Hawkes, who had sd, he wd push for what it was worth, etc., sd Laughlin was out in Colorado, or some place.

Well, I can't worry, etc. Ha. I wish to fuck I cd hear before we take off. One way or the other. The hanging, of such things—what I can't damn well stand.

(I can't see that they wd use same. Even so.)

So, abt it. Will write on Monday, before I take off. Ok.

All our love to you both,
Bob

One note more: that, in keeping the 1st section, as was, my logic: it's beyond, here, "description," i.e., is, more, the eye, in act, as it shifts, to then be caught, by this:

"but out there, on that dirt, in front, directly
before. . ."

Only reason, tho I, also, like same, this first, very much, anyhow. What do you think?

sat april 14 [1951] lerma   R CR—

i've turned, or, so, i figure, it/looks.
suddenly, the past two weeks, my hungers, for these places hereabouts,
seem to have abated. at least, i don't feel, the same, pull

(curious, how
many ways, i take it, we are tropistic. Hadn't thought of it then, but,
was describing to Con the shiftings of such feelings on the road toward,
and away from, Uxmal-Kabah, how, just between the two, one's own
impetus, going north, swings, off from Campeche, and, just there,
around 3 miles either side of each, goes Merida-ways. Or, today, debating, whether to make the run tomorrow, to Merida, for a fine corrida,
Dos Santos, the Portuguese fighter,[144] & the best of Mexico: big thing.
And the deepest reluctance, from the tropistic horror of that road.

But
these geographicals are nothing set against the other planes of tropism,
such as—the above area of turning. I shld, myself, imagine, that,
tropisms are pretty much the controls we were talking abt, back there
some, as of DHL. And it is my notion, that, you can mark a man (as
surely as he was marked at the time of the moon, or, in his intense
enveloping of himself in a flower)[145] by, the degree to which he is, true
to, such, swingings. And that this is a way to be precise about his Holy
Ghost, that, he was registering, in that concept, this high character of
organism.

(Did you ever run into his Fantasia of the Unconscious,[146] a
beautifully exact title, & a wonderfully questing job, where he gets off a
lot of good wild stuff, which, however inexact it may be (and i don't
think Lawrence ever did take the time to bear in, here: example, the way
he lets the Bush and the Pacific, in KANGAROO, the terrors of which he
is most, most responsive to, lets them go, with a few humanistic passes),
is, as first job, prime.)

Fact is, I think the explanation, this time, is simpler, is, that I am
hungry to spend more time on myself! That, again, as so often, when I
have had some outside thing, I want, merely, to be in a position to let it
work in me, do nothing about it, just—like this—write about it, go
about, not do a damned direct thing abt same.

And it could just as well
be here, but for the damned money question, that is, the whole time

here I have taken my way, and kept moving from one thing to another, off & on. Only, all that time, there has been this domination of, here you are for a short time and you better make what use of the ground you can. Which is a killing thing, in the end. Or, now, it seems just so: I feel as though I'd never care a fuck if I never saw or heard of Mayan things again! (It was pointed to me, night before last, when, because I hadn't been in to Campeche all week, I sent a note in asking Sanchez to come out for dinner. Which he did, and it was a pleasure, but, when it came to talking abt glyphs, no, I couldn't even, in answer to his direct question, what glyph drawings I will want for ORIGIN, couldn't answer, couldn't even see, had to try to haul myself up to answer, and, in my confusion, just sd, I don't know, won't know until such time as, if ever, I sit down to write a piece on GLYPHS! And I very much hated to be so casual, for, the lad, is most unhappy because of Pavon's decision, and thinks, I am bitter and gone. Which is, of course, somewhat true, that is, that if Pavon hadn't blocked the wheels, I'd imagine I'd still be going strong by way of the Boston show and the NY book. Or maybe not. Anyway, that, I'd have done, with some drive, the push for dough there, in the States. As it is, I have made only half-hearted passes (ever reluctant to ask such for anything), and got half-arsed answers, so far.

I'm toying with this notion (as you probably guessed, fr a recent letter): shifting base to Mexico City, in about two weeks, or, possibly, earlier, if I don't get off my ass & hit the remaining couple of spots I want to hit before leaving: Labna-Sayil (a pisser of a trip) and Edzna (also, rough) ((to go off to either, I have, first, to get rid of the garapata poisoning which has been keeping me up nights since the Uxmal-Kabah gig!)) (((reason: it settled, no less, in my balls!)))

That is: it amounts to taking the money to get home on, and, though not exactly heading home, making it to Mexico City as carefully and reasonably as possible, there to sponge on someone for an automobile to get to see the Zapotec stuff in Oaxaca, the Toltec stuff in Tula & Teotihuacan, the Aztec circa the City, and, above all, to spend as many days as possible in the Museo Nacional (which, as you probably know, has sucked into itself pretty much all the good pieces surviving, except for the heaviest stelas, the 60 ton babies at Quirigua, and abouts!). For I am in this dilemma (chiefly due to my above reluctance, of course): that if I don't do that shortly, I'll not have the chance at all, will have to creep straight back, by shrimp boat or lumber to Pensacola, straight to the States. And there is this extra advantage:

(1) that, in Mexico City, I might just do better promoting myself a longer time generally in these parts;

& (2) there, I am still in the country if, by any long chance, I do get a 500 or 1000 lift, from, anywhere: and then by god I'd damn well fly straight to Copan, straight to that place, by god!

Another real thing is, that Con, there, can be freer, in the, city, simply because, here, there is no one whom she takes pleasure in. And, there, we do have friends of friends. And, besides, I take it, Mexicans, are more to her taste than Yucatecans: a distinction which is surprisingly right—the Yucatan has only one culture, and that's buried, however great it was, and however sufficient to me, up to this point!

It all sounds not bad, eh? (I guess why I was getting off, abt tropisms, is, that my appetite is up over, Mexico City: 1st time, by god, and, I'd never have dreamed: we'll see, whether, right, or wrong!) Will keep you informed, if, all the above, seems, now that I've sd it, what will be.

Damned just beat, actually, at trying to kick such, as Pavon, Ruz (the boss in Merida), Stromsvik (who makes no offer I come look in on the reconstruction of Mayapan), plus the whole fucking gang of like peoples in the States, to kick them along some new paths, or, at least, get them to give me a look in. The feeling is, fuck em, I have other alternatives. Which is, of course, the way they want it. And I like nothing better than fucking em. But, this time, I don't know: maybe I've got, for my purposes, what I wanted (I know one thing, that, always, it's, go in hard, then, cut, keep it for—sure, years—then, another time, hit. Is best methodology for, me. Which same may be all that is now reasserting itself.

Well, the norther, maybe, but no mail in fr you today. Not that I need anything after that fine letter which still rolls round in my beings like another blood, is, quote, too much!

Love to Ann and the lads,
fr us both

and, please, another thanks to,
Slater, whose, interest, was
very damned nice: he sits on my palate, damn fine. (Ever notice curious
note [*added in margin in ink:*] Dahlberg seems to have had to add to
New Directions XII publications of parts of *Wheel of Sheol*, acknowledging that, it was a conversation in Wash Sq with *Slater Brown* which led
him back to rereading "Daniel" & so, writing, the essay?[147] Wonder, if
SB called Dahlberg on, the fact there was no such, in the book THE
FLEA, itself?

[Littleton, N.H.]
Monday
[16 April 1951]

Dear Chas/

Very damn great having yr 2 in, this noon. The day/
another grey, one, but whether it is just that time, the passage, or a
thing I don't now figure: this weather is what I am after, & very damn
fine.

Let me put it out: a friend I'd known back abt 5 years, & his wife
(new; married about 2 weeks back, now) had called, it was on Sat/ & they
must have started out, just after, up here, coming in about 7.

Well, useless to make much, or too much of it, but that I am, we are,
have slid, beyond the graces, or what must make, perhaps, life for such
as these, possible.

They say, the 2 of them, the wife, such a coldness

from her, it withered me, altogether, such a frigid, a beastly contained-
ness, it was goddamn killing.

                    She must have fallen asleep 3 or 4 times,
in the few hrs we stayed up, after they came in. And, the damn loss :
myself (as I damn well always am, with such things) a madman, running, here, there, every damn where, pulling out bks, reading a half
paragraph, then so red-faced, so apologetic, I wd then lean on it for just
that time necessary to make the whole act: farce, & her, then, so cool
there, sitting on the floor. So damn cool. The face: w[h]ere the eyes,
must have been grey, wd widen, at times, that is, get, bigger, but a trick,
a fucking, trick. And the mouth, a line, somewhat, that is of two edges,
the lips, themselves, having come to a double, so that there is, as even
with a snake, a double presence, of same: the lips, which are one way,
one time; then, one wd suspect, the mouth, at another, is wider, more
large, that the lips, widen, & so, certainly: that sexuality.

                                         And is
perhaps that (?) which got me? No man, it's certain enough, can allow
himself to stay: neuter, in the company of, any, woman. Is impossible.

He: friendly. Just so. Wanted, to understand. And doesn't that damn
well, lead the: dance?

                    They left abt noon, Sunday, again, a wonderful
damn day, very fierce, a sky, way up: these clouds, immense damn
things, with a roll to them, a thickness, & a wind, wd take yr clothes
of[f] yr back, & throw them, to hell & back.

                                Fine, fierce damn day. Got into
me, & seeing them, the car, go jerking, backwards, thru the gate, between the stone, of the walls, seeing that, them, so going, I felt, like a
little dance, a little stamping, & perhaps, some growls, of the deepness,
of my: satisfaction.

                    And did get Dave's kite, &, despite tears, a warped
cross-stick, got it up, so it rode, very fine, over the edge of, these trees.
So goddamn fine/ sight of same, way the hell up there, how she pulled
on, the string, with that wind, the pull of it, the trees, as Dave sd:
bouncing. So very damn fine.

Just that I don't get them, these two, or want to, get them. No part. He sd: how very attractive, the idea of, the "marginal man"—to be there, at that distance, to, observe. . .

Shuddered! And beyond: could not get it, or why? WHY? With, say, even that presence, as, going out these sudden gusts, that grip, of the wind, the day, without distance, beyond it, & you/ them, me: anywhere, any damn where! And he wd put it, make it 'nothing. . . ,' all we got, 'nothing. . .'

His statement: "a very fine play, granting what we have, is, nothing. . ."

DAMN THEM

DAMN THEM DAMN THEM.

Also: reading, after, Lawrence: these 3—The Captain's Doll, The Fox, & The Ladybird. [148]

DAMN THEM.

Kill the idiots, stamp on them, grind them OUT.

Otherwise—just that I put off the trip to Boston. And as much this, as anything : cd not face up to, this kind, these people, as sd city is stuffed, with same. Damn well cd not face, up to it

So, here, as ever. Very damn fine. I figure the poem, this draft now in, has a gain, of the formal, the order, perhaps. I miss the plunge, call it, of the first, the longer.

But is that too damn vague? I can't be as precise as I damn well must be. The shame; that I have that longer, in my head, to fuck up this draft, i.e., that I have that bias.

That, or this above, being how my head now holds same.

Well, let the
letter, just sent, ride for the moment. I.e., will take a day, & sit down to
this, again.

Later/

will enclose here, this last draft of poem, & on same: some
notings, etc. These, again, only yr lad.

Ok. Very damn difficult, to
isolate, even for myself, what it is, nags at me on this. I figure it in the
loss (partial) of that first rush (& this is yr hit, that there is that damn
loss; & to be fought at). Anyhow, the longer: above all, a rush, a
fucking real wildness, of this act: seeing, the thing coming IN. And that
is: beauty.

The shorter: the fix of an order, which is, again, what must
come to hold, hard, call it, to hold, as such can be held: these first
plungings, as in, the longer.

But cannot, or I hate to see it, minimize
any of that first, quickness. I mean, the way it was, so, a rush, & never
one damn second, for breath.

Hence: do figure it so—that if this last, cd, say, be thrown more into, or
back to (but this is not, recall), the longer—wd be then the thing, I
mean, wd bt IT.

Details (in the longer) tho they stretched, ran as far as
any thought wd, even so: the straight run, or what, it is, 'digression' is
all abt. Ok. Here, that same order, ties in the forces, also, makes, of
detail (because its rush now falls under this order) too much the annota-
tion, or too much, that reasonable extension of 'one's thoughts.'

And
these are NOT "reasonable," & they are NOT "thoughts"—I mean,
this is all, of one piece: & action, of either this eye, or, its bull, is ONE.

(And it's there, now, where I figure, the loss: that the bullfight has
grown 'less' (i.e., in the sense of the 'length' of 'digression' it now
pushes) & that this 'digression' also suffers—because of this growing

'less,' on part of bullfight. That is goddamn devious, but do yez get, say, the logic?)

I.e., 1) in 1st case, bullfight, of power, having same, in one respect, because there, altogether literally, the mass, the flood of perception ('digression') it was responsible for; 2) in 2nd (shorter), the curb of same digression now asserts this backward kick against, bullfight, i.e., bullfight not now so apparently pushing this gt/ weight, of the seeing. AND the danger—that, heaven goddamn well forbid—that, reader may, fuck him, take it, the digression came prior, to bullfight. And abt that, there can be NO damn equivocation, i.e., the thing gains, for me at least, in so far as reader, himself, gets the simultaneity, of these 2 things: act/ object: sight/ perception. Well, that much, anyhow, to get into it, this thing that's bugging me here.

Hence, you see, the danger of, that very first word: "yes. . ." Too sure, too, leaning back, much too 'after. . . .'

Think, again, of yr fusing, there, at end: think, quick, of how (writing I damn well must believe it went so) there is NO fusing NO sense of this 'ask. . . ,' till, till, all acts (yrs/ & this bull fight) have come to, fullness. The danger, then, in this first word: that it makes you, going back to—& that, going back, this act of—has not a damn thing to do with this poem. Well, wild words, etc., but you will know.

So this much, then, to break some of it out, & will keep at same & see if I can't get it all to hell clear, because, surely, is what's now the trouble with my comment.

[Olson's typescript enclosed (see photo following p. 100), with note by Olson in ink, a typed note by Creeley at the start, and the rest of Creeley's notes in pencil throughout:]

wed. morn. [11 April 1951]
lad—most sorry, I jumped myself! (now I understand why I slugged in, the whole stuff. wasn't set: here, now, it, is. And thanks, many thanks! What dya say? It digs, no?

[*Creeley:*] (Notes, here, made before the page following. I'm getting torn, on what is (pretentious considering) the logic, formal, & what was that gain in the longer——being, one says: tighten, the other: open up. I say— open up.)

RIGHT THERE IN FRONT OF YOUR EYES

(for R. Cr.)

yes, right
there in front of
yr eyes, god damn
yr eyes, this bull
& this man (these men) can
kill
one another

What one knows, put out, quite simply & quietly out, put out, exactly
I mean OUT
in front of all eyes, including
the bull's, who
runs out so
   lightly, with such
      declaring
         his presence, his
            self

the man, so
careful, such
   preparations (the bull
      only about to find out), the man
         so clothed, such tools, and
            running, at that, back to

so ludicrously the
barricade, the bull, too, smelling

the wood, where an opening is, how
to get out of
here

Whoever
conceived this action, this
thing, this instant declaration of that which you know is all
that constitutes both, what you are and what is going on at all time
as of you or anyone since, and as long as, whatever
it is that it is, is

this bullfight: the bull
so much not animal
(as the word is) his
experience
so very clear, there, his
bewilderment, tries, angers (no
fear, that is, no
way of anticipation, merely
his increasing sense from confrontation that
he is
involved
        (the fourth bull was a doe-like creature who backed off
cow-like

   ((the legs of a bull in the ring are not
    what they are in a field, are
    colt, or
    calf))

   the men (the man)
so much more
animal, so
aware, their
courage (fear) so
most clear, so very much the reason why
we too are

involved, why
we,
here,
are:

      ((the man, down in that dirt, so much
       a scampering, so much (advancing) a
       sort of picked bantam))

                    YET

those horns

that voice repeating   "toro"   "toro"   "toro"

those words, wooing

that head, the plain danger of same

you know you have

been

asked

                    END

[*Creeley's final note in pencil:*]
It's a fucking fine thing, anyhow. Mainly—the RUSH, the CROWD of,
perceptions—can you keep same moving as—simultaneous? That's
where the longer one had gained, in spite of the looseness of same.

One note more: on this Emerson biz, being, only, for my/yr : edifica-
tion.

Well, this, i.e., the line-up on sd bklet,[149] being/ a run-thru of what was, the change, of this thing, from the 1st draft sent in here last October. So:

one/ 1 sentence, the last.

two/ sentence 2 rewritten somewhat; 3rd sentence is either me, straight or a garbling of same—I mean, I know it's me, but can't place it—(I had argued, this abstract biz, in letter answering his 1st draft).

three/ no change   NOTA: #2 & #3 are joined in 1st draft.

four/ sentence 2 is me, I figure—same letter; well, note style of same, as against the rest, particularly, last clause? No other change.

five/ sentence 3, sentence 4, sentence 5: yr lad. Goddamn well NOTE what he does to me, i.e., how sd sentences are thrown in, certainly, without any logic I get. Even buck his sense, as remainder of para/ asserts same. No other change.

six/ new, but? Well, it's way off the beat, as it was supposed, etc.

seven/ same—& E/ at his lowest.

eight/ this is the bitch/ as you sd: look what he does to me—again, my phrase : stands against the rest of the comment, precisely against. No other change here, just that one phrase, added.

nine/ new, & how abt that! I blew up, on this one—just don't make anything, BUT: mess.

ten/ same, but? Idiotic.

eleven/ E/ letting it out, the bulk, the corpus: of the shit. What a fucking drag. No change, is the same, as was.

twelve/ the same.

thirteen/ the same.

fourteen/ some addition here (& on these last, he shifted abt a little, but made no real switch, etc.) This is another damn loss—in much the same sense as is, the form biz. He just don't get it.

fifteen/ again, a hodge-podge, & take it, this is what he had written you. How abt that—what a fucking note, to end on, to be making: climax. Haw haw.

So, that's it. Abt, say, 8 or so sentences added; no basic cuts, no shifts on any of the heads I'd indicated in sd letter of sd 11 pp. All I got was swallowed. I mean, pulled in to the idiocies.

                                        I damn well don't forgive
this.

     Cid, most happily, wrote him one of those horribly honest letters;
very fine. I.e., he nailed him, word by word.

On E/ generally: where we do have him—who else has he got? (Or think
again, of the names he had noted for you, for sd anthology. IS the
give-away.) So don't, myself, worry. Also, what he don't know : I AM
the Machiavel—& that is one bitter mistake, he has made. Ha! I mean,
he's been using me, off & on now, for confessor—& am only biding, the
time. Well, no knives, etc. Don't need same—this boy altogether capable of swinging, altogether by his own hand, etc. Because, look: 1) this
biz of tailing on to, Williams & Ez—can't make same, because he's
riding against a tide, certainly actual, of altogether tangible dislike, of
both gentlemen, & 2) the final allies, call us, he cd be using, he fucks &
even he knows: Hedly, Rubenstein, Greer,[150] et al, do NOT give him
the 'background' he will need to sound his note, etc. I.e., he wants
'group,' that echo of sd 20's, but how the hell is he going to get same,
using a bunch of bleary romanta-cists. Can not be done, & he's shrewd
enough to know same.
                         So, there he is: hating our guts, yrs/mine, but
NOT of sufficient courage, to be out at night, alone, etc. Hence, the way
he swings off & on, etc.
                         Also, he gets to see how Cid is stealing the
march on him—& I got him there, being me, luckily, who had blown
up, at Cid, to him, & so : now my grudging admiration of sd Cid, like
they say. I.e., he don't get, for a minute, what's gone on there. But like
this: a week back, he writes me, he was going to write Sam Morse for
poems, so I answer : gee, what a shame, i.e., Cid just got the pick of sd
new group, & this, is, mind you, NOW, the echo, the kick-back, on
every damn one, i.e. (Cid being now in, with Blackburn), 1/ Blackburn,
2/ Bronk, 3/ Gerhardt, 4/ you, 5/ me, 6/ Pound (as Fang has got some
Chinese stuff for Cid, & that is precisely what, Emerson has never got?),
7/ all the angles, any of us, can now pull in. [*Added in margin:* Emerson
has had *prior* note on every one of these men but Fang—SO, had his
chance and will NEVER let him forget same.

I mean, he's lost his place. Think of it. This mag, of Cid's, begun, damnit, after all of the biz between you & Emerson had taken place, & STILL beating him, altogether, to the punch on this spread, of yr work—i.e., aint it, fucking beautiful, that Cid comes out 2 wks before him, on the mags??? And let me once damn well get to France, & see, there, how this editions biz might go—& we'll have all the damn cards, every damn one. And will run sd idiot to ground, right on his own!

Better: to work a hinge, i.e., a play so that both presses, keep running an easy competition, which it won't be (thinking of his issues, of stuff, to date, etc.). But for one thing, you should see Cid bristle, when Emerson comes into it; or, the other way round! Well, the parallel! Both, with radio programs, both with mags, & if we make it, both with the editions biz! And never, god damn well NEVER, cd one hope for such a damn perfect play-off!

Which is evil, of me. But/ it presupposes, that Cid is worth, a good many Emersons. But also, two mags, going, still better than one, etc.

So I can't damn well but figure: things are going to clear. ONCE Cid's magazine is in Emerson's hands—sd character will SEE what he damn well was sleeping on. That he has lost, as it is, the 1st pitch, & can, as he'll get to see, also lose the 2nd: the bk.

In other words: Emerson, as he has been playing it, with those will make it, I mean even 'write,' 2 yrs, 5 maybe, then O. But Cid/ who has got onto the ones will be sticking. And with such, you damn well cannot hang too close, or too, kind. E/s Folly. It will damn well fuck him yet.

I feel very badly abt the story biz, i.e., that I shift, do shift, on same.

Frankly, the one item, of yr work, where the reaction (mine) has not been immediate, & then held. Hence: my confusion, confusing, of same.

I figure what it comes to: I don't, yet, hold sd story, where I get beyond, incidents, or details, of same. Hence: do shift. As I wd not, holding the whole damn thing.

But where I have no excuses: that I had

not made this clear.

Anyhow, damn well this much—that sd story is no loss, & that, say, it being not, for yr lad, the hit of divers of the poems, or, a gig like GATE & CENTER—what is same, more than the variance (damn well impossible to kick out) of my own damn taste—& this, the flux, as it damn well, makes itself out, proves so, to be.

Presumption, to say loss, anyhow. Presumption, to say more than, exact—I'm of 2 minds on sd story; hence, damn well beware, of my comment.

Well, forgive me; no excuse for same, whatsoever.

(The fact you put that stock, in my word to begin with, showing me how fucking complete my let-down of you, in this instance, turns out; not again.)

Yr notes on the EDITIONS biz: very damn cool. Anxious, very anxious, to get over, & see what cd be done with same. Hoping that some gain is possible, by printing same over there. Well, useless, now, to guess; once there, can see what's what.

If the damn thing can be done, will be the damn: END! Very damn certainly, & have no doubts but that Cid will go with same—for the added substance.

This for now, then; want to get back on, this poem, & will write tomorrow. You note what you think abt, 1st comment, i.e., the letter just out, which was on the biz, of the 1st two/ long & short. And I'll keep on, this one, now at hand; ok.

(That this is a damn real one, no matter which 3 : the one fact.)

Write soon.

All our love to you both/

Bob

[Lerma, Campeche]

tues april 17 [1951]

lad:

yr 1st letter in a week was a shot in the arse. and i figure, today, to do something abt it. that is, i take it you are straight right, on getting PHOTOS, before i pull the hell out—that is, if they, too, are possible, Pavon being, such a fucking idiot.

And I mean photos of Sanchez's drawings. That is, photos of the stones themselves would never, now, be the equal of the, drawings. Even casts. Simply because, to see those glyphs requires just such scrupulous raising of details as he has done: it may be a measure of his care, & dignity, that, after the sketches & photos in the field (three months, I think it was), it took him one solid year to do the finished full size sheets: abt 2 by 3 ft.

There is one profound hitch—and it could be (is now) the death of, the project—that is, from a direct explanatory go-ahead. That is my own profound disbelief in PHOTOS. I fucking well abhor same camera as another machine. Think it reduces, shreds, blunts RETENTION, by this organism, or anyone, attacks, as does all recording instruments, MEMORIA. And thus, the usages AFTER retention. Anyhow, figure, our job (specifically ours) is to retain & then use WITHOUT artificial means of reproduction.

You see, why this Sanchez has been the real biz, is, that, his are drawings. And without them I'm not at all sure I would have fired to these glyphs. (It is a lot like the service Kramer[151] gives me: he translates fr the cuneiform clay, & gives me, thus, the chance to transpose (ex. LA CHUTE). And now that the whole house has come down around my head, I am a little sorry I didn't (not knowing) do the transpositions right here, while, I had the chance to work, with, Sanchez, & the drawings, direct. But it would have only been possible that week Pavon was away (due, again, to Pavon's greed & jealousy, for, he would never let Sanchez work with me while he was there, the cheap shit). And that particular week I had to get inside, as I did, first. (One thing I am glad abt, that, I kept shooting to you what was coming off the top of it. That, at least, is done.)

It is a damned sad biz. For, as I write you, I am waiting for Sanchez to come to lunch: he leaves, tomorrow, for Carmen! With Pavon. Which writes END, at least for the 4-5 months he will, fr here out, be tied up at Carmen, & at Kabah.

(You are, of course, also, profoundly right abt the State & politicks of the thing. Damn funny thing is, that, Pavon saw, some time ago (I just found out) what I had suggested to Sanchez as another notion I would like to raise moneys for, in the States! That is, that, THE GLYPHS OF COPAN, shld only be the 1st! For the same job damn well ought to be done, as soon as possible, for

(1) QUIRIGUA—all inscriptions on that site

(2) PALENQUE—ditto

(3) YAXCHILAN, PIEDRAS NEGRAS, BONAMPAK, that complex, on the Usumacinta River

Wherever, in fact, the art of the glyphs was at its height.

I hunch Pavon secretly sees just such a series as his "life work." And of course it is the easiest little way for such a lazy man as himself to build up a record. For until someone exposes this reading of glyphs for the racket it is—I'd rate it abt, say, Chief, of Decoding Section, Govt Bureau 10—such as Pavon and the rest (there are abt five guys now living who have worked this one for a fare-me-well) will continue to block any other revelation of what this language was.

Now, the politicks: these are ex-Spanish countries, hereabouts. The glyph sites spread over Mexico, Guatemala, Honduras. In fact, they straddle (the chief sites) the very frontiers. On top of that they are fast becoming—due to our American brothers—tourist dollar traps (the present program of reconstructions, all launched, by the way, this very period I have been here—Mayapan (Carnegie), Kabah, Palenque, Bonampak (Mexicans), as well as such things as this biz of Pavon & Sanchez instituting this museum in Carmen—are, essentially, for just that trade—in other words, have nothing whatsoever to do with purposes such as you & I might be interested in.

In other words, the three States are very much interested in any & all. On top of that permissions, in such countries, are fucking well solely political, pay-off, & "side."

It is, of course, "side," which Pavon plays cosy for.

And, in his sense, is right, god help us.

But I have not slept. Your idea—hit him fr above—I have already started. Wrote two weeks ago to a nameless creature who used to be personal friend of Minister of Education of Mexico—and who promised me—10 yrs ago—he'd see I was paid to travel to Yucatan any time I wanted to. Was a dinner conversation. And may not hold. But, I made it as, demarche. On top of that I figure, in Mex City, to do a little operating, even so far as to see what I can do to hit through O'Dwyer.[152]

Fact is, it has all shifted, now, to one boring thing: I must now tie down this fucking Spanish, so that I can, move &, operate. It's a nuisance, and it is hard to bring my will to shift to what is, for me, damned secondary. But there it is.

And have by now layed my eggs in the other birds' nests: have put the picture home to 4 corners in the States, and figure, fr those corners, to try to work out of these Central American narrows:

1 ought to have landed in the Harvard-Peabody lay (nothing for me, there!)
1 has already led into the Viking Fund, whatever, that is—NY (as well as—the news, anyway—to the roof outfit, Am Coun Learned Soc
1 to Moe, including, what the hell's the matter with yr boys, missing on Creeley—saying, he, should have, had it!

1 to Sauer, for, whatever (still figuring he's—though I have felt already (head of Fulbright, for ex.) how very jealous the rest of the fund lads are—including Moe—contra Sauer—still figuring, that, though he is an academic, he has *head*. Never touched him before, and don't ever expect such to move, actually, to do a goddamned thing direct, for another man. But, in this biz, if I am going to euchre Sanchez and my own position on glyphs out fr under (1) professionalism (2) pricks (3) the State, I've got to make it, strong

note, I have entirely gone around, Carnegie (& Peabody, for that matter, the strike, there, going, curved towards, Peabody & Carnegie's enemy, Clyde Kluckhohn, who, 10 yrs ago, laid one home to them for, their, lack of, concept &, methodology. [153]

Which leaves me with two supporting possibilities not yet touched:

(1) publishers: if Emerson definitely is going ahead on PRAISES, & when I know, I can then hit Giroux, at Harcourt, for, possible advance on, book with or without Sanchez

better idea, I still think, is to break this one, all new— and me not knowing them at all—on Bollingen

3rd pub, possibly, Pelligrini & Cudahy (whom I just heard of, before leaving States, through that project of, a tarot book) [154]

& (2) that dame you dreamed up, who, for eyes, would, etc. (know anymore abt her, Crystalball?)

Which brings you up, to date. Had to raise myself (the weekend) against the deepest sort of reluctance. But did it, goddamn it. (I must say, the measure of, Sauer, was, that, writing the gig to him was, the deepest sort of pleasure &, exaction: was really hammering, seeking a prose, to bring him down (don't believe he ever read any of us, including, Barlow, outside, his own specifics: that's what kills off, these men, however, fine).

But what I sat down here today to write you abt, was, how to handle, these glyphs.

> *the best:* Sanchez's COPAN complete, with some photos, just so, the reader (ha!), is constantly reminded, it is stones, one is talking abt (in fact, with, a photo of stela alongside, wherever possible, a drawing
>
> then, any text by me, arises as the discovery arose, fr, those drawings. And in the text, special drawings of those elements of a given glyph which, I take it, need such concentration, such, extrication: that is, e.g., to establish point I have made to you abt balance of nature therein involved, say. Or the full scale of the playing on hands, say. Plus, possibly, analyses, word & drawings, of, how, the composing is, a matter of, the man behind any given stela—the "syntax" or prose narrative

(such requires fullest sort of permissions, not only for drawings but for Sanchez to be free to give me any special drawings necessary, the finest and most pleasurable sort of collaboration—and, on the ground, I'd say)

> *alternative* 1: without Sanchez, drawings, anyway, but possibly (he guarantees this) any *new* things I might ask of him
>
> wld require substituting other persons' drawings plus much more use of photos (fr collections or persons free to give permissions)
>
> and—given my distaste for taking substitutes—most unlikely
>
> *alternative* 2: is, to write a piece, wholly my own, with illustrations reduced to minimum

Aw, shit, I lose interest. That is, if I cannot do it the best way, I prefer to let the whole thing sit, and let what issues, issue, my own way—which is never known in advance, and is not, least of all, to be outlined, goddamn outlines.

Which, unless stake & some little side, is not forthcoming, is, abt, the way it looks now—it's going to be

Please send me, if you can, the clip fr POULTRY NEWS—or the whole thing. And the gig, on, judging, barred birds. For I'm with you, absolute, on yr preference. In fact, just abt the day you wrote that abt literary goofers, Con says I was beefing exactemente. Is one of the reasons I have always cut off, every so often, to some other biz., simply, that, like the lad who preferred his dreams, saying, he gotta a better class of, bims.

> (Fact is, that, if you hadn't been in there, I'd never, the past year, have continued traffick with, same. Never cld see the point of putting up with same, once, they start peeling off, yr skin. Always sd, fuck you. And went off abt, my business: which seems to me, always, the simplest sort of act—do yr own work, and let publishing fall, as, it may. Result, of course, like no dame, is, you get goddamned bored, but, still, by contrast. . . . Ez used to push me, get out, books. And I couldn't buy it, can't, still. Figure, a man can put up with so much of that kind of shit, and he's through. Turn to a new (future) shit-hole: cut a new round board: put the shanty five feet to the north, and spend a lot of time making, the quarter moons or, the clover leafs: move, over

Never did have, such a gig, as, yr birds. So, it's been science or politics, for me, where, I found guys who, were after something, were in there, hard enough, to make it, to make it a go, for me, for, awhile:
> & the work always seemed to freshen—wrote PREFACE,[155] as I guess I told you, when I was being paid, in hotel corridors, by an unnamed foreign power, for, being their brain at, behind, sessions of, the Security Council

> > all because the ambassador was a man who I, for a

time, liked. And then there was Kulikowski,[156] publisher, of OP-
PORTUNITY (ever see the damned thing—for salesmen! 10 cents,
with pix, of Adam, over, some piece of shit for editorial: got good
verse by, involving my life in, his. (My birds seem to have been, men
or, women!) Another was Hannegan[157]—who sold the Browns, you
may recall, for 3 million, was it, his, loot, fr, politicks: liked him,
liked his damned stupidity, and can say for him that, he got out
because, Catholic tho he was, he wouldn't take, Truman going, for
that right biz: rhythm, that's what it was, not at all to do with
intelligence (a cop's son, and, as such, street-wise), but, that easiest of
rhythms, politicks, but, when it's there, the rhythm (Hannegan had
it) it's, well, say, about the level of, Dimag (me, I prefer, old Honus
Wagner, or, among present characters, Boudreau—brains.[158]

But
brains (Roosevelt), then, it's no good, for, when it's that good, it
becomes culpable because it ain't, better, or, the best (which it can't
be, Augustus, or Jefferson, simply, because the discipline, ain't, a
discipline at all, is, sell sell sell, however much, the man, he'll, soon,
be, cheaper.

Or Graham,[159] say, in the other, league. Or Lange
(econometrician).[160] Or a couple of straight Magdalens, professional,
women. Or—ya, a skipper or two, a couple of, fishermen. Or Red
Wing & Blue Bird, they called those two sisters, up, in Yarmouth.

The literary life is Not the life for,

meeeeeeeeeeeeeee!

Love to Ann & the boys,
and yrself
Charles

lerma   thurs april 19 [1951]

ROB'T!   the push on the photos was [what] did it, lad! i broke thru, last
night, after two days of hammering! you see, Pavon had to refuse to let
me take even a photo by myself with my stupid Hawkeye Cartridge!
And that seems to have seemed so pinched an attitude he opened up and
gave me the whole story. So, yesterday, we sat down for a two hr
strategy session (I, finally, getting across to him the tremendous advantages of (1) ORIGIN issue, (2), exhibition, & (3) a push to get, say,
Bollingen, to publish same book)

    I agreed to get for him letters from (1) the editor of ORIGIN no
less, and (2) the director of whatever museum in Boston, asking for the
loan of the drawings, Pavon to present same to his bosses in Mex City,
they to take them to Secr of Foreign Affairs, he to send them to his
Ambassador Tegucigalpa, same Ambassador to wag them under noses
of, probably, a similar string of such characters downstairs, there, until,
the contract with the Honduran Govt is either broken, or, they move,
instanter!

    You see how crazy it is—and all, fr my point of view, *only* to get
the drawings of Sanchez *known,* so that he and I can, alone, collaborate
elsewhere!

I have written Cid, asking him, to go ahead, fast.

One further upshot is, that, the three of us—P, S & I—yesterday—
dreamed up another wonderful deal: it had been my impression, fr
studying, the last two weeks, the plates in morley's THE INSCRIP-
TIONS OF PETEN,[161] that, of all the other sites, Yaxchilan seemed to
have the most & best glyphs. And by god, when I sd it, yesterday, it
turned out, yes! And that Pavon & Sanchez, are the only Mexicans who
have ever been in there (with Giles Healey, the discoverer of Bonampak,
Paramount photographer) in 1945.[162] And that the plot now is, to raise
10,000 $ to finance a year's expedition into sd wilds (sd wilds being, by
god, the toughest there is! what say, eh? Want to come along, eh? Jesus,
rapids, too. Wild real wild.

And gratuitous of me to say, to you, want to come along: how the hell can I invent some reason for me myself to go along, eh?

The point of the expedition being, *another* book, the 2nd of a series of 3, THE GLYPHS OF YAXCHILAN (the 3rd would be a summary of the rest of the Guatemala sites: Quirigua, Palenque, Tikal, Uxactun, etc., none of which are either plentiful or in good enough condition to make such single surveys of, as, Copan & Yaxchilan)

In other words, at the dying end, if the whole thing hasn't jumped up into even more life, and, now, is of a scale (such an expedition, for ex.) to call for a major financial operation from someone, somewhere.

What dya say to that, eh? And where, now, shall I strike in, eh? It better not be just the Bollingen, but the big cheese behind that rat trap, Paul Mellon[163] himself. Which is tough doing, by letter alone, eh?

Can't quite see the moves, yet. Too new. Puzzled. But the proliferation is right, eh? Jesus. Where to turn, to make it! Figure, now, no wonder, United Fruit, American Chicle, etc. are so deeply involved in this business, as well as Govts, and such lumbering bullion carts as Carnegie. What is clear is, that, to keep it clean, to make it possible for me to stay in, it has to be imagined, reached for, the sources of the dough have to be swift, mobile & guerilla—or I go off. And where is same? Believe it exists, simply, if our will exists, there are others who can be drawn after. But where? Texas oil? What abt that, eh? (God damn those oil men of the States who, 40 yrs ago, forever poisoned the spicks against us!)

Still keep wheeling back to Bollingen, that is, that, the operation, as I might imagine it, is, at root, such a combination as Sanchez & myself, that is, the gate is, "art" as entrance to, cultura

& (2) that the discipline, has to be, culture-morphology, not, archeology, that this is what is fresh, in the push for, backing

And so long as the issue of all work is *books* (I'll drive along the path towards (1) The G's of C, (2) the I's of Y, & (3), the Stones of, Guat) I can keep it, clean, possibly, eh?

Or maybe it's wood—lumber—wealth: for Guatemala (I learn fr bo Azar, here) is now become the world's chief backlog of, logs ((funny connect: Sunday fore last, dos americanos, whom I'd chewed the fat with at Uxmal, came in here, to get more. Shortly thereafter, Azar came in. I (to move the whole biz out) sd, let's go to bullfight. Which happened, Azar taking all! Afterwards, too, to his house, for dinner (he's not rich, but generous: and in that way guys are who had to pitch the ball game or wldn't play). So we're sitting there, when, if one of the two Americans doesn't start digging Azar on how's the wood business these days? (Azar buys for a Pensacola Co., which, recently, has been giving him the biz. And he's either going to be thrown out (actually: deported, with Mex politicians charging him with, smuggling!) or he's going to run out.) And I watched one of those switches which burn my arse, of course, but, which also I am prepared for, that, such can take so much of me, and then, because they can't use any more, fall back to their usual pursuits of, say, business: if the better of the two Americans doesn't make Azar a sort of an opening proposition, that, if Azar will lay it out, maybe, in the States, this same bird can get him the moneys to start operations in the Guatemala woods! (Azar, of course, is now a little bit dizzy, and thinks as well, what kind of a character is this olson, to, get into my house, such, surprises: for three days running he was here, taking us to movies! and finally asking, with incredulity written all over it, where, did you meet up with these guys, did you say?) But of course I didn't give a fuck if I never saw same birds again. And ditto now (tho, then, Kentuckian, who made the move, has offered Con his car, when & if we make, Mex City)

What plays straight in to, above is, that, the 1st planned camp (it is such, with radio, doctor, etc etc, which makes for 10000 costs) is to be at Piedras Negras (which ain't so damned far fr Yaxchilan!)

Well, let me shut up dreams. And tell you, how good it's been, to have another letter fr you, the last two days (the Celine). And get the hell back over there to Campeche to keep the heat under Pavon, while I have him heated. And drive it wherever further it can go, eh?

Will keep you posted.

Jesus.

olson

lerma   april 21 [1951] (sat)

lad: yr letter in, last night, on the FIGHT,[164] for which i am damn much obliged. but here's the catch: it's yr SECOND letter on same, and, the FIRST (the one giving me yr first go at same—at the no/ 1 direct to you in form of letter, & the version 2) *has not yet come*

i'm nervous as all shit now that you tell me you value the gig. waited for this morning's mail, figuring, it just got dropped in another bag. but no. last chance is tonight.

well, not to worry you, but, to get off word, that i have yr readings—and they make very good damn good sense to this'un. am slightly hung, not having yr 1st go, but yr critique of version 3 (which i was fatheaded enuf to think was set) ((it was those lock-ups of the sounds which fooled me, and just those you have, yrself, caught, fin oreille![165])) is very great. well, will wait for letter 1 before trying to rework same.

damn pleased, you find it, usable. for still have a hunch it may have been what blew me to hell out of the two month direct push on the maya: it always comes to this, that, if work, that is, verse, does not issue fr my doings (anywhere, any plane, anyone), i begin to tire of same, disbe-lieve, figure, i must be allowing will to replace the center. for surely, in this business, one is stuck, pegged, cut, staked by that one fact: either you have to show or you don't. And if you don't you better call yrself something else, eh?

Sanchez & Pavon have left, today, for Carmen. I have hired a fisherman (30 pesos, or, 4 bucks) to take Con and I in his cayuco to the island of JAINA tomorrow: we are to arise at 4 am! (And this morning, at that hour, the moon was exactly an orange hanging in the west—figure it was so because these days the milpas are burning all over Yucatan, and, the sky is day & night as was the skies of the States last fall, that time[166]. . . very tough heat these days, almost impossible to keep clothes on, and, absolutely impossible to be out, after 10 in the morn, or before 4 in the aft! So (tho I shall feel like some sort of a tourist who runs, when, the heat's, on) it is probably all right that we shall be heading for the heights of, Mex City, eh?

when, i don't know. deep reluctance to leave (that is, burned that the choice is determined, and not, my own). have three more trips i'd like to make in environs: Edzna, Santa Rosa Xtampak, and Labna-Sayil (now that, tomorrow, I shall have taken Jaina down. But these trips are pissers, and take recovering fr, for me. Whether I can make any, or all, will see.

curious, biz, too: that, yesterday, Black Mt wrote to offer me the summer spot (starting July 9). don't know what to do. trouble is, it offers us two months cover (and we'll have zero, on return Wash). and pleasure of Shahn there, in july, and Litz,[167] whom I have never seen, but, whom I take to, as you'd judge fr letter for E Berlin (no, E Baron!), fr the way Litz made some of the lads (chiefly Cernovich & Lafarge) grow. yet, it seems essentially not forward. will toy with it, for awhile, see. could just talk read push write around this maya thing, there. could be hatchin. well. . . .

what is just too much, lad, is, the absolute purity of yr analysis of, emerson vis-a-vis corman! by god that delights my own holdings! and such news! wow. follow you. exact. & much obliged: will cool me, when. and no word fr sd FOOL, makes it look like a—when.

As well yr take, on that, bride: those tricks, eyes, mouth, as, sensuality. Lay her home, one day. For, she's very much the thing (happening here,

& mean, to see the loss fr these other women who (in huipils,[168] with black hair beautifully pulled back to knot above neck—necks the thing, there—and bone combs—no 10 cent stuff—high colors—placed, so placed, the head is. . . And the bodies, what you see, a huipil blowing against, discovering, not, the other thing, the exposing—wonderful working legs, arms, and the hips, fr carrying amporas & babies) but these are few, now, coming in from, the farms. What goes is otherwise, is, the same as, that, fucked out bride of yrn

[*In ink:*] let this go—love—O

lerma   campeche   monday   april 23   51

lad: what a queer one, but it does seem, that, that LETTER, the one,
with, went astray—at least, still, after two more days of mails, it is not,
in: any chance, do you think, it might somehow, fr weight, say, got
shipped along regular mail? but surely yr post office, there, wld tell you,
the stamps were not sufficient for, air. damned curious, it should have
been that one! well, fuck it, just, repeat, fr what you remember, what
you did say. For what I might be able to guess back was the content of, sd
version #1 (the letter): I cldn't, can't, remember much more than the
movement of same, the stagger of it. No matter, only, it teases the
fucking nervous system, such.

Bushed, hoy. And precisely the verb. For, the bush, of Jaina, leaves me
so. Jesus, what a job these lands are, in the sun! Impossible, the way, the
sun drags you down—in one half hr it is eating you, its clawing having
pulled you off yr pins. Wicked. I tried, for awhile, to scratch away at the
walls of the graves (one leaps in to holes which are exactly like the stage
holes into which Hamlet leaps). But there, with what breeze there is
coming fr the sea (and there was good breeze yesterday) cut off, one
can't take more than 5 minutes! I'm telling you, lad, one thing is hugely
proved: one can't touch this Yucatan (or, I'd gather, any place of these
Maya) without full expeditionary equipment. Which, of course, means,
institutions. Ergo, mal.

Any one place requires, instantly, two to three days: that is, all one can
do the first day, is to get there. For by that time the sun is too far up to
do anything but sleep in some place out of sd sun. So that evening, and
the next morning, early, are the only work times. Which means, almost, the 3rd day, for return. All of which is too expensive for the likes
of one sole adventurer as me!

We got away at 5 am, the lad, who was to sail us, having, I guess, spent
too long at the baile the night before, for, tho we were up before 4, the
two of us, he didn't show, until almost five.

                          The run was lovely: 4 hrs,
with a strong following wind, so strong the cayuco, in the hour before

the sun came, was heeled over so, her gunwhale was taking water! And by god if Con wasn't way the hell out in front of me, taking it! And it her first time in a fisherman! Tho I shld say, she knows sailing boats, I, never, previously, having been undersail except in schooners. Wonderful rich sea. And after, with the wind losing that first freshness, under double sail, going like hell across the gulf, straight run, almost due north fr here: a fine lad, 24, 10 yrs fisherman, without grace, but handling his boat confidently.

Hit Jaina abt 9:30, left at 3:00. So it was the meanest part of the day that we had to work. Result: no chance to take away any—to find any—of the great clays with which the whole "island" is soaked: it is, it's whole length & width (approximately a circle, diameter abt half a mile), a cemetery: in fact, the water has intruded on the land on the seaward side considerably, and in the waters offshore one can spot the tell-tale scattering of pieces of pots (literally, as the lady sd, like, rose-petals, literally, color and all—as tho the Maya brought boatloads and threw handfulls as some sort of a gesture of farewell or protection to those, they buried there).

Craziest damn thing ever, this, place: nothing on it otherwise but two sets of double small pyramids at either end of the "island": one to seaward, one toward the land (now, of course, just rounded hills). And not even raisings, where the graves are, as, say, like "ours"! Just a flat island, abt like (with the two raised ends looking, fr seaward, as dunes) coming on the coast, there, abt Ipswich, say! Only difference, that, the shore is, mangrove.

But here's the punch-line: a damned attractive place as place, so much so it occurred to both C & me, was it the reason the Maya (from wherever they came to this jut of land driving out into the sea just here, to bury their, dead) did so come here, chose, this place?

Must find out more. There've been 3 expeditions to dig same, and, the 1st I imagine, found a glyph stone here with the date 652 AD. Which is one of the earliest dates known north of Guatemala. And long before the building of the major cities of the north. Know no bibliography on the place, only one lousy book Pavon & a guy named Pina Chan did, on the

graves, 3 yrs ago.[169] (Figure on this, as on so many things, I shall have
to find out by reading reports in the Instituto Nacional in MexCity,
where, all mss of expeditions are collected.)

I'd guess one thing: if we had gone up there when we first came, I'm
sure I'd have wanted to promote us a singleteam expeditionary force to
live there awhile, and dig. For it has the damndest charm, the place. And
one roofless building at the landing (dating back to Spanish 18th century) in which to live with an ancient well there in which the loveliest
doves (very small, no more than five inches overall) hide.

I slept, awhile, on the return, folded in under the thwarts, out of the sun
which had spent me, and fitting the bottom just like one of its knees: it
was a throwback, for me, to the way it was sleeping, in a schooner's
peak, with the water's sounds coming in through the wood of the planks,
one of those sounds the like of which. . . .

One can buy one of these cayucos, complete with double sails, for 250
bucks! And the rest of the time back Con and I played with the notion of
borrowing some such dough to buy same and to return to the States so!
(Turned out it would take two months, the lad sd, just to get, by the
coast, to Vera Cruz!) But what an idea, eh? And fine, while it, lasted!

Well. Just to keep you, in. Am weak like sick, and so no words, hoy. But
damned happy to have been there: if you had seen any of these small
clay figures they buried clutched in the hands of their dead, you'd know
why. They are intimate, close human things, these—what the dopes
call—"anthropomorphic" figurines. Jesus. Or "zoomorphic"! And two
(here in the Museum) are those I guess I must have mentioned to you:
of the calyx of clay with little humans sitting where the pistil might be.

And no telling what else is there, the place has not been really dug at all:
a couple of halfhearted "trenchings" of the pair of pyramids. And spotted exhumations of, the graves (the graves go right to the mangrove
edge! must have been dug right in salt water!

                                    what bend of mind
motivated this place? from how far did the people come who came here

to bury? how did they come, by sea? for tho the "island" is only more of the land furruled [*i.e.* furrowed] by breakings in of, water, there is nothing inside to indicate any human settlement for great distances. damned funny, the whole, business (and, so far as I know, no other similar example anywhere among the Maya, tho, I should have liked very much to have gone around to the East coast & seen Isla Mujieres, Cozumel, and Tulum, over there, where, the Maya were coastal and thick.

Well, deepest greetings. And

love,

O

[Lerma, Campeche]
Mon aft [23 April 1951]

lad—
    Yr two just in—*including* the one with, yr rewrite, of same
Bull—
    which, on 1st run looks fine to me—Con sez, yes
                                                    & news of
story—await
    ——this, just, to keep you fr boiling over
                        love—
                         O

[Littleton, N.H.]
Monday [23 April 1951]

Dear Chas/

Most wonderful news, & altogether what the hell I was sure
wd break: well/ damn crazy.

This shot (as it now seems worth it): have
written to a lady in this town, one Florence Glessner Lee, who is an odd
one, loaded, with loot, & as looney as they come: hard as goddamned
nails, altogether without blood, but we will see. I.e., simply asked if she
wanted to put loot, into something worth same, & also: the am't/
$10,000.

I don't know : wd say, most certainly, there is not a single
damn reason to expect any response, because I do not know her, or she
me, Olson, or anyone else. But no matter. I.e., will put it out for her, &
suggest you also, write her the brief plan (giving full names of, say,
Sanchez, Pavon, & any other pertinent sources of reference for the scope
& nature, base, of yr plan). I will also take the liberty of telling her to go
to Henry Allen Moe [*added:* also, Sauer, c/o Moe], for check on yr
activities, i.e., he has the letter from you, also has granted you 2
Guggenheims, & should have that reason for telling her good things.
Also, that fact: loot talks to, loot. Ok.

It's a wild damn pitch, but no
matter; cannot go wrong, as either way, what happens, happens, & no
harm. So.

(Her one 'project' has been the hiring of a carpenter to make
models of houses in which unsolved murders took place—these accurate
to the nth detail, & the figures, apparently, made & clothed by herself.
She gave $150,000 to Harvard, I take it, to provide for a room in which
these houses can be put.

I heard this, today, since her carpenter just
dropped dead on the street, one Mosely, & she's looking around for
another.)

Her address: Mrs. Florence Glessner Lee
The Rocks Estate
Littleton [Bethlehem *crossed out*], N.H.

You can never tell.

Well, very damn grand news. I will allow this one out, & back to it, tonight, or tomorrow morning. Damn fine.
Yr lad/
Bob

[*In pencil:*]
*Lay it out cold i.e., 2 pages of
1,2,3. etc. Ok.
("Lots of enthusiasm!")

("Not too
technical!")

Tuesday/
Begin to get somewhat queasy abt this old lady—I mean if it puts you in a fix (such having to address, the open air) then forget it.

But otherwise, wd figure it: simply a concise note, as purposely enthused, as possible.

It's certain enough, that if such cd come, i.e., this old lady's loot, it wd be of that sort you cd best use—simply that the source wd be a good deal more malleable than the big ones.
Well, will send the letter off to her for whatever it's worth—& you can figure it there, i.e., whether or not you want, now, to follow up same with a letter from yrself.

As well—it wd appear to the point, to have an idea as to how this loot, if

got, wd be handled, i.e., wd it take a 'fund,' such a setup, for her to cut
same off taxes, etc.? How wd Mex/ Gov't act?

Well, a shot.

[Lerma, Campeche]

thurs april 26 [1951]:

          damned nuisance, this biz., of mail, apparently,
only coming thru fr the States, it seems, abt once a week: everything
comes in a lump, around the weekend. leaves me very damned bored,
just now, when i find myself casting around. wish very deeply yr story
was in THE HONEST MAN[170] (haven't read yr predications abt it, on
purpose, holding, until I come at the story, new:

                          was lying in bed this
morning, thinking, how much i believe in, the naive, that is, in ripping
away at whatever, as it comes, without knowing, that is, without using,
at that stage, any—say—comparisons. And what a hell of a difference
that makes, how, that is, actually, the gay biz. and at the same time the
serious of it. How, otherwise? Yet my impression is, it damned well gets
lost, mostly, as i observe people, that, shrewdness, overtakes same: or is
it not shrewdness, but, protection, and shrewdness only the shield &
sword. Funny thing too, is, that, it is also my impression that only those
are capable of comparison who go in the naive way, that, comparison is
judgment, and can operate accurately only posterior

also a part of this that wondrous cliche, hang on, for dear life: heard this
way, instead of as, just, keeping on, it sounds (at least this morning) in
my ear as, the profoundest, sense: keep, in there

                             And that the answer
why most don't is, that, it ain't easy: beauty, sd Beardsley, ain't easy,
eh?[171]

(Flash: Rimbaud, in his ma's barn, muttering & groaning those
days, Saison d'Enfer, is not at all the poetic shit of rhapsody, but, a guy
trying, to make it, no? trying like hell to stay with it, hanging
on[172]

    (yr

con-   JECT-
ure, doctrine: WHY

did he give it,
over?

    still puzzles me, despite, my own explanation, that, the time etc.

And interests me, because he poses directly the question of
will: who could argue he didn't have maximum will, yet, at a certain

            point he
did something else, at least shifted
the use of
that will: why?

      I take it, that, involved in the struggle must have been,
for him,
this question of (put it—Menelik vs verse, which
is where i shall exercise my
will?

    Curious, mysterious case, him: contrast Will Shakespeare, who,
without interruption, did what he was led to do, moved directly forward
from lucrece to gentlemen of to henry 4 to hamlet to lear (sound
the gong) to
pericles, and
RETIRED! by christ if that ain't the craziest thing of all, the
perfection of it, the
dramaturgy of his own life & gift through 1234acts, &,
finito, at
56, or,
whatever: cool, like you'd say, real, cool! HOW
come?

At least two forms of, seriousness, and, clearly, I
prefer the

former, take it
that
(at least now, still)
the choice
presents itself:
            that the question lies outside the condition of
one's liver, is (where Rimbaud was) the ultimate one, the USE
of WHAT?
            the easiest (most difficult) answer is no answer the moment
the notion of, is dead, that: the individual is responsible only
to himself[173]
            yet rimbaud saw (no?) that the individual is able to be res-
ponsible to more than himself only by way of
himself, which
renews the
question, for
            the naive use of self (which means, principally, however
interesting are, stars, some others) involvement of, others, which

where the blood is broken, is

complicated (I'd hunch that Rimbaud settled for ma & sis, and the most
            extraneous others, for

                  the sky, grey, leaves, down, and i
                  am full of
                  blood

These two, by the way, seem to me the only modern men who seem to
have got outside the social & class frames, that is, that so much of the
positionalism of Lawrence & Dostoevsky, say, to go where it is hottest,
have these referents of, how *I* am, positionally, on this or that street or,
continent, that, so many of their shots, that we value, are a part of
revolution not a part of, the biz
            (i'm not so sure of the accuracy of what
i am saying when i say it abt dostoevsky just because i have found it
impossible to reread him; yet, this fact in itself is, i take it, evidence of,

same: that is, Shatov[174]—D's "good" was damned close to the inert, and, as such was (the contrast, Alyosha), pivoted on a thing mighty like DHL's dark man, his little silly dark man, that is (D), the peasant—Christ archetype, which is, ultimately, is it not, reference (and distinctly social) rather than knifing in to, relation?

> sure: the posing of it, exactly the words are, Melville, in the chapter THE SPECKSYNDER: God's chosen, or something, the "Divine Inert" (exactly)[175]

((Ez, e.g., gets fucked up, ultimately, by trying to be as free of these drags as Dante was—and coming out all foolish American small bank deposit (but able to travel to Europe) snob, just because *since* Dante (at least, don't know the picture behind him, tho, from the example of Ovid, say, or Catullus, wld judge, the whole thing came in just at with Dante, that, the so-called "Renaissance" was, when you come right down to the mat with it, nothing more than the beginning of the quantitative push, with which all these unhappy comparisons (& denigrations) commence

> (((shld like to see statistics on, how was the population of the west changing fr 1300-1800, as well as the better known biz, of, the leap, tripling, 1800-1950)))

((& Bill, alas, is trapped in that city-biz (as "form") because, i'd take it, he, too, resembles Lawrence & Dostoevsky in, taking it that—despite his medical eye—the lower classes are, potentially, Christs

suffering, as poverty (against it Ez, is stupidity)[176]

> ARE BOTH LIES

so far, that is, as the job other than revolution is

> Which—that offset—I

take a flyer and guess—is the reason why, for so long, so much has been (even of the best) beside the real, point:

> that there is so much

revolution called
for

> Only

its need impedes

the important per-
ceptions, leads
to phoney archetypes like

   "The Idiot" or   Kung Fu Tse   or
   "The Lady-Bird"[177]   and on the other   (the surprise ending)
                                              Buddha (Prince
                                              Gotama)

neither of which come within shooting distance of

   "rimbaud" as,   Medea, or, the
   in his work, him-   or   host of others of
   self   Ovid
          (I leave "shakespeare"—of the sonnets—
          and his personages, out, because, like
          Dante, they, were of the watershed, and
          I don't think are a damned bit of use to us
          on this side—NOT AT ALL—not at all
(and those who continue to fuck around with same two disclose
their total miss)

Which gets us back, in that, now, still, we are not done with the undoing
of quantity, yet, we are, and, as a result, *have* to FIND OUT, which, is
why the choice, still, lingers, has
to be passed
over
      —that rimbaud was right, in the situation, to
        make a sewing circle of,
        ma &
        sis, his
        only answer to
        the iron ring

                                only,
                      his approximation
                      (light—Cezanne's light)

does not get to Ovid's letter of
Medea[178]

It comes out, I see, again, that, he was ahead of, the possible, time,
that is, that, all by himself he fought out the, battle of, the, bottoms!

Could be, could
be . . . .

Am putting away, these days (recovering heart—literally—or lungs,
whichever, fr, the go to, Jaina) book-larnin on, the Maya, just, to
spend time—having no will to do what, god help me, i ought
RAWTHER be doing, eh?
                    And have got (by way of Smith's report on
Uaxactun),[179] some tools for comprehending the displacement in time
of, this people:

mostly architecture (Smith's report) and i'd still give much to have
here reconstructions of Sumerian buildings (photos of same), especially of the Ziggurat of Ur, for, these Mayan buildings still look so
goddamned like those conceptions of, how to get mass into, the verti-
cal:
        it's the flat ramp, set either over or under (the earliest were
carved in, like a sunken ramp—at least on one beauty of a small
pyramid (cut off), building E-VII-sub, Uaxactun) broad level of steps
leading UP, that still strikes me as damned peculiarly like, the Sumerians[180]
        Plus that obsession (the Chinese) of squaring away at, the
cardinal points (agin, Ur, 1st   Peking

Funny thing is, it all comes out like an end & a beginning, this (now)
coming all the way down to, the black dirt, Uaxactun, small clay head,
double-punch, poke-pupil, MAMOM, rolling off, a shovel, there,
1930[181]—for, the point of going over to Mexico is, to see what those
Injuns there were doing which compares to, these Injuns here——and
here I am, here, with this double-punch, poke-pupil ((don't know,
any more than you do, what it means)), back at date Mesoamerica,

these birds call it, some long time ((they don't know either)) ante 278
AD—some hell of a long time, mil-
lenniums, i suppose the word is!

                              well, lad, just
                              to keep in touch!

                                              o
                                        charles

yr rewrite of the poem seems to me wholly
it. So,
have forgotten
same. Only,
a lingering thot, where
who do you think might
be interested in
publishing
same? (Am at a point, fr attrition, where, I don't give a fuck where, or
if ever, print: no ORIGIN
          no GG, no MONTE R, no fragmente
                              NO BOOK! fuck em

Notes

[References to notes in previous volumes begin with Roman numerals designating volume number, e.g., I. 110 and II. 53, etc.]

1 Jonathan Swift (1667-1745), dean of St. Patrick's in Dublin and author of *Gulliver's Travels*, suffered from Ménière's disease, a "labyrinthine vertigo," most of his life.

2 Spanish "sweets" and "books" (or "sweet books").

3 I.e., Batten, Barton, Durstein and Osborn, one of America's largest advertising agencies, founded by supersalesman Bruce Barton (1886-1967). See also *Maximus* I, 71.

Creolin is a disinfecting soap (made from a cresol base), similar to Lysol.

4 After Spanish *sucio* (plural *sucios*), "dirty," "filthy." More properly, as a noun, *suciedad*.

5 The world's first scheduled radio program was aired over station KDKA in Pittsburgh on the evening of 2 November 1920, when returns of the Harding-Cox presidential election were broadcast to an audience listening in on homemade sets. Westinghouse engineer Frank Conrad and an assistant were the announcers (although Bruce Barton later took advantage of the medium for advertising purposes). It would have been the following year that Olson heard the great Irish tenor John McCormack (1884-1945) sing Irving Berlin's "All Alone" with American soprano Grace Moore (1901-1947). The occasion is also described by Olson in an unpublished poem from 14 December 1959 concerning Gloucester inventor, John Hays Hammond, Jr., where the date appears as 1921:

> Jack's a
> cat's cradle/ crystal
> set 1921 with whisker
> catch
>   KDKA Pitts-
> burgh . . . John
> McCormick [*sic*] sang All alone
> by the telephone . . .

6 A household detergent.

7 Book 2 of Stendhal's *Lucien Leuwen*, trans. Louise Varese, p. 373.

8 Ezra Pound, *Make It New*, pp. 304-05

9 *Make It New*, pp. 288-89n.

10 A *medregal*, a spiny-finned fish, like a sea bass or mackerel.

11 See "frigate bird" in *Webster's Collegiate Dictionary*, 5th ed., p. 401, and also "tropic bird" there, p. 1072, both illustrated. In "To Gerhardt, There, Among Europe's Things" (June 1951), Olson will write with different sentiments about the stoning of the birds: "the kids kill / frigate-birds because they have to / to develop a throwing arm" (*Archaeologist of Morning*, p. [90]).

12 See also *Maximus* II, 133; III, 214; and the photo in Butterick, *A Guide to the Maximus Poems of Charles Olson* (Berkeley, 1978), following p. xxxii.

13 *Diccionario de Motul: Maya Español, Atribuido a Fray Antonio de Ciudad Real y Arte de Lengua Maya por Fray Juan Coronel*, ed. Juan Martinez Hernandez (Merida, 1929-30), p. 304, under "chij" (the *j* printed so it looks like a second *i* in Olson's copy): "la orilla o ribera de mar, o rio, o orilla de heredad, boca de pozo, la margen de la escritura, o de papel escrito, de la halda de la vestidura o ropa" ("the shore of the ocean or the bank of a river, or the edge of a piece of property, or the mouth of a well, the margin of a written piece or manuscript, or the hem of a skirt or garment").

14 Alfred M. Tozzer, *A Maya Grammar* (Cambridge, Mass., 1921). See Olson's 20 February 1951 letter to Cid Corman in *Letters for Origin*, pp. 29-30.

15 See also "Letter #72" (*OLSON*, no. 4, Fall 1975, p. 8):

> The gold machine
> which clanks all over Sacramento's
> fields, toward the north fork
> of the American River, a bug
> wilder than movies, or parts

(shitting pissing eating parts)
imagined by Rube Goldberg
of Mars, taking $1,000,000
each year now for the
Canadian syndicate which
—cleaning up after the
Demolition. . . .

Also, Butterick, *Maximus Guide*, pp. 418-19.

[16] John Lloyd Stephens (1805-1852), early explorer of Mayan sites, author of *Incidents of Travel in Central America, Chiapas, and Yucatan*, 2 vols. (London, 1841), and *Incidents of Travel in Yucatan*, 2 vols. (New York, 1843). See also Olson's 8 April 1951 letter.

[17] See note I.51.

[18] Joseph Wechsberg (b. 1907), journalist and musician.

[19] Katherine Ann Porter's *Ship of Fools*, conceived following a voyage from Veracruz to Bremerhaven aboard a tramp steamer in 1931. It was not published until 1962, although portions appeared in magazines throughout the 1940s as well as in 1950.

[20] According to Francisco J. Santamaria, *Diccionario General de Americanismos* (Mexico City, 1942), II, 511, *pontó* is the name in Tabasco (just west of Campeche) for a pelican (*Pelecanus fuscus*) that is found only by chance in interior waters there. Thus here apparently synonymous with *pelicano*.

[21] See the episode from *Sons and Lovers* cited in Richard Aldington's *D. H. Lawrence: Portrait of a Genius but . . .*, p. 61, upon which Aldington comments: "We have confirmation from Jessie Chambers [the real-life Miriam of the novel] that this was a real and not an imagined experience. She was with him not only on this occasion, but on two others, and from what she says it is apparent that the strange mood of frenzy evoked in him by a full moon was more frightening than he indicates. It seemed, she says, as if some 'dark power' gradually took possession of him until 'something seemed to explode inside him.'" As for Lawrence and gentians, see his poem "Bavarian Gentians." Aldington, p. 152, quotes Frieda Lawrence: "When Lawrence first found a

gentian, a big single blue one, I remember feeling as if he had a strange communion with it, as if the gentian yielded up its blueness, its very essence to him. Everything he met had the newness of a Creation just that moment come into being."

[22] Kukulcán is the Maya name for Quetzalcoatl, the Toltec warrior-king, culture hero, and god of Yucatan during the period of the Maya New Empire. His identification with Venus or the morning star is discussed by J. Eric S. Thompson, *Maya Hieroglyphic Writing* (Washington, 1950), pp. 219-20, and especially Herbert J. Spinden, "Diffusion of Maya Astronomy," in *The Maya and Their Neighbors* (New York, 1940), who writes on p. 165, "he [Quetzalcoatl] died on April 5, 1208, and on April 13, eight days later, his soul arose in the east as the Morning Star" (marked by Olson in his copy). The Quetzalcoatl figure had been included in early drafts of Olson's "The Kingfishers" and "The Praises" when those poems were still part of an even longer poem called *Proteus*.

[23] See Olson's March 20 letter, p. 84.

[24] Former student at Black Mountain. See also Olson's 23 February 1951 letter to Corman (*Letters for Origin*, pp. 31-32).

[25] (Sp.) "The Modern Bluebeard," a 1946 film starring Keaton.

[26] Maurice Beerblock (here perhaps confused with Max Beerbohm), translator of Olson's *Call Me Ishmael*. He had previously translated books by Christopher Morley, Betty Smith (*A Tree Grows in Brooklyn*), O. Henry, and Jerome K. Jerome—not a very remarkable or coherent selection.

[27] Carl O. Sauer, "Environment and Culture in the Last Deglaciation," *Proceedings of the American Philosophical Society*, 92 (1948), pp. 71, 75-76; also, his "American Agricultural Origins," in *Essays in Anthropology Presented to A. L. Kroeber* (Berkeley, 1936), pp. 291-93. In "The Gate and the Center," Olson also refers to "Carl Sauer on starch crops and how, where they could be domesticated" (*Human Universe*, p. 17).

[27a] Perhaps an allusion to the film "Time in the Sun" (1940), edited from the footage of Sergei M. Eisenstein's unfinished "Que Viva

Mexico," an account of Mexican peasant life.

[28] Lázaro Cárdenas (1895-1970), revolutionary leader and president of Mexico from 1934 to 1940.

[29] Lawrence and his wife Frieda (nicknamed here after Lawrence's short novel, *The Ladybird*) who traveled in Mexico in 1923-25 while living in New Mexico.

[30] Warren Dodds (1898-1959), famous jazz drummer, originator of many of the techniques of modern jazz drumming.

[31] *The Plumed Serpent* (London, 1926), especially pp. 60-62 and 98-99.

[32] I.e., *igualmente*, Spanish "equally."

[33] For Ceh, the twelfth month in the eighteen-month Mayan year, see Thompson, *Maya Hieroglyphic Writing*, pp. 111-12, where it is suggested that Ceh may have been associated with the god of the eastern sky (a manifestation of Venus). Thompson also reports that Spinden identifies the main element of the glyph as a bundle of sticks representing "the sacred fire which 'was kindled after the ends of important time periods.'" For the Mayan day Akbal, see pp. 73-75 in Thompson. He says nothing, however, about the institution of a "NEW FIRE CERE-MONY" by Kukulkan in 1159 A.D. or thereabouts—which Olson claims (in March 8 letter, p. 48) as his own identification.

[34] See photograph following p. 100.

[35] The tidal river dividing Cape Ann, Massachusetts, flowing into Gloucester Harbor through the "Cut." It is prominent throughout the *Maximus Poems*, as well as one of Olson's earliest poems, beginning: "Between the river and the sea I sit writing, / The Annisquam and the Atlantic / My boundaries . . ." (see also Butterick, *A Guide to the Maximus Poems*, pp. 125-26).

[36] Olson had written the Middle American Research Institute at Tulane University on February 24 for "an ARCHEOLOGICAL SITES IN THE MAYA AREA *map* in a scale 1:500,000" that he found referred to in *The New World Guide to the Latin American Republics*, eds. Earl Parker Hanson and Raye R. Platt, 2nd ed. rev. (New York, 1945). The Institute's director, Robert Wauchope, sent the section covering the Campeche area on March 5.

[37] Olson had also written Corman, 21 October 1950, that Barlow's "main job, right now, is a life of Montezuma" (*Letters for Origin*, p. 7), although no fruits of the project appear to have been published.

[38] A solar eclipse, 31 August 1932. Olson wrote an account, "The Moon was two seconds late in keeping her engagement . . .," which was published in *Svea* ("The Swedish Newspaper of New England"), 7 Sept. 1932. The dark filters mounted in a cardboard frame that he used to view the eclipse—a device manufactured especially for the occasion—are among the poet's memorabilia in the University of Connecticut Library.

[39] Spinden, "Diffusion of Maya Astronomy," p. 165.

[40] English critic and semanticist (1893-1979), whose *Principles of Literary Criticism* (1925) and *Practical Criticism* (1929) were influential in shaping the New Criticism. More immediately relevant is that Richards extolled the usefulness of English as a "world language" (his later *So Much Nearer* from 1968 is subtitled *Essays Towards a World English*). His *Basic English and Its Uses* (1943) offered improved international understanding through communication and what he and C. K. Ogden called "Basic English."

[41] Attributed to Louis XIV at age 17, addressing the Parliament of Paris in 1655 ("*I* am the State").

[42] See also Olson's letter to Corman, 6 March 1951, in which he speaks of "the blueberry time, simpliccimus, Thoreau-time"; also, the editor's introduction to *The Post Office*, pp. ix-x. A notion apparently derived from Sherwood Anderson. Olson writes to English author Ronald Mason, 21 June 1953, commenting on Anderson: "Anderson has no personal time—never cld leave the blueberry time of the States (his own childhood, to say, 14 ****I think I am drawing on a book most essential to a comprehension of him: the Many Marriages. Do you know it? My memory is, one of the loveliest passages in him is, going for blueberries, in that book." Olson goes on to speak of "the great turn from blueberries, to sour grapes: date, 1900 (?—it happened before 1918, but that War confirmed all the muck-rakers, the 'literary' radicals . . ." And he adds the next day to Mason: "What I have herein called the blue-berry America which went sour, seems to me to stem from Whitman, from that hope and, a good deal, from that passiveness that place encourages,

when it is too big to tie down and so is apt to sail off to India! like Europe did, in the dream of Columbus—all the way through to Woodrow Wilson . . ."

There is no episode or mention of picking blueberries in Anderson's *Many Marriages* (New York, 1923), but see perhaps the theme of town vs. country there, pp. 43-45. *Winesburg, Ohio* begins with berrypickers returning from the fields, though in a later chapter the berries are described as "red, fragrant" ones, not blueberries. The same berry fields occur in Anderson's *Poor White* (New York, 1926), but those are acres of cultivated berries (raspberries are specified), harvested by the townsfolk. Anderson does describe there (p. 46), however, what could well be taken as Olson's sense of "blueberry time": "In all the towns of midwestern America it was a time of waiting. The country having been cleared and the Indians driven away into a vast distant place spoken of vaguely as the West, the Civil War having been fought and won, and there being no national problems that touched closely their lives, the minds of men were turned in upon themselves."

Again, in writing to Edward Dahlberg, 24 July 1950, Olson tells of touring Civil War battle sites in the countryside around Washington: "It is very weird, how much it was Anderson's blueberry America that was the time & people of these frightful places of slaughter. And how they sit now, as they did, 100 years ago, a few monuments, but crops, fishing rivers, the same stone bridges, & wilderness roads . . ." (*Sulfur*, no. 2, 1981, p. 151).

43 Friedrich Ratzel (1844-1904), German geographer. Edward Dahlberg writes similarly in *Do These Bones Live* (New York, 1941)—which Olson had read in manuscript—p. 21: "'Universal History is Monotony,' said Ratzl."

44 I.e., *zopilote*, Spanish "vulture." See also Olson's 18 February 1951 letter.

44a Usually attributed to Goebbels' colleague, Hermann Goering (1893-1946).

45 Blake writes in the "Argument" to his *Marriage of Heaven and Hell*: "Without Contraries is no progression. Attraction and Repulsion, Reason and Energy, Love and Hate, are necessary to Human existence.

From these Contraries spring what the religious call Good and Evil"
(*Poetry and Prose*, p. 181). In the title to his *Milton*, he also has en-
graved (in reverse): "Contraries are Postives / A Negation is not a Contrary" (*Poetry and Prose*, p. 415), and in *Jerusalem* (section 17) he
writes: "Negations are not Contraries: Contraries mutually Exist" (p.
452).

See also Olson's letter to Corman, 18 May 1951 (*Letters for Origin*, p.
54): "I have fed as much on a remark of Blake's as on any single remark
of any man: Oppositions are not true contraries." See also "This Is
Yeats Speaking" (*Human Universe*, p. 99); the early version of "Human Universe" in Glover, "Charles Olson: Letters for Origin," p. 269;
and the final version, *Human Universe*, p. 4.

46 Cf. Spinden, "Diffusion of Maya Astronomy," pp. 162-63: "It seems
that the drama of nature was partly explained by the conflict between a
Jaguar God of the clear sky, the sun, the moon, the stars and the dry
season, and a Serpent God of the clouded sky, the storm, the lightning,
the rain and the wet season of the year" (marked in Olson's copy). For
the lines that follow concerning the weather coming from the west, cf.
"The Dry Ode" (*Archaeologist of Morning*, p. [42]): "The movement
is, generally as, as weather / comes from the west," and also, more
obliquely, *Maximus* I, 36: "Weather / comes generally / under the /
metaphrast."

47 Spanish "snail," "spiral shell"—from which the Mayan observatory
was named (see notes IV.16 and V.49).

48 See note III.8.

49 "Diffusion of Maya Astronomy," pp. 174-76. The Caracol or astronomer's building at Chichen Itzá was so named by the Spanish because of its winding passages, twisting like that of a snail's shell to the
top of the observatory (see fig. 32 in Sylvanus Griswold Morley, *The
Ancient Maya*, Stanford, 1947, p. 328). See also Olson's 8 April 1951
letter, p. 133.

50 See Spinden, "Diffusion of Maya Astronomy," p. 166: "on page 47
of the Codex Vienna is a rather well-known picture of the grotesque
Quetzalcoatl as Venus God supporting, Atlas-like, the starry sky and the
waters above the sky . . . The accompanying date is Year 10 House Day

2 Rain, the god himself bearing the designation Nine Wind." Also p. 168 there: "The same Venus God labeled Nine Wind descends from heaven on a spiderweb bearing the Venus Staff . . ."; and again p. 176, where Spinden reports that "One Rain" bears a "Venus staff."

51 George C. Vaillant, *The Aztecs of Mexico* (Harmondsworth, 1950), plate 59.

52 Edward King Kingsborough, *Antiquities of Mexico, comprising facsimiles of ancient Mexican paintings and hieroglyphics, preserved in . . . the Borgian Museum at Rome* (London, 1830-48).

53 *The Ancient Maya*, pp. 71-72.

54 "The Birds," "Death and the Summer Woman," and probably "Cantar de Noit," all published in *Origin*, no. 2 (Summer 1951). Creeley now encloses "The Birds."

55 See also "people want delivery . . .," *Maximus* II, 97. Susumu Hirota (b. 1898), Japanese-born painter, made his home in Rockport, Mass.

56 Spanish "head."

57 The Vienna Codex?

58 Spanish "mountainous region."

59 Spanish "country dwellers."

60 Imported into northern Yucatan during the New Empire II period (A.D. 1194-1441). "Plumbate ware has a beautiful lustrous finish, almost a metallic sheen, and varies in color from a brilliant orange through terra cotta and tan to lead gray . . . (Morley, *The Ancient Maya*, p. 399).

61 Pelasgus was the eponymous founder of the prehistoric Pelasgians, the earliest inhabitants of Arcadia. See also "A Bibliography on America," *Additional Prose*, p. 12 and note p. 83 there; and Olson's 8 August 1951 letter to Louis Martz to come. For Waddell, see Olson's 27 July 1950 letter (II. 84) and notes II. 46 and 58.

⁶² The Tlascalans. See Prescott, *Conquest of Mexico*, p. 225.

⁶³ Paperbound volumes of local archeology published by Campeche's own Museo Arqueologico, Etnografico e Historico, including Raúl Pavón Abreu, *Metodo Para el Calculo de los Jeroglificos D, E y C* (1948), with drawings of glyphs, apparently by Sanchez.

⁶⁴ Also, Chih-t'ung Fang. Chinese scholar at Harvard working on a dissertation on Pound's *Cantos* ("Materials for the Study of Pound's Cantos," completed in 1958). He also contributed an introductory note to Pound's *Confucius* (New York, 1951).

⁶⁵ See especially Morley, *The Ancient Maya*, pp. 309-10; also Thompson, *Maya Hieroglyphic Writing*, pp. 201 and 217ff., esp. 218 and 221 (although in identifying the morning star as female and saying she was born "from the balls of, father, the sun," Olson has superimposed the classic Greek myth on the Mayan).

⁶⁶ Not, apparently, Rimbaud's own words; see, however, Wallace Fowlie, *Rimbaud* (New York, 1946), p. 42: "Many men wonder what lies beyond sin, but when, on persevering, they discover that it is despair, they retreat to sin or to chastity. But Rimbaud moved on to the despair which lies beyond sin and then sought what lies beyond despair." Also used by Olson in, among other places, "Materials and Weights of Herman Melville" (*Human Universe*, p. 114) and "A Bibliography on America" (*Additional Prose*, p. 4).

⁶⁷ Menelek II (1844-1913), emperor of Abyssinia for whom Rimbaud ran guns and traded contraband. See also Olson's 26 April 1951 letter.

⁶⁸ Keats writes of "negative capability" in his letter to George and Thomas Keats, 22 December 1817 (*Poems and Letters*, p. 277): ". . . it struck me what quality went to form a Man of Achievement, especially in Literature, and which Shakespeare possessed so enormously—I mean *Negative Capability*, that is, when a man is capable of being in uncertainties, mysteries, doubts, without any irritable reaching after fact and reason. Coleridge, for instance, would let go by a fine isolated verisimilitude caught from the Penetralium of mystery, from being incapable of remaining content with half-knowledge. This pursued through volumes would perhaps take us no further than this, that with a great

poet the sense of Beauty overcomes every other consideration, or rather obliterates all consideration." He writes of the "Wordsworthian, or egotistical Sublime" in his 27 October 1818 letter to Richard Woodhouse, (*Poems and Letters*, p. 336) (and see "Projective Verse," *Human Universe*, p. 51).

[69] The original title of Lawrence's *The Man Who Died*, in two parts (see esp. *The Escaped Cock*, ed. Gerald M. Lacy, Los Angeles, 1973). See also Olson's 1 October 1950 letter and "The Escaped Cock," *Human Universe*, pp. 123-25.

[70] See Thompson, *Maya Hieroglyphic Writing*, p. 218, on *caan* as "sky." Olson wrote on the same day to Robert Wauchope, director of the Middle American Research Institute at Tulane, concerning a "correction" to the map he had sent (see note 36 above):

> It is a correction, I think, to what yr map shows for the environs of Seybaplaya, specifically, today, CHUN-CAN. Or so I was told, last night, by natives of Seyba, is the name of a set of ruins I went to, by my nose, yesterday (I had spotted this pyramid, from the bus to Champoton. . . .
>
> I make point of this, because, from a first examination, this ruin is of some importance. For example, against the bottom of the pyramid there is a good size hieroglyphic stone (with its worked face in against the hill). And two stones, alike in size, abt 7 ft by 3, which look suspiciously like stela (though, if they are such, the faces are in the earth, and I had no crowbar, and was alone). Also sections of columns.
>
> But what is perhaps of more importance is the rest of the complex farther in the country, approximately east by south: 1st, a series of houses, apparently, abt a kilometer and a half fr the pyramid, and (2), a small pyramid another like distance farther in, and all, seemingly, on the same axis. . . .
>
> In any case, this, for what it is worth. (The wagon-road directly in to the pyramid, leaves the highway precisely at the kilometer sign, 40) (And the name CHUN-CAN means, "Trunk of the Sky"—which, indeed, it is, surveying, as it does, from its high, sharp top, the whole coast from Ensenada to Seybaplaya.) (The top is no more than 12 ft by 6 ft.)

In the margin of his carbon copy, Olson added: "CHUN-CAN (Seybanos say, al tronca del cielo / trunk of the sky) but Martinez sez, CHUN-CAAN . . . otherwise is, as it stands, TRUNK OF THE SERPENT. Martinez also sez, fr the sea and is called MUCHIL, which he does not know the meaning of."

Wauchope responded, 9 April 1951, that the Institute had very little information about the site, welcoming Olson's report.

[71] See note III. 34.

[72] Unpublished poem by Creeley (Corman will write to Olson ca. April 1951 that Creeley won't let him print it, "wanting more out of it than whats achieved").

[73] Arnaut Daniel, Provençal troubadour, praised by Dante and Pound; practitioner of *trobar clus*, the "hidden" and "close" or subtle style of composition.

[74] See especially Morley, *The Ancient Maya*, pp. 141ff.

[75] See Olson's 25 October 1950 letter (III. 131-32).

[76] From Dahlberg, *The Flea of Sodom*, p. 19: "The greatest profligacy comes from tedium. The garage proletariat will blow up the earth to make his existence less monotonous."

[77] See also "Human Universe," *Human Universe*, pp. 6-7.

[78] I.e., a "greased slide"—Pound's term. See note IV. 24.

[79] See also Olson's 16 May 1950 letter and note I. 10.

[80] Hamlet says to Rosencrantz and Guildenstern (II.ii.316-21): "What a piece of work is a man! how noble in reason! how infinite in faculties! in form and moving how express and admirable! in action how like an angel! in apprehension how like a god! the beauty of the world, the paragon of animals!" In his copy of *The Complete Works of Shakespeare*, ed. George Lyman Kittredge (Boston, 1936), p. 1163, Olson has marked the entire speech (in which Hamlet also expresses his disenchantment with man), adding in the margin: "typical of me as I was: trouble with Hamlet he could never add anything to me, for I was he." See also "Beginning of 3rd Inst," *OLSON*, no. 10 (Fall 1978), p. 17.

[81] Wauchope (b. 1909) was director of the Middle American Research Institute at Tulane since 1942 and author of *Modern Maya Houses, A Study of Their Archaeological Significance* (Washington, 1938). See note 36 above and the portion of Olson's letter to him, note 70. Lothrop (1892-1965) was curator of Andean archeology at the Peabody Museum, Harvard, and author of *Tulum: An Archaeological Study of the East Coast of Yucatan* (Washington, 1924), in one volume only, done for the Carnegie Institution. Olson wrote him on 19 March 1951 for advice concerning "the sea, & its effects upon Maya economy, culture & art":

> I sense, too, that I ought to be much more precise about what I mean by the "sea," as well as what I mean by its "effects." What I have in mind is, basically, an essay in culture-morphology, I should imagine. For example, how come that the introductory glyph has, so often, abstracts of fish alongside the head? Why was the caracol so much a principle of design? Is there a relation between the quality of the work done at Jaina and its location? Was the need for protein and fat to be added to the maize diet any force in the movement of the peoples north into this peninsula where there was both hunting & fishing? How extensive was the trade in fish and salt? What is the reason that Quetzalcoatl-Kukulkan is associated so closely in legend with the sea? Was it merely the attraction of the "exotic" that led to the painting of those murals of the sea and fishing at Chichen, or was it more a registration of an importance they recognized which we have not restored?
>
> These, of course, are the reaches, the easy beginnings which may or may not turn out to be the worked ends. I take a risk in leading to you with them, without your knowing my own work, knowing, that I'd not say one such word in print until I had exhausted all scholarship on the subject, and added what I could of my own to that scholarship. But I respect you, have fed on you, and am happy to write you. I do hope you will be able to write me back.

He adds in a postscript: "If I did no more than call expert attention to a couple of valuable sites, on the coast, I should feel excused!"

[82] Apparently in M. Wells Jakeman, *The Origins and History of the Mayas* (Los Angeles, 1945), pp. 62ff., esp. pp. 71-76. E.g., on p. 73 Jakeman writes: "When they [the Quiches] rose up to come from there, from Tulan-in-the-Ravine, the first captain was Balam Qitze, by unanimity of votes. And then the great father-priest Nacxit [identified in a note as one of the titles of Quetzalcoatl] gave them a present called *Giron*

Gagal." (This has been identified by Adrián Recinos as a stone—see *Popol Vuh: The Sacred Book of the Ancient Quiché Maya*, trans. Delia Goetz and Sylvanus G. Morley, Norman, Okla., 1950, p. 205n.)

For Tula, Tullan, and Tulapan (Tlapallan in Jakeman), see also, Morley, *The Ancient Maya*, p. 88 (where Tula is underlined in Olson's copy), and Recinos' *Popol Vuh*, p. 205 and n.

83 See Jakeman, *The Origins and History of the Maya*, pp. 166ff. For Waddell, see Olson's 27 July 1950 letter and note II. 46.

84 Earnest A. Hooton, "Skeletons from the Cenote of Sacrifice at Chichen Itzá," in *The Maya and Their Neighbors*, pp. 272-80 (recommended in Olson's bibliography for *Mayan Letters, Selected Writings*, p. 126).

85 Olson apparently first learned of this technique while researching the South Pacific as part of his Melville studies, as notes from Robert J. Casey's *Easter Island* (Indianapolis, 1931) in his notebook "#3" from 1939 indicate (Casey, p. 32, briefly mentions Polynesian "charts of ocean currents with sticks of wood"). The Russian explorer Otto von Kotzebue first described similar charts made of shells and strings in use by the Marshall Islanders (*Voyages of Discovery in the South Seas*, 1821).

86 Jean-Louis Barrault. See also Creeley's 29 June 1950 letter and note II. 16.

87 Nicola Cernovich, who had danced Olson's poem "Pacific Lament" (*Archaeologist of Morning*, p. [5]) and for whom Olson would write "Applause" and the dance-play "Apollonius of Tyana" upon returning from Mexico.

88 Bernadine DiYulio had also been in Olson's "Verses & Drama" course at Black Mountain College in the summer of 1949.

89 Dallam Simpson, editor of *Four Pages* (see note I. 11), and probably John C. Rowan, who contributed to *Four Pages* from Cheshire, Eng.

90 Elizabeth "Ibby" von Thurn, a friend of composer Frank Moore, was staying in the Olsons' Washington studio while they were in Mexico.

91 Author of "The Infix in Maya Hieroglyphs Infixes Touching the

Frame," in *Proceedings of the Twenty-third International Congress of Americanists*, pp. 193-99.

92 Clifford Odets' 1935 play, set in a Bronx tenement.

93 Poems by Samuel French Morse and William Bronk, respectively. Morse's "Creatures Like Chameleons" was published in *Origin*, no. 1 (Spring 1951), pp. 13-15, while Bronk's "The Mind's Landscape" appeared in *Origin*, no. 3 (Fall 1951), p. 129.

94 From Thompson, *Maya Hieroglyphic Writing*, pp. 230-31.

95 See Olson's 5 March 1951 letter. Apparently, the glyph of the *xoc* fish, "a large mythical fish identified with both the shark and the whale," discussed in Thompson, *Maya Hieroglyphic Writing*, pp. 38, 78 *et passim*.

96 Pound's retort to Eliot. See also Olson's 25 May 1950 letter and note I. 40.

97 Thompson, *Maya Hieroglyphic Writing*, p. 219. Also, pp. 72-73 there for Imix as a water lily.

98 *Maya Hieroglyphic Writing*, esp. pp. 172-73 and 220.

99 Olson's information here is again from Thompson, pp. 23ff.

100 *Maya Hieroglyphic Writing*, p. 23.

101 See Thompson, *Maya Hieroglyphic Writing*, p. 6: ". . . the intensive excavation of Uaxactun, which erected its last stela at 10.3.0.0.0 (A.D. 889), failed to produce a trace of metal"; also, A. Ledyard Smith, *Uaxactun, Guatemala: Excavations of 1931-1937* (Washington, 1950), p. 68.

102 See fig. 60 (and frontispiece) in Thompson, *Maya Hieroglyphic Writing*, p. 59, and pp. 142ff., esp. 146-47.

103 See Olson's 28 March 1951 letter in *Letters for Origin*, pp. 41-42.

104 Alfred M. Tozzer (1877-1954), professor of anthropology at Harvard and curator of Middle American archeology at the Peabody Museum. See also note V. 14.

105 The 1913 Armory Show (held at the Sixty-ninth Regiment Armory in New York) introduced modern art to the American public. Frobenius' "cave" exhibition, held in 1937 (not 1928) at the Museum of Modern Art, consisted of facsimiles of materials in the Research Institute for the Morphology of Civilization, Frankfurt am Main, founded by Frobenius in 1923. See the catalog, Leo Frobenius and Douglas C. Fox, *Prehistoric Rock Pictures in Europe and Africa* (New York, 1937). See also *Letters for Origin*, p. 42.

106 See Morley, *The Inscriptions at Copan* (Washington, 1920), pp. 102-07 and plate 13 for Stela 7, and pp. 334-38 for Altar T.

107 Undoubtedly "the magnificent full hieroglyphic tablet found in the 1949 excavations under my friend Alberto Ruz's direction," mentioned in Olson's application to the Wenner-Gren Foundation, "'The Art of the Language of Mayan Glyphs,'" *Alcheringa*, no. 5 (Spring-Summer 1973), p. 99.

108 Olson's reluctance to review Edward Dahlberg's *Flea of Sodom* (Norfolk, Conn., 1950). If death is what is meant by a "going out," the third loss is possibly F. O. Matthiessen's suicide in March 1950, which Olson bemoans in his poem "Diaries of Death," written shortly thereafter (*Some Early Poems*, Iowa City, 1978, pp. [17]-[18]).

109 Published in *Origin*, no. 1 (Spring 1951), pp. 5-6, 42, 53-54, and 61.

110 "O my son, arise from thy bed—work what is wise." From the Babylonian creation epic as translated by Samuel Noah Kramer, *Sumerian Mythology* (Philadelphia, 1944), p. 70. Originally sent Corman by Olson with his 1 March 1951 letter (see *Letters for Origin*, p. 34; also p. 45 there).

111 The unpublished "l'education sentimentale: anglo-saxon class," beginning:

> Come la rena quanda turbo spira—
> Whom hell refused, walk this void:
> Like Dante's sand the leaves circle
> Whipped by a turbine wind . . .

The original is among Blackburn's papers at the Archive for New Poetry, University of California, San Diego.

[112] I.e., Pound.

[113] (Paris, 1942). Bérard (1864-1931) was also a senator in the French government, a member of the Socialist-Radical party, and an authority on foreign affairs. The main themes of his *Les Phéniciens et l'Odyssée*, 2 vols. (Paris, 1902-03; rev. ed., 1927), which influenced Joyce's *Ulysses* and Pound's *Cantos*, are summarized in his *Did Homer Live?* (New York, 1931).

[114] Bérard, *Did Homer Live?*, pp. 145-46. It is not that Etna could not be seen from a ship, but that the mountain, "towering over all with its snows or gleaming fires, never appears outlined on the horizon."

[115] The term, meaning Greek and Phoenician sailors' charts, is derived by Pound from Bérard (see *ABC of Reading*, pp. 43-44) and recurs throughout the *Pisan Cantos*. It is glossed in Canto LIX: "not as land looks on a map / but as sea bord seen by men sailing."

[116] See Bérard, *Did Homer Live?*, pp. 108-12 and 120; also, p. 157 for Corfu as Ship Rock. See also "A Bibliography on America," *Additional Prose*, p. 9.

[117] *A Study of Classic Maya Sculpture* (Washington, 1950), p. 2: "Even a cursory glance shows a preponderance of motifs in which a single human figure is dominant." See also Olson's letter of 27 April 1951 to Corman, *Letters for Origin*, pp. 46-47.

[118] In late February or March 1938. Olson mentions having "had dinner with Whitehead last week" in a March 1938 letter to Dorothy Norman, publisher of *Twice A Year* (at Beinecke Library, Yale University). Again, in a 1968 conversation with the editor, he told of the occasion, a small dinner party held in the exclusive Louisburg Square section on top of Beacon Hill when he was a tutor at Harvard, recalling the formality of the dinner and of Whitehead. Olson told a similar story to Charles Boer and John Lobb: "Lobb asked you if you had ever met him [Whitehead]. You said you had. It was at a party in Boston, when you were a student at Harvard. You went up, you said, and tried to speak to him about his work, but the man was 'too formal to let anybody talk to him about his work at a party' " (Boer, *Charles Olson in Connecticut*, Chicago, 1975, p. 107).

[119] See section VI on non-Euclidean geometry in "Geometry," *Encyclopaedia Britannica*, 11th ed. (New York, 1910), XI, 724-30, identified (by initials) as being by Bertrand A. W. Russell and Alfred N. Whitehead. Olson notes in the margin of his copy, p. 725: "by B. Russell & Whitehead!"

[120] See especially H. S. M. Coxeter, *Non-Euclidean Geometry* (Toronto, 1942), which Olson had read in the Library of Congress; also Coxeter's *Regular Polytopes* (London, 1948). See also *Muthologos*, II, 72.

[121] Bernhard Riemann (1826-1866), the German mathematician, first set forth his geometry of spherical space in "Über die Hypothesen, welche der Geometrie zu Grunde liegen" (1854). See Coxeter, *Non-Euclidean Geometry*, pp. 11-13, and Russell and Whitehead, *Encyclopaedia Britannica*, XI, 726-28. See also *Muthologos*, II, 101 and n.

[122] Bolyai János (1802-1860), actually, son of Bolyai Farkas. See also Olson's 27 May 1950 letter and note I. 46.

[123] Louis de Broglie (b. 1892), discoverer of wave mechanics, brother of Maurice de Broglie (1875-1960). In *Letters for Origin*, p. 11, Olson writes: "NATURE TAKES NOTHING BUT LEAPS / (de Broglie brothers)," referring to de Broglie's revision of Linnaeus's—also Leibnitz's—observation that *"Natura non facit saltus."* Max Planck (1858-1947), German physicist, formulated the quantum theory.

[124] Dutch astronomer and mathematician, Willem de Sitter (1872-1934). Olson had read his *Kosmos: A Course of Six Lectures on the Development of Our Insight into the Structure of the Universe* (Cambridge, Mass., 1932) in November 1946, according to entries in a notebook from that time. Years before, while an undergraduate at Wesleyan University, he had attended a lecture by de Sitter entitled "The Size of the Universe," given as part of the school's centennial celebration in October 1931. Olson told the story one class at Buffalo of walking late into the lecture from debating practice and comprehending immediately, to his own amazement, all that de Sitter had to say. Notes taken during the lecture survive inside the front cover and flyleaf of the poet's copy of Foster's *Argumentation and Debating*, which he apparently had with him that evening. See also *Maximus* II, 131, and Butterick, *Guide*, pp. 420-21.

[125] Karl F. Gauss (1777-1855), pioneer of non-Euclidean geometry.

[126] See note I. 66.

[127] (1892-1947), professor of biophysics at Columbia University since 1926, specialist in vision and light reception. Among his books were *The Retinal Processes Concerned with Visual Acuity and Color Vision* (Cambridge, Mass., 1931). He contributed an essay entitled "Vision II: The nature of the photoreceptor process" to *A Handbook of General Experimental Psychology* published by Clark University (Worcester, Mass., 1934), when both Olson and Graham were teaching there. See also *Letters for Origin*, p. 7.

[128] Leo Frobenius (1873-1938), Africanist and founder of the Forschungsinstitut für Kulturmorphologie in Frankfurt am Main. See also I. 60, II. 80, and note V. 105 above. Bronislaw Malinowski (1884-1942), Polish-born anthropologist, led exhibitions to New Guinea and Melanesia, notably the Trobriand Islands. He was the author of *Argonauts of the Western Pacific* (1922) and *Myth in Primitive Society* (1926), quoted in Jung and Kerenyi (see III, 135-36, and note III. 78).

[129] Alfred North Whitehead, *Science and the Modern World* (New York, 1925), p. 158: "On the materialistic theory, there is material—such as matter or electricity—which endures. On the organic theory, the only endurances are structures of activity, and the structures are evolved."

[130] See I. 147 and note I. 131.

[131] American philosopher (b. 1895), best known for her *Philosophy in a New Key* (1942).

[132] *Incidents of Travel in Yucatan*, I, 434—a section entitled "Vestigia Phallicae Religionis Prout Quibusdam Monumentis Americanis Indicantur." Stephens comments on Kabah having been "more richly decorated" than Uxmal on I, 370. See also Olson's 10 June 1951 letter to Corman, *Letters for Origin*, pp. 57-59.

[133] Anthropologist Clyde Kluckhohn in his survey, "The Conceptual Structure in Middle American Studies," in *The Maya and Their Neighbors*, pp. 41-51. He writes specifically, p. 42: "To begin with, I should like to record an overwhelming impression that many students in this

field are but slightly reformed antiquarians. To one who is a layman in these highly specialized realms there seems a great deal of obsessive wallowing in detail of and for itself." See also Olson's 17 April 1951 letter and note V. 153 below.

[134] *Incidents of Travel in Yucatan*, I, 226-32.

[135] See Olson's 4 August 1950 letter (II. 93) and note II. 71 (also "The Gate & The Center," *Human Universe*, p. 21). See also the summarization of the Omaha "rite of the vision" in Jane Ellen Harrison, *Themis* (Cambridge, Eng., 1927), p. 69.

[136] I.e., Richard Wirtz Emerson, editor of *Golden Goose*. The "Bro. Aspirin Box" mentioned next paragraph is Emerson's *Frère Vital's Anthology* (see note IV. 18).

[137] See Olson's 25 October 1950 letter (III.134) and note III. 75.

[138] Apparently a typescript of an unpublished collection of poems.

[139] "Slydynge of corage" (slippery of heart): Chaucer's *Troilus and Criseyde*, V. 825.

[140] Douglas C. Fox, "Frobenius' Paideuma as a Philosophy of Culture" (in six parts), *New English Weekly*, 9 (3 Sept.-15 Oct. 1936).

[141] Carl O. Sauer, "Environment and Culture in the Last Deglaciation," *Proceedings of the American Philosophical Society*, 92 (1948), 65-77.

[142] Creeley wrote at the top of the manuscript, "This is really—a *diatribe*—as sd all good stories BE."

[143] "A Note on the Objective" (see note II. 40), published in *Goad*—edited by Howard Schwartz—no. 1 (Summer 1951), pp. 20-21.

[144] Famous bullfighter, Mañuel dos Santos (b. 1925).

[145] See note V. 21.

[146] D. H. Lawrence, *Fantasia of the Unconscious* (London, 1923).

[147] In a note prefacing "The Wheel of Sheol," one of three excerpts from *The Flea of Sodom* (1950) appearing in *ND 12: New Directions in Prose and Poetry*, ed. James Laughlin (New York, 1950), Dahlberg writes, p.

252: "It was after a conversation, in Washington Square, with Mr. Slater Brown, regarding the fiery, prophetic Wheels, and knowledge as an inflamed Roman vice, that the author reread *Daniel* with increased rapture and wrote this little apocalyptic essay."

148 Three short novels published in one volume under the title *The Captain's Doll* (New York, 1923).

149 *Frère Vital's Anthology* (see note IV. 18).

150 Leslie Woolf Hedley, Richard Rubenstein, and Scott Greer, poets published earlier in Emerson's *Golden Goose*.

151 Samuel Noah Kramer (b. 1897), noted Sumerologist. His translations of fragments of the epic of Gilgamesh in "Heroes of Sumer," *Proceedings of the American Philosophical Society*, 90 (10 May 1946), pp. 120-30, were the basis for Olson's poem "La Chute" (*Archaeologist of Morning*, p. [65]).

152 William O'Dwyer (1890-1964), U.S. ambassador to Mexico, 1950-52; former mayor of New York City.

153 Kluckhohn writes again in "The Conceptual Structure in Middle American Studies," p. 45: "Even the Carnegie Institution's well-known and justly praised scheme for a many-sided attack by specialists drawn from varied disciplines is but an extension of the received system, an improvement of method of intensification and intellectual cross-fertilization"—a passage marked by Olson in his copy. See also note 133 above.

154 See note IV. 59.

155 "La Préface" (*Archaeologist of Morning*, p. [43]), written in 1946 while Olson was working for Polish interests at the United Nations.

156 Adam H. Kulikowski (1890-1966), Polish emigré and consultant to the O.W.I. Olson wrote the poem "For K," revised as "Trinacria" (*Archaeologist of Morning*, p. [11]), for him.

157 Robert E. Hannegan (1903-1949), chairman of the Democratic National Committee who served as Postmaster General in Truman's cabinet until November 1947, when he resigned to purchase the St. Louis Car-

dinals (not the Browns) baseball team, which he sold shortly before his death for a reported one million dollars. See also "Maximus Letter #28," *OLSON*, no. 6 (Fall 1976), p. 15.

[158] Joe DiMaggio (b. 1914), New York Yankees batting champion, 1936-51; Honus Wagner (1874-1955), batting star of the Pittsburgh Pirates, 1900-17; and Lou Boudreau (b. 1917), shortstop and later manager of the Cleveland Indians, then with the Boston Red Sox.

[159] See Olson's 7 April 1951 letter and note 127 above.

[160] Oscar Lange (1904-1965), professor of economics at the University of Chicago, 1938-45, and Polish ambassador to the United States, 1945-46.

[161] Sylvanus Griswold Morley, *The Inscriptions of Petén*, 5 vols. in 6 (Washington, 1937-38); especially II, 341-607, on Yaxchilan. See also *Mayan Letters* bibliography (*Selected Writings*, p. 126).

[162] Giles G. Healey, who stumbled on Bonampak in 1946 while making a documentary film of the Maya for the United Fruit Company. See "Maya Murals," *Life*, 27 (21 November 1949), pp. 80-84.

[163] (B. 1907), trustee of the Andrew W. Mellon Foundation.

[164] I.e., Olson's poem "Right There In Front of Your Eyes," revised and later published as "This" (*Archaeologist of Morning*, pp. [27]-[28]).

[165] French, "fine ear."

[166] See Olson's 29 September 1950 and 8 March 1951 letters, and note III. 8.

[167] The painter Ben Shahn (1898-1969), whom Olson had known in Washington when both worked for the O.W.I., and dancer Katherine Litz (d. 1978), who had taught the previous summer at Black Mountain.

[168] Loosely fitting, sleeveless cotton blouse of the Indians of Mexico.

[169] Román Piña Chan, *Breve Estudio Sobre la Funeraria de Jaina, Campeche* (Campeche, 1948). Raúl Pavón Abreu was director of the Museo del Estado in Campeche.

170 Possibly the name of a magazine then being planned (see Creeley's 1 May 1951 letter to come).

171 See note I. 100.

172 See, e.g., Enid Starkie, *Arthur Rimbaud* (New York, 1947), p. 270, concerning the composition of *Une Saison en Enfer* (1873): "when members of the family went by near the barn where he [Rimbaud] shut himself away to work, they could hear sobs and groans issuing forth from it as if he were in agony, and shouts and curses of rage as if he were in battle with an enemy."

173 Cf. *Call Me Ishmael*, p. 119: "The Pacific is the end of the UN-KNOWN which Homer's and Dante's Ulysses opened men's eyes to. END of individual responsible only to himself. Ahab is full stop."

174 Character in Dostoevsky's *The Possessed*; Alyosha, following, is one of the three brothers in *The Brothers Karamazov*.

175 Chapter XXXIII of *Moby-Dick* (Constable ed., I, 182): "God's true princes . . . the choice hidden handful of the Divine Inert." See also *Maximus* I, 122, and "Equal, That Is, to the Real Itself," *Human Universe*, p. 122.

176 See Olson's 25 May 1950 and 27 March 1951 letters, and note I. 40; also, "David Young, David Old," *Human Universe*, p. 107, quoting Pound as the sly "Fox": "What the Fox said to Mr. Eliot one fine day: 'It ain't Original Sin that done us in, Possum, it's o-riginal in-nate stupidity!'"—a position which Olson rejects in *"April 24 1959"* (*OLSON*, no. 9, Spring 1978, p. 15): "The original sin / is inadequate means, not innate / stupidity."

177 The novels by Dostoevsky and Lawrence, respectively.

178 Letter XII of Ovid's *Heroides or Epistles of the Heroines*, in which Medea writes to Jason "the day she learns the bastard is taking up with another dame" (Olson to Monroe Engel, 8 April 1949). Pp. 11-24 in Henry T. Riley's translation (London, 1879), which Olson had acquired in 1949.

179 A. Ledyard Smith, *Uaxactun, Guatemala: Excavations of 1931-1937* (Washington, 1950).

[180] See Oliver G. Ricketson, Jr. and Edith Bayles Ricketson, *Uaxactun, Guatemala: Group E—1926-1931* (Washington, 1937), pp. 67ff., especially figures 33-35, 55, and plates 30 and 33.

[181] See Smith's account of the first digging at the pyramid temple E-VII-sub in his *Uaxactun, Guatemala*, p. 4: "We all gathered around to watch. The first floor was pierced, a second, a third. Nothing between them but footings of mare and limestone chips. Then, from a meter down, there came out a shovelful of black dirt. As it fanned out over the growing heap there rolled to the bottom a little brown object. George [Vaillant] leaned over and picked it up, brushed it clean—and whistled. We passed it around. There could be no doubt what it was: the hand-modeled clay head of a crude human figurine, with the double-punch and poke-pupil eye that is one of the hallmarks of the Archaic cultures of the Guatemala highlands and of Mexico." Mamom refers to the earliest pre-Classic phase of Mayan archeology (Smith dates the Early Classic period as beginning in 278 A.D.).

I. Index of Persons Named in the Letters

Adams, John, 52
Ainsworth, Evelyn, 42
Ainsworth family, 42
Anderson, Sherwood, 113
Arnault, Daniel, 80
Augustus (Octavian), 169
Aunt Vandla (Vandla Hedges), 22
Azar, 62, 172
Barlow, Robert H., 14, 47, 166
Baron, Eleanor, 93, 94, 174
Bartók, Béla, 93
Barton, Bruce, 14, 15
Beardsley, Aubrey, 182
Beerblock, Max, 35
Benedict, Ruth, 85, 86
Bérard, Victor, 117, 118
Beyer, Herman, 95
Blackburn, Paul, 59, 60, 79, 114, 115,
    116, 124, 137, 160
Blake, William, 53, 75, 76
Bolyai Farkas, 127, 128
Boudreau, Lou, 169
Broglie, Louis and Maurice de, 128
Bronk, William, 96, 97, 137, 160
Brown, Slater, 38, 39, 43, 48, 54, 55,
    56, 57, 59, 66, 71, 78, 83, 84, 92,
    95, 97, 103, 108, 110, 117, 124,
    135, 151
Buddha, Gotama, 186
Burns, Robert, 76
Cagli, Corrado, 93, 94
Cárdenas, Lázaro, 37
Carlos, 32, 48, 61
Catullus, 185
Céline, Louis-Ferdinand, 172
Cernovich, Nicola, 93, 174
Cézanne, Paul, 186

Chaplin, Charles, 93
Christ, 76, 77, 89, 185
Cole, Thomas, 20
Columbus, Christopher, 62
Confucius, 49, 52, 186
Corman, Cid, 16, 20, 21, 33, 34, 35,
    42, 44, 45, 46, 59, 60, 73, 80, 87,
    94, 95, 101, 108, 109, 114, 115,
    122, 124, 136, 139, 140, 141, 160,
    161, 170, 174
Cortés, Hernando, 58, 71
Coxeter, H. S. M., 128
Crane, Hart, 113
Crosby, Caresse, 88
Cunningham, Merce, 94
Dahlberg, Edward, 50, 96, 113, 151
Dante, 49, 51, 97, 185, 186
De Sitter, Willem, 128
DiMaggio, Joe, 169
DiYulio, Bernadine, 93
Dodds, Warren ("Baby"), 38
Dostoyevsky, Fyodor, 184, 185
Drake, Francis, 96
Drohan, John, 61
Duncan, Robert, 113
Duns Scotus, John, 49
Eberhart, Richard, 60
Einstein, Albert, 128
Eliot, T. S., 138
Emerson, Richard Wirtz, 20, 35, 60,
    80, 115, 137, 138, 146, 158, 159,
    160, 161, 166, 174
Erigena, Johannes Scotus, 49
Fang, Achilles, 76, 160
Ferrini, Margaret, 139
Ferrini, Vincent, 46, 60, 114, 115,
    137, 139

Fielding, Henry, 19
Fox, Douglas C., 139
Frobenius, Leo, 15, 103, 109, 129, 139
Fourier, Francois, 51
Galileo, 59
Gauss, Karl F., 128
Gerhardt, Rainer M., 29, 34, 77, 116, 141, 146, 147, 160
Giroux, Robert, 138, 166
Goebbels, Joseph, 53
Goodman, Joseph T., 108
Graham, Clarence H., 128, 129, 169
Grant, Ira, 39, 40
Greer, Scott, 160
Guggenheim, John Simon, 110
Hannegan, Robert E., 169
Hanson, Kenneth O., 79
Hardy, Thomas, 19
Hatson, Constance, 60
Hawkes, John, 147
Healey, Giles G., 170
Hecht, Selig, 129
Hedley, Leslie Woolf, 160
Hernandez, Juan Martinez, 23
Hirota, Susumu, 61
Homer, 52, 75, 76, 77, 118, 120
Hooton, Earnest A., 90
Horton, T. David, 20
Hoskins, Katherine, 60
Jakeman, M. Wells, 90
James, Henry, 19
Jefferson, Thomas, 169
Jonson, Ben, 96
Joyce, James, 49
Juan Pablo, 63
Keaton, Buster, 34
Keats, John, 76
Kingsborough, Edward King, 58
Klee, Paul, 129
Kluckhohn, Clyde, 166
Kramer, Samuel Noah, 109, 114, 130, 163

Kukulcán (Quetzalcoatl), 31, 33, 38, 43, 45, 47, 48, 51, 52, 55, 56, 57, 58, 59, 61, 67, 78, 89, 90, 103, 108
Kulikowski, Adam H., 169
Lafarge, Timothy, 174
Lange, Oscar, 169
Langer, Suzanne, 130
Laughlin, James, 139, 146, 147
Lawrence, D. H., 31, 37, 39, 75, 76, 77, 124, 148, 153, 184, 185
Lee, Florence Glessner, 180, 181
Litz, Katherine, 94, 174
Lothrop, Samuel K., 88, 134
Louis XIV, 50
Lobachevski, Nikolai I., 127, 128
Malinowski, Bronislaw, 129
Mao Tse-tung, 37, 52
Martinez, 13, 35, 62, 82, 86, 90, 108, 119
Marx, Karl, 51
McCormack, John, 15
Medici family, 110
Mellon, Paul, 171
Melville, Herman, 37, 52, 75, 76, 96, 120, 128, 185
Menelek II, 75, 183
Moctezuma II, 47
Moe, Henry Allen, 29, 165, 166, 180
Moldovan, Sacha, 61
Moore, Grace, 15
Morley, Sylvanus Griswold, 58, 66, 106, 170
Morse, Samuel French, 95, 96, 97, 137, 160
Mosely, 180
Nietzsche, Friedrich Wilhelm, 51
O'Dwyer, William, 165
Ovid, 75, 185, 186, 187
Parkman, Francis, 37, 52, 128
Pavón Abrue, Raúl, 78, 86, 101, 102, 108, 109, 126, 127, 134, 149, 150, 163, 164, 165, 170, 173, 174, 177, 180

Piña Chan, Roman, 177
Planck, Max, 128
Porter, Katherine Ann, 28
Pound, Dorothy, 94
Pound, Ezra, 19, 20, 25, 49, 50, 51,
    62, 71, 94, 97, 100, 111, 118, 123,
    132, 138, 160, 168, 185
Pratt, 41
Prescott, William H., 52, 71
Proskouriakoff, Tatiana, 121
Rainier, 94
Ramon, 45,
Ratzel, Friedrich, 51
Rexroth, Kenneth, 113
Riboud, Jean, 28, 29, 45
Richards, I. A., 49
Richardson, Samuel, 19
Riemann, Bernhard, 127, 128
Rimbaud, Arthur, 75, 76, 77, 183,
    184, 186
Ringer, Gordon, 20, 117, 137
Roosevelt, Franklin D., 169
Rowen, 94
Rubenstein, Richard, 160
Russell, Bertrand, 127
Ruz Lhuillier, Alberto, 150
Sahagun, Bernardino de, 58
Sanchez, Hippolito, 36, 37, 73, 74, 89,
    95, 101, 102, 103, 105, 107, 108,
    112, 126, 127, 132, 137, 139, 149,
    163, 164, 165, 166, 167, 170, 171,
    174, 180
Santos, Mañuel dos, 148
Sauer, Carl O., 35, 88, 129, 139, 166,
    180
Schwartz, Horace, 146
Segovia, Andrés, 94
Shahn, Ben, 174
Shakespeare, William, 76, 96, 183,
    186
Simpson, Dallam, 20, 94
Smith, A. Ledyard, 187
Spinden, Herbert J., 48, 55, 108

Stephens, John Lloyd, 25, 52, 126,
    133, 135
Stromsvik, Gustav, 36, 89, 150
Strzygowski, Josef, 129
Swift, Jonathan, 13
Tagore family, 29
Thompson, J. Eric S., 103, 104, 108
Tico del Saz, Joaquin, 15
Tozzer, Alfred M., 23, 46, 104
Truman, Harry S., 169
Vaillant, George C., 58
Vasquez, 62, 63, 64, 65, 92, 113
Viereck, Peter, 122, 124
Waddell, Laurence Austine, 67, 89,
    90, 130
Wagner, Honus, 169
Wauchope, Robert, 88, 134
Wechsberg, Joseph, 28
Whitehead, Alfred North, 123, 127,
    128, 129, 130
Williams, Paul, 34, 94
Williams, Vera, 94
Williams, William Carlos, 49, 50, 51,
    71, 72, 110, 138, 160, 185
Wilson, Edmund, 110

II. Index of Works by Charles Olson and Robert Creeley Cited in the Text

Robert Creeley:
"The Epic Expands," 146
" 'Guido, vorrei che tu e Lapo ed io,' " 146
"Hart Crane 2," 146
"The Hawk," 79
"Helas," 79, 80, 81, 146
"Le Fou," 146
"Littleton, N. H.," 146
"A Note on Objectivity," 146
"The Poor Season," 81

Charles Olson:
"Adamo Me," 45, 140
"Bigmans," 50
Call Me Ishmael, 71
"The Gate & The Center," 33, 35, 44, 45, 59, 114, 115, 162
"I, Maximus of Gloucester, to You," 115
"The Kingfishers," 54
"La Chute," 146, 163
"La Préface," 168
"The Moon Is the Number 18," 16
"Origo—Dreme—Imago," 137
"The Praises," 34, 54
The Praises (proposed book), 35, 115, 116, 137, 138, 139, 166
"Right There in Front of Your Eyes." *See* "This."
"The Story of an Olson, & Bad Thing," 140
"This," 142-44, 156-58
Y & X, 104

Printed February 1983 in Santa Barbara and Ann Arbor for
the Black Sparrow Press by Graham Mackintosh and Edwards
Brothers Inc. Design by Barbara Martin. This edition is
published in paper wrappers; there are 750 hardcover trade
copies; 250 hardcover copies have been numbered & signed
by Robert Creeley; & 26 lettered copies have been
handbound in boards by Earle Gray & are signed by
George Butterick & Robert Creeley.

GEORGE F. BUTTERICK studied with both Charles Olson and Robert Creeley at the State University of New York at Buffalo, where he received his Ph.D. in 1970. He is Curator of Literary Manuscripts and Lecturer in English at the University of Connecticut, and lives with his wife and sons in the nearby mill city of Willimantic. He is currently preparing a definitive edition of Olson's *Maximus Poems* and, more slowly, writing a biography of the poet. His essays and reviews have appeared widely in journals, including *American Literature, Credences, Iowa Review, New England Quarterly, Paideuma, Review of Contemporary Fiction*, and *Sulfur*.